M000313427

DANCING WITH MY FATHER

Dancing with My Father

Leif Anderson

University Press of Mississippi / Jackson

www.upress.state.ms.us

The University Press of Mississippi is a member of the Association of American University Presses.

Copyright © 2005 by University Press of Mississippi

Walter Anderson artwork (pp. 22, 26, 32, 38, 42, 46, 50, 54, 58, 62, 66, 70, 74, 78, 82, 86, 90, 94, 98, 102, 106, 112, 116, 120, 124, 128, 132, 136, 140, 144, 148, 152, 156, 160, 166) copyright © by the Estate of Walter Anderson

All other artwork copyright © by Leif Anderson

Manufactured in the United States of America

FIRST EDITION

Library of Congress Cataloging-in-Publication Data
Anderson, Leif.
Dancing with my father / Leif Anderson.
  p. cm.
 ISBN 1-57806-722-7 (cloth : alk. paper)
 1. Anderson, Leif. 2. Children of artists—United States—Biography. 3. Anderson, Walter Inglis, 1903–1965. 4. Artists—United States—Biography. I. Title.
NX512.A544A2 2005
 700'.92—dc22

2004017356

British Library Cataloging-in-Publication Data available

To the truthful child in all of us,

who weeps when we would be too mature and competent,

who rages when we forget how to play,

who hides when our feelings seem unacceptable

to those we love,

who leaps for joy at a smidgeon of heartfelt response

FOREWORD

Oh strange and lovely world where
Weavings of the light and shade
Dapple the paths our faltering feet
Step gently, softly, seeking out
Some glimpsed, elusive truth.

—*Agnes Grinstead Anderson*
letter to Leif Anderson, 16 May 1982

In these vignettes a daughter searches for her father, turning the pain of absence into compassion and love. The father is legendary painter Walter Anderson (1903–1965), and the daughter who confronts his emotional and creative legacy is Leif Anderson (b. 1944): dancer, poet, graphic artist.

One of the happiest periods of Walter Anderson's uneasy life came in the 1940s when he lived in Gautier, Mississippi, with his wife Agnes Grinstead Anderson (Sissy) and their four children. At Oldfields, a coastal farm on the Mississippi Sound, Walter Anderson reconnected joyfully with art, nature, and language after years of severe mental illness, and created an astonishing number of drawings, paintings, carvings, and prints. Those years were his only prolonged experience of family life. Mary (b. 1937) and Billy (b. 1939) were old enough, back then, to remember him as "marvelous playmate," and it was at Oldfields that Leif was born and given a name that challenged her, years later, to "journeys of exploration" ("a name can become an ideal to attain, a reason to go on striving"). Sure that she would be a boy, Walter Anderson named her for Leif Ericsson, one of his favorite adventurers. In 1946 or '47, when Leif was two or three, and John, the fourth child was less than a year old, Walter Anderson announced that he would move by himself to Ocean Springs in order to devote himself entirely to his art. He divided the last fifteen years of his life between seclusion in his cottage (where he earned a meager living as decorator for Shearwater Pottery), bicycle trips across the South, journeys to Costa Rica and China, and long periods of meditation and creation on Horn Island, a patch of wilderness in the Gulf where he drew as close to herons, gallinules, and other winged creatures as he ever had to his children. As adolescents in Ocean Springs, Leif and her siblings saw little of Walter Anderson. It was clear they were not welcome in his cottage, and although Sissy surrounded them with love and taught them compassion and admiration for their father, they sometimes felt embarrassed by his odd behavior. Even in a town as tolerant as Ocean Springs, he was known as an "eccentric," a "hermit," or a "crazy artist." Over the years, the absent father would become an overwhelming presence in the children's lives.

In these pages, Leif Anderson defines her own complex relations to a "fly-away sort of father," a person "unto himself," who "lived in a far-away place, no matter where he was. . . . That I once had a father sometimes seems a dream." Believing that "the hard things" are "equally worthy to be told," that life is a "dance of light and shadow," and that "contrast beguiles," she does not hesitate to admit that when she was young and her father was away, she slept more soundly and breathed more easily. "One could play with abandon; no fear of sudden encounters." Lovingly, she remembers his courtly manners and decorous gifts (pens, books, and above all, flashlights, wrapped in brown paper, "to Leif from Bob," one Christmas after another). She listens to him—and speaks to him—in the places he loved. She stares at the "found objects" and mementos he collected in his cottage or considers the meaning of a vase, presented to her by Sissy, on which he painted a double vision of his infant daughter. She can imagine her father as winged spirit ("Birds") but, just as easily, as the "ogre" who lived on the edge of the woods at Shearwater ("Remembering Fairyland"). He was always, she writes, a "wild and wayward artist" of a father, one who "found us when he wanted to" ("Bequest," "Immortalized"). Rather than resentment or self-pity, what these pages reveal is an awareness that—as Walter Anderson once wrote—"beauty is born of the rain": that hardships help make us what we are; that "the flaw that one curses can turn out to be a blessing," allowing one's gift to flourish. Each of these vignettes is an act of forgiveness and acceptance, of him and of herself.

The acceptance came gradually over the years, with a growing sense of burdens and conflicts shared with the father and with other family members. First among them is the struggle between the artist's need for freedom and the demands of family life: the urge to abandon the "normal" world. "The heart seems torn in two at times by difficult choices. . . . How can I be in this world and fulfill my deepest needs?" Another shared burden is the tug of familial—particularly maternal—expectations. Sissy's loving encouragement of her daughter's gift and "great dancer dreams," her unshakeable belief that Leif was a "torch-bearer" like her father, are a reminder—though a distant one—of Walter Anderson's struggle with the "fierce expectations" of *his* mother, Annette McConnell Anderson, who had put aside her own career as a painter to raise children whose lives would be devoted to art ("Choices"). A challenge unmentioned—but amply surmounted—in these pages is one shared by Leif with her mother and siblings: not to be overwhelmed in their own creative pursuits by the greatness and abundance of Walter Anderson's work. Two things helped. One was the realization that, although "creatives have reputations for floating in unreality," art depends on "groundedness"—on habits of working and *making*—the hard, steady pursuit of one's craft. "To face each day supported, not by the dictates of a reliable outer framework, but by a chosen obedience to an inner necessity, one has to have one's feet on the ground" ("Grounded"). Walter Anderson taught his children still another reassuring lesson, one he had learned from his mother: the spiritual discipline of creation—of "realizing" beauty in wood or clay, on paper or canvas—matters more than the objects produced. The dance of creation ought to weave itself like prayer into everyday life.

"Only dance," Walter Anderson once wrote, "brings one within leaping distance of one's reward." And it is in dance, her chosen art form, that the daughter most easily finds the absent father. The memories are indelible, sometimes painful. On the one hand, his solitary dancing at night in the cottage, the music turned loud, the children afraid of a "drunken frenzy," praying that he would *stay* there, in a world of his own ("Dancing with My Father"). On the other, the Walter Anderson who caught the world's music in color and line: the father who carried her as a baby into the water at Old-fields (her artistic christening) and danced with her in the waves; painted her in ballet costume; gazed down at her as she practiced in the Ocean Springs Community Center. (He was on a step ladder, absorbed in his great mural. "Was he even aware that I was there? Did he know that his youngest daughter worked with passion-ate devotion—as he did—to perfect her art?") Still later, toward the end of his life, he sits unexpectedly in the audience beside Sissy, his suit spattered with paint, at one of his daughter's performances in New Orleans—an act too precious to forget. Sissy had told her daughter of Walter Anderson's "Terpsichorean feats": he was agile enough to perform a triple *tour en l'air*. Leif caught that "creative exuberance" and pursued her art until the forms of ballet gave way, after his death, to a style she called "Airth," where levity and gravity—poles of her father's art—melded into a free-form dance of her own. Some of the vignettes and sketches ("Cat Wisdom," "Inspiration," "Messenger") want to rise from the page into movement, the daughter's lines reaching toward those of her father.

They reach and sometimes touch, and word and image remind us that he too was lonely in his art, that "artistic flights may be overrated," that the "very private father . . . mostly bereft of intimate companionship," "must have suffered greatly at times; fulfillment must have been partial." The Oldfield years and the later, less frequent contact with the family must have left him hungry for ordinary companionship and warmth, as though (one of his sons remarked) his wife and children had abandoned *him*, unwilling or unable to accept the reality he offered. This too awakens the daughter's compassion. "With all of his brave adherence to the artist's path, the adventurous life, he still had moments when all he wanted was loving reassurance," moments when he must have felt as vulnerable as the bunny in *Resurrection Rabbit*, "love and fear all mixed together in the creative breast." When a "large, strangely patterned snake" appears in their woodland playground at Shearwater ("Fairyland"), Walter Anderson emerges with a smile from his cottage. As she watches him stroking its scales, the daughter senses that the snake is *him*: beautiful, feared, mostly unwanted.

Like any memoir, the vignettes bring private moments into public view. The "familial" becomes familiar, and personal memories turn into collective ones—a process that fascinates the daughter as she stands in an exhibition of her father's work at the Smithsonian Institution, celebrates her mother's brave memoirs (*Approaching the Magic Hour*), or reflects on the meaning of the Walter Anderson Museum of Art. It is odd to see so many people love her father so effortlessly, without thinking what it was like to live with him or near him. "People who didn't know Daddy fall in love with him through his art. They get to love him as I wasn't allowed to do. It seems cruel, and I'm sometimes mixed up in response to it." This too the daughter comes to accept, glad to share his "legacy of love and beauty." Such communion leads to a final irony: "For one who was driven to escape his human family," Walter Anderson has had "a strangely unifying effect on all of us."

Christopher Maurer

ACKNOWLEDGMENTS

First I would like to thank my father for being inimitably who he was, and for returning spiritually to bless the writing of these pieces. Then my mama, who supported my creative efforts through thick and thin, and eventually became my best friend. My sister, Mary, hugs me when we both need hugs, and reminds me of the courage of my convictions. My brother John mysteriously sees my father in me and loves us both. My brother Billy surprises his "weird" sister by happily welcoming her into his home, and reminding her of her need for family. I thank my whole family at Shearwater, and am eternally grateful to my children, Moira and Vanja, and my grandchildren, Olivia and Wyatt, for pulling me out of my isolated otherness to give me grounding love. This reminds me to include my furry companions, Music, Star, and Sunny Day, for their mostly patient and always unconditional love. I am also thankful to my friend Lou Ann, who tirelessly listens, blesses, and encourages. My friends at the Walter Anderson Museum of Art are much appreciated for their interest and for opportunities to share these pieces through performance. Many thanks to Christopher Maurer, whose e-mails cheered me on throughout this process. Joan Gilley, dear friend and curator of the Walter Anderson estate, helped me to select the drawings for this book. Special thanks to the University Press of Mississippi, to John Langston, Carol Cox, and to Seetha Srinivasan, my elegant and affirming editor.

DANCING WITH MY FATHER

Revelation

I STAND IN A ROOM full of art in a well-known museum. As my father's fame grows, I stand in the midst of his art in a distant room. I feel small and exposed; it is all so familiar, and yet so strange. People exclaim over Daddy's paintings. His energy fills this space. People are hungry for large ecstatic bites of my father, and also of me. They see me as symbol. My father's success is obvious on my smiling face, on the clothing I wear. His designs cascade across my body. See this living, walking fragment of my father's greatness. Touch me, hug me, ask me questions, whether you hear my answers or not. A symbol is safe. But just beneath the surface of attractive, accessible daughter of Walter is Leif: the strange, the vulnerable, the one who blurts out truth, who feels and can't help sharing what she feels. In a dance, if you're lucky. Keep your distance from a woman in a room full of art who is more than she seems. She carries a child around the room; a child called Leify whose father left to create the art you admire.

Behind the beautiful images is a desperate tortured man, as well as a genius. Though I try, as you speak of my pride and joy in my father's success, I cannot see only the wonder of attainment. There is too much missing from this story of real pain, real loss, real sacrifice. Oh Mama! My childhood memories are more than memories. I live the whole story. I may embarrass you, for strange realities prod my surface calm. My father's art in a distant room is too close for comfort; the child's emotion may erupt, despite the woman's smiling wonder, her efforts at playing the part that pleases. This woman may have to carry a weeping child from this room of perfection . . . hide her away that she not disrupt the celebration. For God's sake, keep her tears from smearing the paint!

But what if the child is the missing fragment of her father's revelation? Who is brave enough to bring her back, tears and all, to express her father's humanity? His weakness? His need? Really, the man was a father, too. Not only an artist. And his children are still here. Leify?

Dancing with My Father

I REMEMBER MY MOTHER speaking of Daddy's Terpsichorean feats. Because of her, a sort of raw Nijinsky leaps through my mind. Her tale of his wild cavorting around my baby self continues to reenforce the bond his early departure from my life still threatens. Later, my own ecstatic dancing to Beethoven, Brahms, and César Franck would evoke those firmly instilled memories. I can understand his affinity for Beethoven's Seventh Symphony, can almost see his half-crazed romping on the Oldfields porch, down the bluff to the water's edge, and out the long pier.

Oldfields, our family's home in Gautier from 1940 to 1948, stands for a brief early closeness in my mind. I was born at the center of this period, and perceive it as a golden time, if steeped in mystery . . . hinting of terrible things as well as joyous. A very young child is ripe for lasting impressions, and whatever I don't remember consciously, my unconscious carries, releasing periodically through creative means, or through inexplicable bouts of emotion. My passion for the dance may reflect an earlier passion shared with my father. As I dance, I may reconnect with the earlier bliss of dancing with my daddy. Later encounters are less than blissful, tainted by separation and strangeness: my father becomes an alien presence, best kept on the fringes of my mother's re-created life for her children. He couldn't belong any more than we could belong in his rarified world of reclusive artist. He seemed tormented by brushes with normalcy. And we were tormented by sounds from his cottage at night: loud music and louder stompings of his feet. It could mean a drunken frenzy, and everyone silently prayed he would stay where he was.

Yet there were surprising islands of connection that enriched regardless of discomfort: modeling for my daddy in a ballet tutu, standing in fifth position with graceful arms as he spoke of seeing Pavlova dance *The Dying Swan*. Or fluttering moth-like to Debussy's *Claire de Lune* as he watched, each of us pretending he wasn't there. I shall never forget his visit one spring, seeing him perched on a chair arm in the sitting room of our house at Shearwater. I had been making garlands of fallen azalea blooms, and I came in to find him and Mama quietly conversing. He made an effort that day to share my dance again, speaking of movement that springs from stillness, inviting me to move for him. My efforts, so loaded with desire to please and be loved, probably fell short. The room was soon empty of all but the pungent scent of his cigarette smoke . . . and, of course, Mama and me, and my quest for dance. Ballet obsessed me for a while. My studies in New Orleans with Lelia Haller led to performances in her company. I was sixteen when my father came to see me in the ballet *La Péri*. I was in the corps, one of many undulating chiffon-clad nymphs behind a scrim. It was all very otherworldly; the dance and my father's presence—his paint-spattered suit, red tie, and wine-laden breath.

Yet his efforts count with me. They were few, but well-meant. And I know that leaving his haven of art and nature was no small thing. Probably his preferred reality affected me deeply, even as I followed an art inclined toward contrivance. It would all soon collapse: my ballet dream would dissolve in the wake of unmarried pregnancy, be replaced by a free-form dance inspired by Isadora Duncan. In the same year, Daddy's breath would escape his body, perhaps to travel through air and merge with my breathing dance, never to leave me. My dance would forever after spring from stillness.

Birds

M Y FATHER'S BIRDS are not distant objects that I can quietly admire. They are lodged deeply in my soul, inciting sudden and irrational compulsions to take flight. I am capable of choking on my father's birds, and equally capable of joyous careening, epitomizing creatures he loved without reserve. I can be wing, curled or thrusting . . . one with the wind's erratic or calm dance. Keening with a winter gale, I can call Daddy forth, tempt the courage of a small man in a small boat to bridge the gap between mainland and paradise, gravity and flight.

Sometimes you have to sit still to fly—squat on your haunches, grounded by paper and pen. Inspired detachment allows the soaring to happen. Flying is more mysterious than feathers and hollow bones, elegant motion responsive to currents of air. Later the paper demanding your absorption reveals your essence, and a minute portion of that which you long to fathom.

Dear Daddy . . . what a terrible quest! Thank heaven

for the immensity of your belief, your persistance in the presence of unbelievers. I continue to learn from you, Daddy. Frustration can turn in an instant to clamorous heart-bursting courage. Then I dare the chaos of raucus utterings, clatter of earthbound wing; I am ready to catch an errant updraft and ascend. Order finds me through my willingness, makes sense of who I am. Am I one of your birds, left behind in your haste to complete the quest? You always were a fly-away sort of father.

So what is a daughter to do, left behind in the midst of discarded plumage? Essence is everywhere; brilliant portions of a father's quest surround, distract, overwhelm. I am sometimes afraid of suffocation, must strive to avoid a premature burial in . . . Feathers? Feathers elude control; the slightest breath can send them in all directions. Lighter than air, they make love to the atmosphere. Playful as fairy sprites, they drift from great heights to land in an open palm like a kiss. They exude an aura of otherworldly bliss, hint of an unseen messenger, hovering.

Are you near, and listening? You understand my

plight, as well as you do my flight. You remember how fearful a loving embrace can be. You still know that fighting for air, for space, for freedom to move unhindered by others' agendas is instinctive and often necessary. But you want me to conceive of something more, perhaps a strange companionship, unhindered by the old unwieldy efforts to escape. You want me to shrug off the feathers not lending themselves to flight, and don the brave new plumage of my destiny. You know me capable of rising to the surface of old dreams, of sending my gaze far beyond familiar horizons. Is is time to take wing once more, my father?

Yes, my daughter. Fly . . .

Resurrection Rabbit

June
1959.

I TREASURE A PAINTING by my father called *Resurrection Rabbit*. It is beautiful; the colors are gathered like jewels to express one moment in the artist's life. But I see it as a personal expression. I am sure of my father's identification with the rabbit. His role is often that of a creature humbled by a vision, receiving grace through the natural world. How could he not believe in resurrection? Intensely human, his chosen work brings him face to face with his own transcendance. Yet, there is another reason for my treasuring. Written on the back in Daddy's hand is a date.

In 1953, at the age of nine, I am hardly capable of treasuring my father's reality. It keeps him distant, makes him strange—in fact, deprives me of his presence and his love. I compensate by dancing butterflies and birds, trees and windswept islands, wildflowers and waves. Now and then, the artist returns to paint his child, but never the father.

Perhaps this is why, as a woman, I look at the date with more emotion than I do the painting. I sense the man in the curving stroke of his pen. I feel his desire to remember this experience. By the simple act of recording the year, and the month of June, he returns to me the gift of his humanity. I am with him in the joy and pride of a job well done. Seated beside him, sharing the warmth of a summer day, I see him smile. I also see that the rabbit is no longer present . . . only my daddy silently gazing into the light. But he knows I'm here. He knows that I now understand the struggle involved in being human and feeling compelled to create: the heart seems torn in two at times by difficult choices.

I turn the painting over, and we look together at this scene of resurrection. Now I can feel the small, quick thump of the rabbit's heart—love and fear all mixed together in the creature's breast. Oh Daddy! Yes! Resurrection isn't a onetime thing; it goes on and on. For this is the gift of a father to his beloved child. How can I thank you, Daddy? I can believe!

Harvest

THESE DAYS, I have the urge to commune with my father as never before. In these fall days one hundred years beyond his birth, he is accessible. The sky, so brilliant a blue, seems open to my gaze. The crimson splash of leaf invites my heart to reach for his, as though he reaches, too, from another place, another time. No barrier divides us now; I can see through his eye, and he likes what he sees through mine.

I see the waters of the Sound being blessed by molten sunlight. This reminds me as I walk on the morning beach that he is present. His love slips over the water with the sun, bringing my day into focus, cooling my brow. His hand is touching me, guiding my mind, my heart, my body to express new ways of being. I can move freely in my father's world, realize his world with expanded sensibilities. My father may be teaching me something new, not only to me, but to him. Together we may be finding the courage to share the intense reality of our perceptions.

Already we know what it is to *be* an artist, shutting

out the world for the sake of creating. We know that being is the only way that a flower can unfurl. For my father, it is a season of unfurling. Could it also be for me? I feel so as I witness the effects of his long, hard seedtime. A kind of autumnal abundance spills from the fertile center, affecting me as I open to the flow of climactic happenings. I have no choice; control is minimal; the wave is released. Thankfully, this cascade of creative energy is benevolent. Joy springs from acceptance and cooperation. I ride the wave, convinced that my daddy loves me. And I love him . . .

Bequest

A T THE TIME of my birth, my father painted a vase with my baby image. Of course, his perception infused the design; he has given his daughter wings. I have taken his act to mean that my coming was celebrated, even rejoiced over. Yet the vase conveys a message of ambivalence to me—a mixed response.

Two winged babies grace the surface of the pot's circumference. One face appears to express such tenderness and vulnerability. The strokes of his brush are softer, more rounded. And the small child gives herself to the artist's eye, willingly merges with her daddy's purpose. No questioning mars the conjunction of mind and heart. But the other child's features may withhold trust, harbor suspicion of the man's objectives. The demeanor is that of a tough little kid who knows what it is to have a wild and wayward artist for a father.

I look at this vase that my mother placed in my hands after Daddy died, and I realize the prophet who foresaw the balancing act that his child was doomed to, or blessed with, depending on one's perspective. I feel that he willed me this: the vase and its mystery. I believe that in our first encounter as father and daughter, a current of understanding passed between us. No simple emotional rush of love, but a complex array of components infused his creation. Often I've thought I might find the most valuable part inside. Does the naked, untouched interior contain the greater truth? After all, it *is* a vessel. It must have an inner life . . . a secret reason for existence.

Peering inside, I see darkness first. But, tilting the vase toward the window, I see circular indents marking the path of the potter's hands. When I touch the ridges, a memory blooms in my mind of my uncle's leaning figure, his eyes on the rising clay, watching the elegant miracle of formation. Is my daddy waiting nearby? I tilt the vase further, and circles of light overlap the original lines. A dance of shadow and light is born. A secret reason becomes a sacred reality.

Cat Wisdom

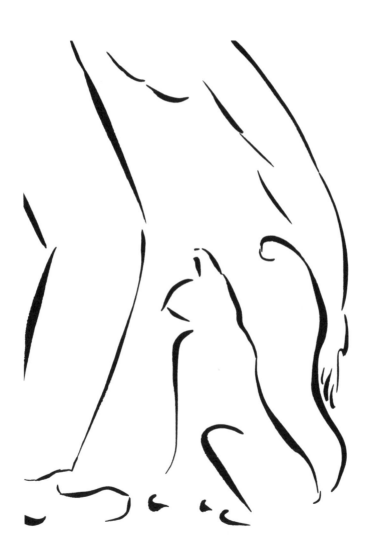

I WOULD LIKE TO HEAR my father's laugh. Could this happen if I were to walk on all fours, assume paws and a perfectly curving tail? If my look is mostly benign, and often amusing? If I keep my face clean, my whiskers sensitive and shining? I shall place my cat feet with infinite care on the path that he travels. I shall sense my father's delight in my flawless form. My ears will prickle and twitch at the scratch of his pen upon paper. My timing will be beyond reproach as I suddenly pounce upon beetle or lizard, suddenly bat at a butterfly's passing.

Was that a chuckle . . . low and rich . . . ruffling my fur with pleasure. This thought pulls me close to his human warmth. His trouser leg yields to my firm appeal. The artist's fingers set down his pen, descend to my arching back for a long slow stroke, and another. Delicious! I move away, my small heart pulsing against my ribs. Being a cat, I know the importance of dignity, and respectful sharing of space. I know to save something for later, perhaps when the evening fire leaps on the hearth.

At dusk, the man almost relaxes, settling in his chair to read. The lamp lights his book, and halos his graying hair. He takes a few swallows of wine and places his glass on the floor. I am good at waiting. My patient cat mind is watchful, aware of each delicate moment drifting by. When the scene is set, I spring with certainty onto my father's knee, tamp the pages of his book, turn my green-gold eyes to catch a smidgeon of lamplight, and finally emit a perfectly pitched me-yooow.

My father's laugh erupts into the night-quiet room. I almost flee. But this is what I came for: my daddy's laughter. I hold my fear, observe its subsidence, and look at the mouth of the man, now gently smiling. His eyes are soft with gratitude as he pulls me close. A brief fierceness is felt; I must practice cat patience again, curb reaction. And soon, his surrender allows me to lower my weight, to drape my body across the expanse of his lap. He leans his head back with a sigh, lets his large rough hands come to rest upon me, and I purr.

Souvenir

Entrance to
Village.

cream
chartreus
o omeslts

salmo
pink

WHEN I WAS A LITTLE GIRL my daddy went to China. He was always going to faraway places. He lived in a faraway place, no matter where he was. But this time he was going to China; his goal was Tibet. Did he long for austere mountains, ancient wisdom, monks with their heads in the clouds? If he did, he didn't tell us. He just left a scrap of paper attached to his screen porch door. By then, I was used to his leaving. It made little impression—except, perhaps, some relief was felt. For a while life would be more relaxed, less inclined toward watchful nervousness. One could play with abandon; no fear of sudden encounters. Sleep would be deeper, more peaceful.

I know now that Daddy didn't make it to Tibet, that he suffered great hardship, lost his passport to thieves, had to beg for food. I also know that he painted some marvelous watercolors. I have seen and felt the rich reds, blues, and yellows of his China paintings. They declare his location; "I am a Chinese lobster" is a clear proclamation. They declare that the artist, Walter

Anderson, is free of familiar inhibitors, free of the usual elements defining and sometimes threatening existence. His inner farawayness merges with his outer circumstances, bringing him close to himself in a new way. Colors/passions/forms are less careful, more bold.

I vaguely remember that Mama and my grandmother had to help him get back home. I may remember a small doll in a red dress. But I'm not sure that came from Daddy; it would have been out of character for him to bring back a souvenir/gift to a little daughter. It may have been a dream. That I once had a father sometimes seems a dream. It's all so far away . . . that time. And I have traveled far, myself. I, too, have been an adventurer, have stood upon foreign shores and proclaimed myself a dancer, a poet, a woman in a red dress, have relished the unfamiliarity of a Paris street. I have felt at home, merged with my inner farawayness. Possibly, I am the gift my daddy brought back to me from his travels afar.

Christmas Flashlights

THEY WERE WRAPPED in plain brown paper, torn from the showroom roll that my aunt Pat used to wrap pottery for Shearwater customers. The slender oblong packages were unmistakably from Daddy, handed out from beneath the tree along with others, brightly colored and Christmassy. They were probably laid down thoughtlessly in favor of these more enticing shapes and sizes. We knew they were flashlights; the presents seldom varied from year to year. On a rare occasion an old, used book was the strangely conceived gift to a child. Some years a pen was proffered; some years nothing.

Always across the paper wrapping my gift was scrawled: for Leif, from Bob. I thought nothing of this, or of the fact that my cousins' were marked in a similar way. This was the way he was. My father was not my father in any obvious sense. It was only later, when no more flashlights came my way, that I took to calling him Daddy. Only then was I free of the one who called himself Bob, and could claim the close relationship I missed while he lived.

Now I can seek him out when I need the light shined on some aspect of his presence in my life. And he willingly reveals the truth. At least, the truth of now. I can almost see him walking the path to my house, one of those infernal flashlights held in his hand. He seems to look for me, seems to be glad of my fearless going to meet him. The familiar figure wavers, in and out of focus; the outline of his hat is vague. Yet the light he holds out to me is substantial; the transfer is possible. I believe he wants to walk with me on the path I now tread, wants to share the glow of illumined memory. The strength of the beam going out before us increases. The things he invites me to see are potently real. All the little unloved flashlights of the past seem gathered into one extraordinary torch. And I am shown the most enticing gift of all: my father.

The Gentleman

Franco-
Flemish –
á gentleman

M Y FATHER TIPS HIS HAT to ladies as he pass-
es. His rickety bicycle becomes a noble steed,
and shabby, paint-smeared clothes turn into elegant
attire. The ladies suddenly hold parasols, housedresses
are replaced by ankle-length gowns, eyes startle and
glance demurely down, and hearts do a fluttery dance
instead of the usual dull plod.

I've seen this strange phenomenon, taken pride in
my father's gentlemanly ways. Once upon a time, I
looked without wincing at my daddy's strangeness,
glad for his old-world courtesy and his assumption of
polite regard. If he did take notice, and favor you with
courteous attention, his interest was real; his admiration was a serious and stirring thing. You wouldn't forget it if he kissed your hand and called you *"tres belle."*
Especially if you were a girl in your sixteenth year.

I was a reader of books, a natural romantic, and my
father was the sort of character that held me to the
page. Reading of him in a novel or biography, I would
have wanted to know more about his courage and his

view of the world. I would have identified with his differentness, and his determination to fulfill an inner cause. I would even have seen through his eyes a prospective painting—its placement of form, collusion of color, harmonies of line—and felt his need to translate what he saw. And I would probably have fallen in love with his tragic nature, understood his inability to fit in with the world's idea of sane and responsible. No doubt I would have gathered my skirts and leapt to the back of his horse at the slightest invitation, eager to accompany his isolation and his ecstasy.

But he was my father, as remote as he was mannerly and charming. Back then, he was never safely ensconced in the realm of literature, accessible to a dreamer of a daughter. Life has its limits when it's happening. It's only when it becomes a "once upon a time" that one can freely respond to the tipping of a hat.

Choices

M Y FATHER'S MOTHER was not affectionate. Nor did she seem maternal, though she became "Mère" to all our family. Her love tended toward the dutiful and was often dominating, but she loved her Bobby with the kind of passion usually reserved for a personal vocation. She taught him that art and the making of art were of prime importance; creative pursuits were the highest form of human expression. His early talent for drawing was praised and encouraged, and my father learned to put art first. His painting became a necessity, something he could not live without. Mère also proclaimed that the writing of seven hundred and fifty words a day was essential to stimulate and cleanse the mental palette. Daddy's writing was less disciplined than that. He did his island logs, chronicling his trips. But usually his thoughts seemed to wing their way onto paper: brief statements of rhythmic intensity, poetic observations containing effortless wisdom.

I am sure that my father loved and admired his

mother, and perhaps the "Bobby" in him wanted to please her, wanted to meet her fierce expectations. But his need to escape her control increased as he matured and sought his own way. The phone that she had installed in his cottage was quickly yanked from the wall. And her growing need for his attention earned her at least one physical assault. Her nurturing of his artistic talents may have given him wings and a taste for freedom, but her later attempts to cage the gift only sent him on more determined flights away from her.

I understand Daddy's need to escape his beloved mother, and the rest of us. He had to clear his mind of external chatter, and the distracting requirements of being in a family. Yet I continue to ponder the initial absence of affection, and the role it played in later choices. The natural craving that such an absence creates must swirl in the depths—seeking, seeking for the touch that never comes. My very private father must have suffered greatly at times; fulfillment must have been partial, regardless of blissful, transcendant highs that sprang from the making of art.

Brothers

M Y GRANDMOTHER claimed she knew the secret of having all boys. She thought she was rather too old for dealing with daughters. Peter came first, then Daddy, and finally Mac. Naturally, I knew the brothers later on. My uncle Peter was a potter with magical hands. I admired him, but his wry sense of humor was never humorous to me. Daddy, like me, was a middle child, noticeably off balance in the normal world . . . gifted, solitary, difficult. And then there was Mac.

Mac seemed to epitomize things I lacked in a father figure. He worked at a regular job and came home dependably to wife and daughters. He was accessible, and he was calm. Even his art, which he did as a matter of course with no big show, evoked a peaceful mood: the beauty and harmony to be found in everyday things. Walking into the back two rooms of the showroom put one in mind of Japanese tea rooms or Buddhist temples. Mac was safe space; a calm still center in a frequently chaotic world. In Mac's house a tired little girl could find rest on a hot summer afternoon, piled with her cousins on a roomy bed, reading Nancy Drew mysteries beneath a cooling fan.

I imagine that the obvious balance of his younger brother roused shame in my father at times. Poor daddy; such strong feelings. Unsharable feelings. And mysterious urgings toward revelatory art. It must have been hard when brotherly love would surface and tempt him to reach for someone who might understand, should understand. Intensity would have been met with a cool sort of kindness. Yet during the years beyond my brilliant father's passing, a surprising brilliancy erupted from the quiet one. The conduit seemed to expand; Mac's colors intensified. Mac's forms became bolder and slightly more abstract. They were brothers, after all.

The Barn

For MOST OF MY CHILDHOOD, we lived with my grandmother in the Barn: my mother, my brothers, my sister, and me. It really had been a barn and carriage house, which made it different from other houses. My uncle, aunt, and cousins lived in a large spacious home overlooking the water. The Barn was dark inside, though the outside shone whitely with pretty green trim. Inside, the boards of the walls were unpainted and dingy with age. Shadows were everywhere. Whatever light came in was filtered through ancient panes of glass. Upstairs was a loft.

I never thought of the Barn as Daddy's home. He lived down the road in his cottage, where azalea bushes grew tall and gangly and Cherokee roses ran wild. The vines of the roses had thorns a half inch long. There, in forbidding seclusion, he painted, living a life mostly separate from ours. He did come to visit his mother now and then, and he came to see Mama in the night. I could hear them climb the stairs to the loft, and then I tried not to hear. My grandmother made attempts to include him in family life by having strange suppers; we all sat around the table my daddy had carved and ate tuna, boiled eggs, and mayonnaise on iceburg lettuce. We sat in acute discomfort and awkward silence. The adults made efforts at conversing, but even art and books didn't ease the strain.

The soirees were more successful. My daddy sat in the glare of a hanging bulb and read from his logs. Island paintings were spread on the table for friends and family to view. Sometimes a pianist played. I remember sitting on the dusty stairs to the loft, squirming because I felt so much like dancing. I looked at my father, sitting with one leg crossed over the other, his body curved over the spiral notebook on his knee. His dimestore glasses softened his face, and he almost looked real—I mean like someone's father reading bedtime stories to his children. Drowsiness made me feel safe and sort of normal. But he never was there the next morning. It all seemed a dream.

Daddy and the Showroom

Shearwater Pottery

Unloading the Kiln

A S AN ADOLESCENT GIRL, I worked in the Shearwater Pottery showroom on weekends and after
school. The fifty cents an hour was mine to spend on
myself; it seemed a wondrous amount in those days
when my mother stretched her schoolteacher salary
over twelve months. She had to provide for a family of
five; Daddy was unto himself. I knew my father was
paid by my aunt from the showroom take. The agree-
ment was that he decorate ten pots a week for ten dollars. And often he did deliver the quota. I know
because I saw them appear in each firing. The designs
were unique to Daddy, depicting nature in swirling
evocative lines: blues and greens, or starkly dramatic
black, brown, and white. They stood out effectively
among the smoothly shining glazes of his brother's
work. But they sold slowly.

Not everyone saw what the artist realized with a few
strong strokes. I liked it when I could tell the rare person who noticed the pots about my unusual father, his
trips to Horn Island, and his love for the creatures,

birds, and waves that adorned the pots. It was quite another thing when Daddy appeared in his shabby, paint-smeared clothes with his awkward, preoccupied air. His hair might be thick with salt water. His feral animal smell made his elegant manners surprising. He slipped away quickly, leaving me disturbed—and relieved. Sometimes I found small scraps of paper scrawled in his hand: "I.O.U. $2.00. BOB" might be the message for my aunt.

One time Daddy came when a truly interested customer was inquiring about block prints. He was in a surprisingly jovial mood, glad to share his creative process; he would paint a print then and there for the customer's delight. Inspired and impulsive, he fetched his paints, laid out the print upon the floor, and proceeded with abandon to brush on color. Whether pine tree, bird, or fairy tale, I don't remember, but I do remember my father's impromptu performance before a stranger and his astonished daughter. Me!

Winter Bathing

I GREW UP ON THE COAST of Mississippi, swimming every summer in the Sound. The Sound is inland from the Gulf of Mexico; little water as opposed to the vast far-reaching waters off the islands. There are ripples instead of surf most days, inviting locals and tourists to long white beaches for harmless play. I was forbidden to swim until May, and waiting was sometimes difficult.

My daddy ignored all rules; if he felt like swimming, he swam. But he called it bathing. It could easily be on a winter day that my father set out for the marshy beach at the tip of our twenty-four acres edging the harbor. On one such day he invited me. I quickly donned my bathing suit and ran after him. How could I not? He was my father, wanting me with him. I had to try, for the sake of a longtime desire to be worthy of his companionship. But Daddy was no one's companion. And though I followed him into the icy water, and slapped my arms, as he did, to circulate blood and distract from the stinging, heart-stopping immersion, I was horrified, miserable, and ashamed of my goose-bumped skin. He laughed at my tremulous hooting, splashing, romping, and called my attention to winter-blue sky, wind-chased clouds, and small ducks cavorting nearby.

My father took pity, eventually, for he turned, walked up from the beach, and left his frozen, towel-clenching daughter at her mother's door. Whether or not he noticed my tears or my careful thank-you, he was gone. And I was alone in the bathroom, burning my legs on the little gas heater, permitting my teeth to chatter, my heart to break, my eyes to spill hotly into my cold wet hair.

Recalling that long-ago winter day (I must have been eleven or twelve), I wonder if he was seeking to recapture an earlier time, when he carried the baby Leif to the water's edge, proud of his gleeful newborn who never flinched at the rippling waters of the Sound. But Daddy, why didn't you remember? I was born in May. It was in early summer that we first bathed together. Not winter. Not winter, Daddy. Why couldn't you wait until May?

Messenger

Last night i dreamt of a painted bunting, perched in the branches of a tree I stood beneath. I admired its colors, marveled at its nearness. And it came closer, leaning its rosy feathered breast against my face. Its soft weight surprised me, but I reached one finger to stroke its small head and it nuzzled my cheek. My heart warmed and beat faster. The bird was so beautiful and trusted me. But why didn't it fly? I began to wonder if it was hurt, and left it to find my sister, who knows about birds. But she was pushing a cousin's wheelchair up a hill. I rushed back in time to save the small bird from a fascinated cat. It was tiredly hopping over the ground, and again I wondered what was wrong, why it didn't fly away. I picked up and cradled the bird in my hand. It snuggled, settled, and gazed at me. Could it want love more than flight? Rest more than bold migrations to other lands?

This dream makes me think of my father: that rare bird of brilliant color and flight. I remember him telling in his logs of his longing for a gesture of trust from a small bird, and of the bird's compliance. I think of Daddy's chosen isolation, yet he reached out for a sign of love from a fellow creature. With all of his brave adherence to the artist's path, the adventurous life, he still had moments when all he wanted was loving reassurance. And the creature came close and gave to him what he needed. He was touched and his heart was warmed. Perhaps all the world grew soft and warm, before his resolve took hold once more . . . to continue the rarified existence, mostly bereft of intimate companionship.

Do I dare suggest that my father's spirit is reaching out now to this daughter who lives in a similar isolation, perhaps to convey a valid need for close connection? Could he even be saying that constant flight, however beautiful and inspiring to others, can be exhausting? Could artistic quests be somewhat overrated? Could solitary island sojourns be escapes from what we most desire? We: my father and me. Are we both brightly painted birds in sore need of rest and signs of love?

Mary

M Y SISTER MARY is Daddy's first child, my father's other daughter. Daddy was sick when Mary was born, his mind in terrible confusion. Perhaps he was only then discovering his alien status in the world. Perhaps it was too much to bear. He was hospitalized in Baltimore, his wife ensconced in rooms nearby, when along came Mary, a round sweet-faced child, a gift of precocity and wonder, a small fiery spirit to warm the bleak hearth of her mother's existence.

Later, when Daddy was less shocked by who he was, he lived at Oldfields with Mama and Mary and Billy. He even managed to share his reality with his young children, and my sister absorbed his obsessive fascination with nature, his heart-shaking love for birds, and his need to know all there was to know of the ways of nature and the habits of birds. The long walks with Daddy, Mama, and little Billy, learning to see and to hear (Walter Anderson style) never left her. Imprinted on the little girl's impressionable mind, they continue happening in the woman's present.

I am the richer for this, for every now and then, I am privileged to walk with my sister on one of her favorite trails. Always after one of these walks, I see things more clearly, am more acutely sensitive to the charms around me: the flash of bright yellow and black in the branches above my head, the branches themselves that tell stories I might have missed, show me dances I may have forgotten. Surely my father returns to me through my dear Mary's fierce determination to live her life fully, and lately even in her passion for painting. But Mary shares; she wants me to know her vision while she is still warmly present. Mary has hugs for her little sister. For yes; I do tend to feel very small at times, in awe of Mary/Daddy. And if my heart breaks a little when she walks away, entranced by something I cannot yet see, she always returns.

Haven

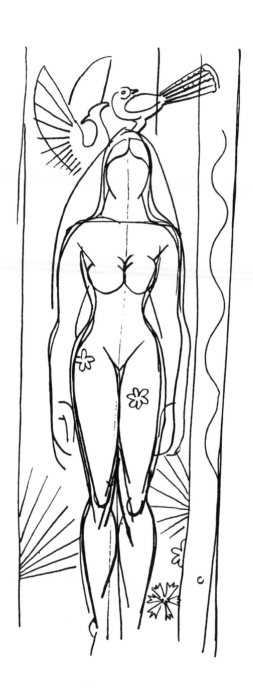

HORN ISLAND became my father's haven, the outer answer to his inner question: how can I be in this world and fulfill my deepest needs? He found his way to the strange and marvelous connection that would last a lifetime. And the island received him, welcomed him, encouraged his longing for union with what he saw. The object of his desire was nature in its purest form, miraculously untouched by the incursions of blind humanity. The Island Goddess appears to have chosen this man with his eyes wide open, all of his senses straining to realize what was before him. Here was one who, even in the heat of his partaking, never lost his awe for the revelations granted him. His patience matched his passionate need to possess—to translate, through drawing and painting, his experience.

Of course, he was tested: hard work, discomfort, and even danger are expected in an untamed environment. But the time there was also beneficial; the demons raised by struggles to comply with mainland demands could subside, rest easy as he went about the physically demanding tasks of living in the rough. Such peace came over the man as he lost himself in the beauty of a gnarled tree graced by nesting cormorants. Birds flew for his spiritual delectation. And small creatures scampered and played close to his wanderings. Dunes yielded to his explorations, allowing long grasses to part and reveal surprises for the man-child to discover. His raptures must have been worth the ravages his large form inevitably committed now and then, out of eagerness.

Daddy's existence exemplifies the human potential for islanding. My own way has been mostly internal: small excursions into the center of my ocean self. I live in the world among family, friends, and the tamer sort of creature, dogs and cats. Birds tend to remind me of my need to fly, sometimes inspiring a drawing or dance. Lately, I look to my father more frequently, almost praying for his kind of courage to enter, claim, and carry his child to an island haven of her own.

Inspiration

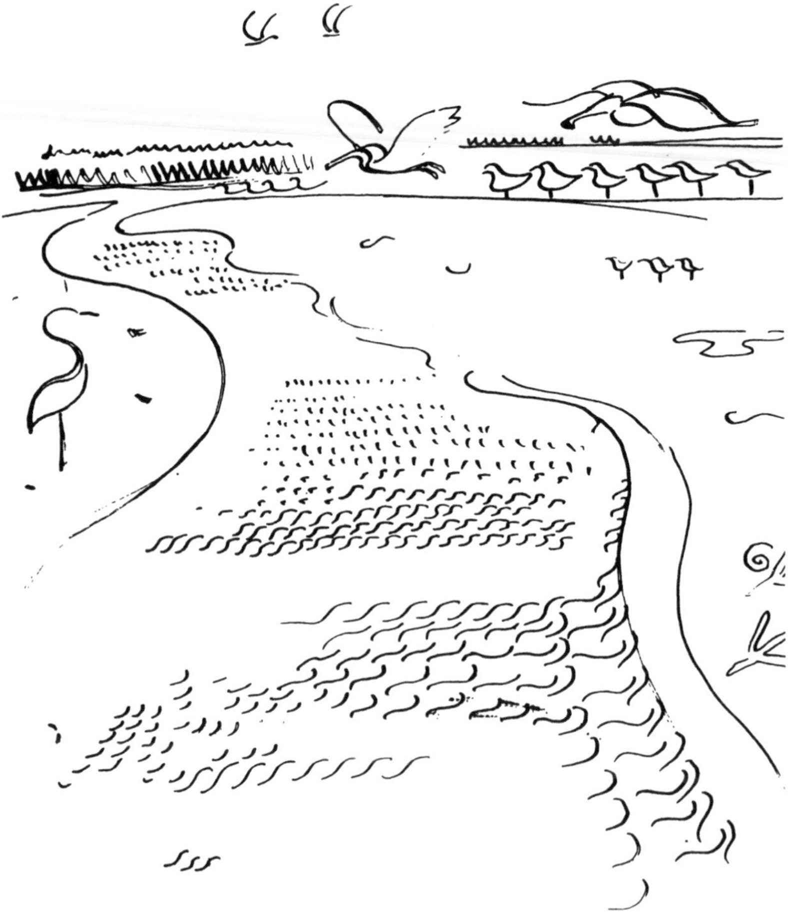

O N A WINTRY, bone-chilling morning in November, I think of my father weathering a surprising cold front on the island. Perhaps not quite prepared for penetrating winds, he huddles near a fire made up of damp drift gathered hastily. The wood smokes, causing him to cough. His nose drips, and his hands are chafed and sore. It takes some time to realize beauty on such a morning.

Does he look rather longingly toward the mainland as he sips his too hot, too sweet coffee from a jar? Does he imagine the cozy possibilities of his cottage with its flaming hearth? Does he even remember the warm soft closeness of beloved wife on a rare sweet morning of gentle conversing? Does he shake himself reproachfully, bring back reality and challenging convictions, direct his disciplined eye to the scene around him, summon the urge to paint what he sees? I can almost hear his low voice mutter: "C'mon Bobby; paradise waits; wake up and see what you see."

The mudflats attract his attention, tides sucked out

by the cold. Curious birds walk the rippled sand in search of tidbits exposed by providence. Great blues stand awkwardly poised in perfect trust; the long S curves of feathered form invite the artist's appetite for line. Small terns and pipers also beckon, and once more the islander overcomes discomfort and the pull of softer pleasures. He rises to the task, joins his chosen friends, and goes in search of his daily bread.

I, too, am drawn to mudflats exposed by harsh winds. Countless times I have walked the suddenly naked sands stretched out from familiar shorelines. Their strangeness pulls me; the secret surfaces, usually hidden by water, are like new land to explore—not forbidden, after all, to feet accustomed to plodding, repeatedly, the same terrain. Out on the flats, birds flying at my approach, I seem to breathe more freely, my lungs attaining unlimited capacity. My body lightens, restored to surprising potential. For flight? At least, for inspiration: a sense of "I am!" and "I can!" I relate to my father's courage in braving cold days with fortitude and a warm heart.

The Naming

M Y FATHER named me Leif, and challenged me to Life. I was going to be a boy, named for his favorite voyager of the moment: Leif Ericsson. Drawings of the Norseman, and his great winged serpent of a boat, littered the floor in the months leading up to my birth. Leif the Lucky, son of Eric the Red, captured my artist father's imagination, and so I was named.

My arrival in feminine form did nothing to change his decree, though Mama would stubbornly call me Leafy for my first few years. Obligingly, I danced, blown about by wayward winds, but to Daddy I was Leif, his brave explorer child, destined for new worlds. I could never choose between the two. I was drawn to wayward winds, letting them dance me into ecstatic states. But I did learn, eventually, to harness their power, merge breath with body, and purposefully dance the strange new worlds I discovered in myself.

My father's naming challenged me to continuous journeys of exploration. I never could say Leif without thinking Life. LIFE in capital letters beckons me onward, won't let me rest for long on whatever laurels I may have won. A name can become an ideal to attain, a reason to go on striving, a longing to be the soul my father recognized and named. It can even instill the courage to move beyond my origin, discover the woman who lives beyond the man, and complete the journey. True courage is of the heart, requiring love. To step out is to conquer fear by affirming love. As a woman named Leif, I embark once more, with love for the adventure.

Oldfields

THE PLACE WAS BEAUTIFUL. Perched high on a bluff overlooking an untamed shoreline, it must have been lovely to see from the water. Imagine the view from my father's skiff as he sailed slowly in from a three-week stay on Horn Island. Sunset time; a rose-gold glow over everything. He raises his eyes to the elegant house, shimmering whitely in the softening light. Green shuttered windows grace the front porch, and seem to peer out at him, causing some slight discomfort. It could be that someone is watching and waiting. His beloved Sissy, or the old man, her father. The man shakes himself, and gathers his recent experience of islanding like a protective cloak around him. He looks for and sees his children at play near the swing. The ancient oak to the left of the long, sprawling porch looms maternally; its low-hanging branches surround and nearly conceal the small bright figures. Leif, the littlest one, is watching the somewhat reckless swinging of Mary, her older sister, pushed by their brother, Billy. She turns her head, sees her father's sail and his blue-clad figure waving. He thinks he hears her outcry: Daddy! Daddy's coming! But it could be the clamoring gulls. She's pointing now, and the others come to stand beside her, mesmerized by the sight of the man, the boat, the crimson sky behind him.

Oldfields was not a negative spot for my father. After all the troublesome years, the dreadful hospitalizations, it has to have given him time to recuperate. Work in the garden was good. The farmlike environment provided subjects for painting and drawing. And beach walks, turning up Indian arrowheads and pottery, must have soothed his soul. He was very prolific in those years, and was moved to share his creative exuberance with his children. Life-sized puppets in the attic won the awed delight of his offspring, who already showed some evidence of giftedness. Mary, with her crayons. Billy, with his strange capacity for love (especially of his mother). Then Leif: I danced. It must have been very good, at times. He must have gained strength in this simple environment, been prepared for the terrible choices that would have to be made.

Walter Anderson had to leave; his wife and children

would have to suffer. And all of us would cope the best we could with the artist's need for solitude, and time to create. Sometimes I think that my father's decision made my own present life inevitable. The daughter, too, must struggle passionately with creative drives, choose paths that might be painful for those who traveled with her, love desperately and irrationally, and always leave. I learned from you, Daddy, that one has to live to the best of one's ability. And the flaw that one curses can turn out to be a blessing, enabling the gift to flourish and come to fruition. But Oldfields, Daddy, along with the image of your homecoming, will always remain for me, your littlest girl, the place where it all began.

Billy

WHEN I WAS A BABY, and Daddy still lived with us in the large plantation house on the bluff overlooking the sound, we were almost a family. I had a mother, a father, a sister, a brother, and Grandpa. We often ate meals together around the large polished table in the dining room. It was strained at times, with everyone trying too hard. Except Daddy. It wasn't in Daddy's nature to try or to lie. You always knew what was going on; his face and his actions reflected his pre-occupations. His moods were served up with the dishes of food and could end up strewn chaotically about. Hunger could turn to indigestion rapidly. Daddy was wildest nature, ridiculously unsuited to confinement.

My brother Billy has always seemed to be Daddy's opposite, and mine. Totally suited to family life: faithful, committed, dependable, absolutely devoted to wife and children. Nothing could be better than a meal with everyone gathered around. Billy, the hub of a perfect wheel. But I remember moments of intense emotion, when anger or anguish were spewing hither and yon. I have felt the effects and doubted his love. Fortunately Mama knew her oldest son from way back, knew his capacity for tenderness, and even his childish gift for noticing things that others might miss. Once when I felt bruised, sore, and unloved, my mother told me of Billy holding his tiny sister before the fireplace in one of Oldfield's vast chilly rooms. Flames danced in barely contained release, and little Billy sat mesmerized, gazing at the same flames dancing in baby Leif's eyes.

Effortlessly, my mother implanted a source of comfort that would outlast her physical presence. And she made me more willing to know my brother, to remember that he too lost a father and lived through the years of estrangement and the pretense of normalcy. He tries but he never lies. And he loves his sister, if he doesn't always recall his delight in the dancing flames.

Compensation

I N MARCH OF 1947, my brother John was born.
Daddy had left, and into our lives came Johnny, a
tiny cherubic version of his father. A treasure, a distraction, a miracle of consolation in an arid world. I
had a little brother, a friend. Yes, he was small, but I
helped my mama take care of him, told him I loved
him, and he grew. His nose grew longer, like Daddy's.
And his head was soon covered with golden curls. His
nature was mostly sweet, and we all adored him. Even
Daddy, when he rode his bicycle from Ocean Springs
for a visit, had to admire his beauty and self-assurance.

We were still at Oldfields. Grandpa Grinstead was
still alive. And Susie, large, generous, and kind, looked
after Johnny and me while Mama taught school. When
Daddy came, he was like a rapturous whirlwind, catch-
ing us up, infecting us with ecstatic energy. There was
no controlling us when Daddy was there. Mama must
have wrung her hands, knowing the effect of soaring
highs on the psyche. And she knew who would deal
with the aftermath of those joyous, wild rides on the

tail of her husband's kite. She would have to console, distract, and reassure her three fallen angels. Johnny was small, not as likely to fall. Mama was his primary influence; he was constantly bathed in the calm glow of her stability. But he looked like Daddy.

As the years go by, my brother resembles my father more; the gold in his hair has darkened, his features grown craggy. And he sports a Horn Island beard. He is even at home on the island, guiding others that they may love nature in a Walterly way. Yet wise providence still endows him with his mother's soft charm, her quiet assertion. Have I mentioned that my brother John dances with me at the slightest invitation? I reach my hand, and he merges most mysteriously with his sister's cavorting. Unreserved in his loving support of the flights of my body, he accompanies my ecstasy as my father might, yet grounds and stabilizes like my mama. And I am blessed by knowing that though I may sometimes feel loss, nothing is lost.

Community Center

THE MURALS were painted when I was ten. Often, when Daddy was painting, I was present. This was because I took dance in the large spacious room. Once a week I practiced my pliés, piqué turns, and leaps with the other little girls. Daddy would be on a ladder in his usual messy attire. His odd-shaped hat would be on his head, and often a cigarette hung from his lip. He worked absorbedly, plying his brush with incautious energy. Paint splashed about as the murals took form. He seemed unconcerned, unaware of all but the inevitability of his design.

I wasn't comfortable, having him there; it heightened my self-consciousness. I couldn't forget his presence, couldn't help peeking over at him, as I waited in line to do arabesques across the floor. I never saw him looking in my direction. Was he even aware that I was there? Did he know that his younger daughter worked with passionate devotion to perfect her art? Like her father? It was probably good that he did not see how awkward I was in those classes. He had painted me when I felt more free, more one with nature, and more me. He must have known who I was, underneath the ballet facade. Perhaps we had a secret understanding, but all the stuff of living obscured the truth.

After I left the ballet behind me, after my father had died, I may have become the dancer he knew me to be. For I rediscovered the spacious room, performed there, and even taught children that they could dance birds in flight, flowers blooming, and setting suns. His murals must have guided, inspired, and encouraged our gestures. And many times since I have stood before his dallying eagles and been born anew as dancing daughter of Walter, no longer self-conscious or unsure, but strong in the knowledge of mysterious partnership. In these later years, when I walk into the glory he created, I can sometimes see his ladder still standing across the room. Only now, my father descends, and we dance as one.

Remembering Fairyland

ACROSS THE ROAD from my father's house is a small untamed woodland known as Fairyland. I don't know how it came by its name. As a child I simply accepted that it was there: a place of mysterious beauty, and the abode of fairies. I played there with siblings, cousins, and special friends. My brothers tended to build forts or private clubhouses, or to swing upon thick trailing vines, a la Tarzan. I wasn't above an occasional Jane-like swing, but for me the aura of mystery was foremost. I knew they were there, hiding and watching, possibly hoping, as I was, for contact. Picnics in Fairyland always evolved into carefully laid out feasts for the unseen inhabitants; tables of bark were set with acorn cups and dried leaf plates to hold drops of lemonade and sandwich crumbs. Our senses alive with possibility, we basked in the sunlight filtering through the tall pines.

Yes, life was delicious in Fairyland. It was freedom in the truest sense of the word; nature as refuge, inspiration, and an expanded sense of self. And at its edge lived its guardian, or ogre . . . depending on the tone of the day. Even then we knew that Bob Anderson had preeminence over such a realm. Any sort of wilderness was his domain. So, on those days when we had thoroughly absorbed the ambiance, we dared to approach him. One day, encountering a large, strangely patterned snake, we informed the man who rather resembled the creature in skittish fearful beauty. I remember him kindly emerging from his lair to identify (perhaps to protect) the snake. He stroked its scaley back, tolerated our squeamish laughter, then stood back to watch it slither away.

I live now in those woods that inspired my childhood years. The cottage where Daddy lived is visible through the trees and thickly grown underbrush guarding my home. It holds less mystery these days, as does this tract of land. Yet, I do still think of it as Fairyland, and wonder at inexplicable happenings. So I lead my grandchildren into its sun-dappled depths, encouraging their belief in fairies. I can only tell them of their great-grandfather's fearlessness. I shall never pet snakes!

Mama's Gift

I never knew that my mother loved my father until he was gone. His presence had been so peripheral, and she so private about her feelings. Any intimacy they shared tended toward furtive, half-secret meetings that we were not meant to know about. When I think of it now, it seemed an unhealthy way of doing things, bound to instill in their children a sense of shame: there must be something wrong if they never touched one another openly. Why would parents hide their love if it was really love, and not some fearful thing that might be harmful for us to witness? Some things were fearful, but surely not all.

Surely not all . . . I know this now. For my daddy's passing seemed to release my mother from years of containment. Her admiration and almost worshipful love were allowed to bloom as time went by. She called him forth in poems reminiscent of Rumi's ecstatic phrases. He appeared to her as she walked on the beach of his beloved island. Every bird cry, every sunlit tree, every fragrance carried on every breeze brought him closer and made him more worthy of her revealing, even to us. Mostly through creative outlets. She and I shared our writings through letters, for I was frequently far away, pursuing my dance. This was a means through which we shared surprisingly personal things. Poems transformed, so secrets could be revealed artistically, acceptably.

Gradually, I came to know my mama, was let to see the woman who felt so deeply that when she finally formed those feelings into words, she sang. And mostly, she sang of her lover: her partner in life. When I read her book, *Approaching the Magic Hour*, I wept at the realization that my parents were truly in love. How could I not have known? Here were her brave revealings of their relationship. Their whole relationship: nothing hidden anymore. The hard things were equally worthy to be told, their love more apparent through the telling. And we are there! The children! We are part of their magic hour, too. And all is well.

Immortalized

CHILDHOOD SUMMERS at Shearwater could be heavenly in tone. With my siblings and cousins, I basked in the long free days, and the heat. We took numerous dips in the cool salt water bordered by marsh grass. I remember hours of make-believe, acting out stories we loved. It might be Robin Hood, my brother's favorite. My preference was Peter Pan. The secluded beach was conducive to mermaid scenes. The water lent buoyancy to imagined tails and long flowing hair. The lost boys were always going off with Peter in search of Captain Hook. We frolicked and forgot them, and were startled to see a hatted figure approaching. It wasn't Hook; it was Bob, my daddy. And he carried his clipboard of paper, pencil, and paints. We were the ones who were lost—or found, as the case may be. We were at his mercy . . . for a while.

My father found us when he wanted to. Sometimes we were flattered, enlarging upon our importance to his work. But other times, we couldn't wait to escape. Staying in the hammock past the period when it felt like a pirate ship made us uneasy. And we got hungry, perched in the oak tree near our cousins' house, our small supply of dewberries dwindling. He captured us as we set out in pirogues to explore the harbor. There's a painting in which I look like an Indian maiden, wielding the paddle, straightbacked and proud. Sometimes we were rewarded with sour lemonade, and sometimes he asked me to pose (just me), and later brought me a box of Elmer's Fiddlers. The candy was far more appreciated than the lemonade.

I am now aware that many of those summer paintings burned on his hearth. But a few still exist and remind me of a special time. The freedom and pleasure of childish play is quickly evoked by a glance at those renderings. The girl whose father seemed hardly a father returns as I look, and she tells me to see what the artist saw, and be glad.

Wings

I HAVE EXPERIENCED the wonders of Horn Island. As a child, I was carried out among cousins on my uncle Peter's boat: a wonderful, home-built, raggle-taggle sort of boat, used for shrimping, fishing, and family outings. Its bow was my favorite spot to sit; poised above waves, I could see forever. I loved the salt spray cooling my skin, and I loved the wind that blew everything ordinary back toward the mainland. One felt clean and new by the time one reached the island.

I knew it as my father's special place, but we never saw him while we were there. We children would play in the fresh green surf, or search the beach for unusual shells. I thought angel shells were the very most beautiful shell in the world. As large as my hand, wing-shaped, they were white, crisscrossed with a feathery pattern, and conjured up heavenly feelings when I held them to the sun so the light shone through. They were fragile, easily broken, and I may have identified with this aspect of the shell. The hard-packed sand at the water's edge was fine for dancing; waves made a musical accompaniment like none other.

On these trips, I must have realized a little of what drew my father seaward again and again. Freedom lived in the atmosphere; you breathed it in and couldn't help doing what you loved the most: dancing for me, and painting for Daddy. I can see my daddy striding the beach, or drawing among the sea oats and dunes: leaning his back against warm rough pine bark, inhaling beauty and letting it flow onto paper. The sky feels close, and the birds. It is all so uncluttered and pure.

As it came time to leave, I might pull on one of Daddy's block-printed dresses over my damp bathing suit. Designed by Daddy, sewn by Mama, printed with simple motifs, they had tiny wings. These dresses from Oldfields days became shirts as I grew, but they never lost their magical effect. Nor has my father's island.

Grounded

Feb – 22.

CREATIVES have reputations for floating in unreality. It's true that what they espouse hints of magic and mystery, having little to do with what the larger world calls real. People like Daddy are labeled "hermit," "madman," "eccentric." Because they don't live as others live, or accept the routine that makes the world go round, they are blamed, ridiculed, barely accepted as members of society. They are driven, as Daddy was, to greater extremes and further isolation, and rarely helped to do what they are born to do. Some do it anyway, and anyone who doubts the groundedness necessary for such a life should try it. To face each day supported, not by the dictates of a reliable outer framework, but by a chosen obedience to an inner necessity, one has to have one's feet on the ground. Walter Anderson did this, maintaining this reality for most of his lifetime.

I am my father's daughter, and though I may have more contact with "reality," I think I know something of the discipline required to enter the arena of mystery, where rewards seem intangible and are often slow to come. Transcendant bliss is not an everyday affair; one keeps on keeping on. It is a job done out of commitment to something not easily grasped. Yet it requires motivation, and the use of physical tools to suit the art form. Tools require maintenance and replenishing, require venturing into normalcy and risking distraction. Then one must find one's way back home, reacclimate to solitude, and regain focus. This can take days. And doubts can assail before strength of will and devotion of soul can mesh again with the purpose of creating. Then the fragile moment comes when the brush approaches and finds the paper ready to receive. I know what it takes to carry on, what it means to see an image reflect something deeply true. Then a quiet joy can arise from a job well done. My own experience tells me these things, but my father comes to me in such moments and tells me it's worth the effort. The smidgeons of satisfaction, the tiny islands of realization, the briefest awareness of the harmonious whole. These are reward enough.

Final Journey

IN 1965, my father weathered a hurricane on Horn Island. (Mama said later he'd always wanted to.) The early fall storm came late in the season; Betsy surprised us. And Daddy, enjoying monarch butterflies and goldenrod in paradise, welcomed the sky's sudden shift from intense autumn blue to white-gray expectancy. Here was his chance. He raced with the winds, did battle with pelting rains, and managed to move his camp to high ground. Finding a sturdy and willing pine, he tied himself securely for the duration.

None of us could imagine what Daddy experienced during those raging hours, whether he was exhilarated or terrified. We only knew that he stayed with the storm, and survived. A waking must have occurred as the fierceness subsided. Drenched and exhausted, loosed from his ties to stand on shaky legs, the islander must have seen unspeakable turmoil. His beloved was ravaged: sand torn from her side, trees ripped from her breast, debris strewn indiscriminately over her surface.

Dead birds, too. And small mammals. His friends. His Goddess would never be the same. Nor would he.

My father was ill; cancer was wreaking havoc on his lungs. He tended to discount physical pain and so had ignored the twinges he suffered when lifting heavy objects. But after Betsy, back at Shearwater, he couldn't deny the torturing cough, the blood. On a Sunday morning in mid-November, he knocked on the door of his former studio, where I lived with Mama; I was expecting my firstborn child. Hidden, I heard him tell Mama he needed a doctor. After that, his decline was rapid.

On November 15, my beautiful Moira arrived, and initiation into motherhood eclipsed my father's passing. Ensconced in a state of blissful adoration, I missed the funeral. Even Mama's grief was lost on me. I recall her quietly rocking the baby, tunelessly singing, and, behind her, Daddy's painted saints, weathered as the boards of the walls were weathered. The saints endure, and my father has to be smiling, amused at the way life goes on happening, while he is free.

Morning

M Y MOTHER RAISED ME to lift myself up, to look for the bright possibility in all situations. She wouldn't let me sink to the lowest ebb. She conditioned me, and I took up where she left off. Yet all the fairy stories and great-dancer dreams would never erase the fact that my father left, and though he came back he would never *be* back. I could re-create him by making beauty and idolizing nature. I could romanticize our original connection. But my truthful subconscious repeatedly told me how I felt about my father. The cries of a small child continue to echo in my psyche, calling her daddy to come and telling him go away. The constant hope that I'll meet him around the corner, and the fear of that meeting, are one with my existence. It is part of what makes me who I am. But . . .

How can I find a way to mourn my father's passing? He keeps returning. Even death cannot be believed in. He left all this glorious art behind him: the art that he loved more than me. And people who didn't know Daddy fall in love with him through his art. They get to love him as I wasn't allowed to do. It seems cruel, and I'm sometimes mixed up in response to all this. So now I tell stories, and truth emerges from my memories. I share my daddy's humanness with the world, and even partake of the love the world holds for my father. But how can I mourn?

To be honest, some mourning comes from the telling of this. The heart softens, stretches, and opens; moisture comes to the soul. I am what I am. Perhaps this is what needs saying. Nothing can distract from my father's genius, or from the world's readiness for what he left behind. Possibly, even the hard things will be welcomed. On this earth there are shadows lurking among bright splashes of light. Contrast beguiles. Dear Daddy, if I hate you for making me love you so frightfully much, I love you for bequeathing me feelings so tautly clear, and intense. Maturity teaches me, through my tears, that morning sometimes brings mourning. And mourning can lead one forth into a whole new day.

Evening

RAIN DROPS FROM THE SKIES in a soothingly delicate rhythm. I am all smoothed out inside, blessedly clean from my day of solitude. And thankful. I am able to see my life in an undistracted way. No stressful confusion or eagerness to please mars my vision. Strange to know this as evening darkness obscures the world. Strange to see beauty expansively with my mind's eye. I realize the trees are yet standing around my house; their green still holds true, and their silvery forms in naked relief. It is winter, after all, with minimal evidence of growth. But the rain seeps thoroughly into their earthbound roots, cleansing and easing the hold of the earth a little. I somehow feel what the trees are feeling. Like toes, the tender endings of deep-born roots wriggle happily into the moist wet ground. I know the relief that comes with the rain.

My father wrote: "Beauty is born of the rain." And if I had not been born of my father, would I know beauty so well? Could I sense so strongly the tree's experience, identify with nature's joy? I think not. I continue my father's relationship with the natural world, as though I am rooted in his awareness. I cannot escape the fact of his choosing to merge with the earth that bore him. I embody that merging, even as his other creations embody that merging. If I sometimes forget, in my eagerness to belong among fellow humans, I am always reminded. Mystery finds me as certainly as my father might if he chose to visit his daughter and calm her questing.

His coming would be as delicate as this present moment. Spirit would mix with rain, or with tears, and still my frustrations. He would bring me to listen to whisperings softer than that of the rain outside, until I heard the message of infinite love. It would be the same voice that breathes patience into the trunks of trees as they grow. And I would grow patient, like a tree, and know it was he.

Artifacts

Objects found at Graveline
April. 28.

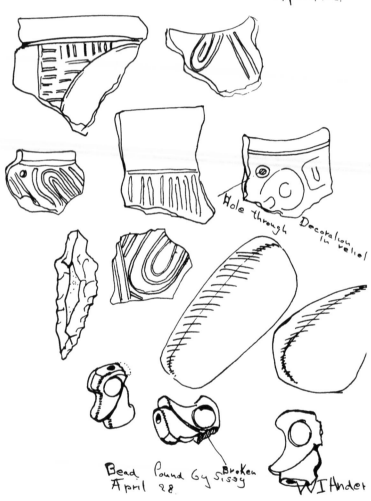

Hole through

Decoration in relief

Bead found
April 28.

found by sissy

Broken

WI Ander

ARTIFACTS? I prefer to call them mementos: objects picked up by my father over many years of island sojourns, brought home and cherished as reminders of a place so loved. He lived among the shells, bones, and other oddities that caught his eye, that stirred his heart with awareness of some creature lost. No more bright life to startle the eye, yet his love for them still enlivened the brush, the paint, the artist's task.

Remnants of what has been engage the imagination, bring the human psyche to a state of awed familiarity. We take possession, forgetting that life coursed here. Walter Anderson walked on the floors of his house, lovingly placed the beautifully patterned shell, the stone crab claw, the bottle transformed by the sun's harsh rays into glowing newness. Found objects, recycled through still lifes, were blessed by the artist's gaze and his reverent handling, then finally left behind when he closed the door of his cottage for the last time.

Over the thirty-eight years since his death, I have

opened the door countless times, walked into my father's private domain as though I belonged, as I never did during his lifetime. The mementos reside there, amazingly comforting to a daughter who slowly comes to know her father. I am less disturbed by the life mask hanging on the wall. The plaster features are almost welcoming, as I look for the living man among his artifacts, and find my father.

And my son. For my bright-eyed laughing Vanja lives in the cottage now, greeting my approach with open-armed delight. His black-and-white cat wanders out in hopes of a little extra food. And Christmas lights are strung in December. A garden stands in a clearing among the azaleas. The Cherokee roses are only a memory; no more thorns.

The Present

THE WALTER ANDERSON MUSEUM OF ART is dedicated to my father's memory, designed especially to house and display his lifework. The low gray building is elegantly placed at the center of Ocean Springs, adjacent to and joined to the Community Center, where his once-reviled murals can be viewed. The large room continues to be utilized for community functions.

The museum is lovely and practical, designed by Ed Pickard to let the light in judiciously. Exhibits shift, but a plentiful amount of my father's art is always displayed. The effect is exquisite. The art, and the natural world it evokes, radiates from the walls, inducing a state of quietude and reverie. One is slowly prepared for entry into the little room. Walter Anderson's day is encapsulated in this small space: morning, midday, afternoon, and night are blended into an indivisible wholeness. The visitor, standing at the center, becomes creator and creation, if so willing.

My experience of the little room is uncanny. I feel

that I have known this room forever, have never not been allowed to enter this magical realm; it is imprinted on me. The element of secrecy (his padlocked door) seems ridiculous now. I am at home in this celebration of life and light, knowing intimately every animal, flower, insect, and bird. I see the brilliant violets, greens, blues, reds, and yellows wherever I am. The mere thought of my father's little room brings to mind its vibrancy. The frolic of goats, slinking of cats, opening of morning glories, and waking of moths can never be fully absent from my consciousness. If I strive to shut it out at times, as I once did Daddy, my father's vision calls to me in my father's voice; calls me to embrace and be embraced by this legacy of love and beauty.

This embracing must be inclusive of all things associated with the living, growing world still springing from the artist's soul. Perhaps, especially, the people, and what the people are bringing about in Daddy's name. Miracles still occur because my sister, Mary, curator for many years, saw what was possible, and worked tirelessly toward a mysterious goal. Finally the momentum was such that she said bon voyage, and turned toward her own desire to paint and write. Now many are involved: family members, those employed by the family, and the large staff at the Walter Anderson Museum of Art. For one who was driven to escape his human family, Daddy has had a strangely unifying affect on all of us. For me it can be a positively familial experience to enter the museum on Washington Avenue. The atmosphere tends toward warmth and conviviality. And I am always welcome in my father's new home.

Motif

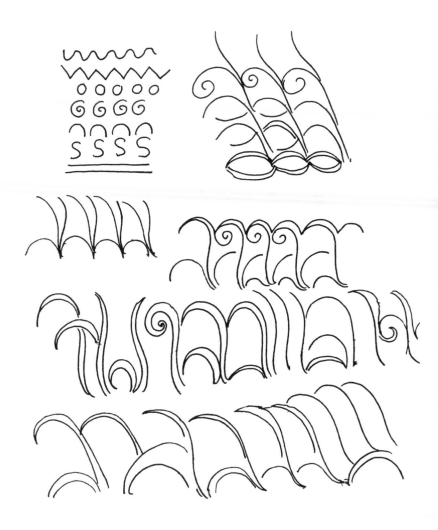

I THINK THAT MY father's favorite motif was the spiral: the point become line that circles, opens, and evolves to infinity. You can hold a spiraled shell in the palm of your hand, but you cannot stop the spiral from unfolding. By its very nature, it tells of more to come; it is unending.

I see this happening as the centennial celebration of my father's birth moves beyond his birth date. The effect put in motion by the Smithsonian Institution exhibit that opened in September 2003 travels on, even as the exhibit travels on to other museums and galleries. Awareness increases. It is evident in the written comments of visitors to the exhibit. To quote my father's words, which gave the Smithsonian show its title: "Everything I see is new and strange." First-time viewers of Walter Anderson's works often say: I have never seen anything like this. This is so new to me. This artist. Where did he come from? Well . . . I say that he came from the center of his favorite motif. And the people who exclaim and wonder are standing at a new place on the spiral's path.

As am I. My father seems to dance before me, tantalizing, beckoning, inviting with open arms. Open! Never closing, stopping, staying, or obstructing. His invitation is completely spacious, infinite and unformed. I may dance, unpressured by what has come before. I may dance new worlds into being, if I like. The way is open. For my father is a spiral, and so am I.

Books on the life and work of Walter Anderson (all from the University Press of Mississippi): *Approaching the Magic Hour: Memories of Walter Anderson*, by Agnes Grinstead Anderson, 1989; *The Art of Walter Anderson*, edited by Patricia Pinson, 2003; *Birds*, by Walter Anderson, with an introduction by Mary Anderson Pickard, 1990; *Fortune's Favorite Child: The Uneasy Life of Walter Anderson*, by Christopher Maurer, 2003; *The Horn Island Logs of Walter Inglis Anderson*, edited and with an introduction by Redding S. Sugg, Jr., 1990; *A Painter's Psalm: The Mural from Walter Anderson's Cottage*, art by Walter Anderson, text by Redding S. Sugg, Jr., rev. ed. 1992; *A Symphony of Animals*, by Walter Anderson, with an introduction by Mary Anderson Pickard, 1996; *Walls of Light*, by Anne R. King, 1999.

CLATE MASK

CONQUER

THE

CHAOS

The **Six Keys** to Success for Entrepreneurs

SECOND EDITION

WILEY

Published by John Wiley & Sons, Inc., Hoboken, New Jersey.
Published simultaneously in Canada.

For general information on our other products and services or for technical support, please contact our Customer Care Department within the United States at (800) 762-2974, outside the United States at (317) 572-3993 or fax (317) 572-4002.

Wiley also publishes its books in a variety of electronic formats. Some content that appears in print may not be available in electronic formats. For more information about Wiley products, visit our web site at www.wiley.com.

Library of Congress Cataloging-in-Publication Data

Names: Mask, Clate, author. | John Wiley & Sons, publisher.
Title: Conquer the chaos : the six keys to success for entrepreneurs / Clate Mask.
Description: Second edition. | Hoboken, New Jersey : Wiley, [2024] |
   Includes index.
Identifiers: LCCN 2023047938 (print) | LCCN 2023047939 (ebook) | ISBN
   9781394217380 (hardback) | ISBN 9781394217403 (adobe pdf) | ISBN
   9781394217397 (epub)
Subjects: LCSH: Small business—Management. | Small business—Growth. |
   Success in business. | Strategic planning.
Classification: LCC HD62.7 .M3797 2024 (print) | LCC HD62.7 (ebook) | DDC
   658.4/06—dc23/eng/20231207
LC record available at https://lccn.loc.gov/2023047938
LC ebook record available at https://lccn.loc.gov/2023047939

Cover Design: Wiley
Cover Image: © Dimitris66/Getty Images
Author Photo: © Allie Renee Photography

SKY10064695_011224

To Charisse and our kids, who have seen the ups and downs of entrepreneurship as we have lived it together, every step of the way. I love you guys and I love living our family Mission together. Keep going, keep serving, keep growing.

CONTENTS

FOREWORD

There is nothing more inspiring than sharing a well-told story of transformation. Especially when it's written by the ones who experienced it as this book describes. And most especially when the transformation of the ones who experienced it led to the transformation of hundreds of thousands who benefited from participating in the outcome of that story.

This book is about such a transformation. The story of Keap.

I'm Michael E. Gerber, creator of the E-Myth and author of the E-Myth books—now 34 strong.

I met Clate Mask years ago, when Keap was Infusionsoft. He and his partners had come to a point in their company and their lives when the question was not only what to do, but should we?

In short, the chaos Clate speaks about here had turned into doubt. Doubt about whether their original idea was worth pursuing any longer. I've seen that doubt in the faces of literally tens of thousands of clients of ours at Michael E. Gerber Companies and E-Myth Worldwide. Not only a state of chaos, but a state of confusion—confusion that puts everything into serious question.

It was just that state that I saw in Clate and his partners when we met. Are we in the right business? Are we doing the right things? Are we really up to this job we've created for ourselves? Is it really worth all the trouble?

I invited them and their senior managers to join me in The Dreaming Room™.

I remember their faces when they were done. It's astonishing when a Dream comes alive in one's day-to-day experience. Clarified with a Vision, a Purpose, a Mission. It was astonishing to see the dramatic shift in Clate's state of being, and his partners' as well.

What had brought them together to found Infusionsoft had, in only a few intense days in The Dreaming Room™, amalgamated into a new, visceral understanding that, lost in the chaos, now had somehow become clear, vital, renewing.

They told me as such when we met later on.

It wasn't as though they had discovered something that wasn't there, in Infusionsoft, before—it was that, in the chaos, they'd simply forgotten it.

In The Dreaming Room™, they told me, they remembered it. They remembered why they'd become entrepreneurs. They remembered how it felt there, at the beginning, The extreme joy of it. The extreme delight of going out on their own. The immense pleasure they shared in creating the future, of designing a business to transform the lives of small business owners, to provide their clients with the experience they themselves were living, through the technology they'd been applying so originally, so well.

It was that vitality I saw in Clate's eyes as he spoke to me about what they thought of as the new Infusionsoft. It is that vitality you'll see in Clate's story as you come face to face with your own, as you read what follows here, as you come face to face with your business's reality. As you come face to face with the truth underlying the reason you created your company perhaps not that long ago. And yes, the chaos. And the chaos that clouds it up. And the confusion that comes from that chaos.

It's not only that inevitable confusion that Clate describes so well in this book, but also the intense joy that comes from seeing through it.

There's nothing like a truly great book, I say. Enjoy what follows, because you're reading it!

—Michael E. Gerber

PREFACE

About 14 years ago, we wrote *Conquer the Chaos* to teach small business owners how to grow a successful small business without going crazy. The book was a *New York Times* bestseller, and entrepreneurs all over the world told us how much it helped them. We shared it with our customers and used it as the foundation of what we teach to entrepreneurs. Our company grew to over $100 million in annual sales, with over a hundred thousand users and 2,000 partners who teach and serve our customers. And yet for all the success of the first edition, it was incomplete. Furthermore, some of those original strategies have morphed and needed to be updated as the world changed.

And a lot has changed in 14 years. Digital marketing has become a necessary part of small business success. Work-life balance is completely different in the new world, with COVID rewriting the rules entirely. And yet work-life balance is actually *tougher* for entrepreneurs today than it was 14 years ago. In addition to the market changes, we've learned so much from serving entrepreneurs at Keap. Our methods have evolved. Our products have evolved. Automation has evolved. And now AI is changing everything.

Small business owners need the revised edition of *Conquer the Chaos* now more than ever. The world has become so chaotic. It is incredibly challenging to grow a successful business when the business dominates your life. The Lifecycle Automation method we've pioneered has been a total game changer for small businesses. The work-life balance techniques are critical for balanced growth, with business *and* personal success. The Leadership section comes from years of practicing and teaching a model that creates great results in great places to work. I'm excited to share important updates to the book that will be appreciated by original readers and new readers alike.

This is no minor revision. The six strategies from the first edition have been reworked into the Six Keys to Success. There is more emphasis on the execution of the entrepreneur's life plan and how it ties together with the business strategy. The revised edition is more practical, more concrete, and more balanced in its approach to business and personal success for entrepreneurs. It is born out of lessons learned working with entrepreneurs for another 14 years since my co-founder and I wrote *Conquer the Chaos*.

Speaking of my co-founder, Scott Martineau has taken a product role at Keap so he can focus exclusively on product development for our customers. That's his passion. He liked the idea of a revised edition and he liked even more the idea of not having to co-write it. He fully supports the Six Keys shared in the book. Scott continues to be a great business partner and friend.

I should also note that Scott's brother, Eric, the other co-founder of our business, is back at Keap, after leaving the business for a tumultuous season. Such are the ups and downs of entrepreneurship. It's great to have Scott and Eric doing what they love at Keap: building game-changing—no, life-changing—products for entrepreneurs and their teams.

The bottom line is, since we wrote *Conquer the Chaos* about 14 years ago, we've had a lot of experience with the Six Keys to Success. We've never put together all Six Keys and taught them succinctly in one place. We've practiced them ourselves and we've worked with our customers doing the same. We have observed *what* works and *why* it works. As we've studied and practiced the Six Keys to Success, we have refined them and distilled them into actionable steps all entrepreneurs can take to improve their business and personal life. We are so excited to share these powerful keys with you.

HOW THIS BOOK WILL LEAD YOU TO SUCCESS

This book does not contain stuffy research or theoretical models that only make sense in a classroom. Each of the Six Keys to Success is based on real-life entrepreneurship, with practical examples and stories from over two decades of living and teaching this stuff. We live and prove the Six Keys to Success every day, as do our customers and entrepreneurs everywhere, sometimes almost accidentally. Sure, we stumble at times and lose our edge with one Key or another. But we are practitioners of the Six Keys to Success. And we have experienced and seen more than enough results to know these keys work for those who use them to unlock business and personal success.

In Part 1, "The Entrepreneur's Quest for Success," the first three chapters present the real story of small business ownership. They include the fear, the pain, the ego, the overwhelm and the emotional struggle. They also include the thrill, rewards, and triumph of small business ownership. In Chapter 1, "The Entrepreneurial Revolution," you'll learn why millions of individuals choose to become entrepreneurs, even though they might know the struggles they'll soon experience.

Chapter 2 lays out the entrepreneur's "Quest for Success." You'll learn about the Hierarchy of Success, the real definition of success for entrepreneurs, and the stages of small business growth.

In Chapter 3, you'll learn what small business chaos is, why it happens, and how it can block our success or even destroy us as entrepreneurs. We'll cover "The Dark Side of Entrepreneurship" and how it shows up in the extreme, as well as the more subtle ways it affects us if we're not careful. You'll come to realize we can and must conquer the chaos to achieve the success we want as entrepreneurs and we'll introduce the way to do it: the Six Keys to Success for Entrepreneurs.

In Part 2, Chapters 4 through 6 cover "The Personal Keys to Success." In Chapter 4, we dive into "Mindset"—the one that entrepreneurs must cultivate to win. This is the mental stamina and emotional capital entrepreneurs need to rise above the chaos and discouragement that are commonplace in entrepreneurship. Successful entrepreneurs are intentional about protecting their mindset and fueling their positive energy so they can achieve peak performance.

Chapter 5 covers "Vision." But we're not talking about the business vision. Here, we're talking about the personal vision entrepreneurs need, the Life Vision that provides meaning and direction to your business pursuits. Building a small business is incredibly demanding. Without a clear Life Vision, the chaos of the business will almost certainly knock your priorities out of whack. Your Life Vision enables you to build a business that serves others while protecting what matters most and propelling you to achieve your most exciting business and personal goals.

Chapter 6 is about "Rhythm," which rounds out and ties together the three Personal Keys to Success for entrepreneurs. One of the amazing things about entrepreneurship is the "lab for life" the business provides to help you become your best self. This key is about creating a natural and exciting flow in your daily, weekly, monthly, quarterly, and annual execution, which ties into your Life Vision, to help you become your best self.

In Part 3, "The Business Keys to Success," Chapters 7 through 9 explore the Business Keys to Success, starting with "Strategy." Most small businesses start with big goals and dreams, but the daily grind of running a business can douse the flames or diffuse their efforts across too many "priorities." Successful entrepreneurs have a way of doing the right things at the right time instead of constantly running their business in a reactive, firefighting mode. They know what to say no to. In this chapter, you'll learn how to set your Company Strategy and your Customer Strategy so you can proactively build a successful business.

In Chapter 8, we hit "Automation," which is the big time-saver that unlocks the ability to grow the business and maintain an enjoyable lifestyle. As I always say, "The fortune is in the follow-up." Lifecycle Automation (LCA) is a proven method for automating the follow-up process in your Customer Strategy so you can grow sales and save time. Simply put, it's a systematic way to get and keep customers by creating great business relationships. LCA is the great game-changer for small businesses, making it possible to get off the "trading-hours-for-dollars" hamster wheel and build a profitable, enjoyable business that brings balance to your life through the power of automation.

In Chapter 9, we cover "Leadership," which makes it possible for entrepreneurs to have great impact and freedom and achieve their highest goals. Many entrepreneurs want to keep the business small because they don't want to lead a team of people. But that limits their income and impact. The truth is, leading your team to achieve a shared vision for the business is a skill any entrepreneur can learn. And when successful business owners learn how to go "from entrepreneur to CEO," their success and freedom soar.

In Part 4, "Putting the Keys into Practice," Chapters 10 and 11 show you how to put into practice the Six Keys to create sustainable success. These chapters focus on how to implement the Six Keys, with proven tips and tricks to "keep going, keep serving, and keep growing."

In these Six Keys to Success for busy entrepreneurs, you will discover there is a better, more productive way to run your business. You'll learn that balanced growth really is possible. And you'll discover that by implementing these Six Keys, you can conquer the chaos, making it possible to find the time, money, control, impact, and freedom to live life on your terms. That's the joy of being an entrepreneur. Let's get started!

Part 1

THE ENTREPRENEUR'S QUEST
FOR SUCCESS

"The difference between the great and good societies and the regressing, deteriorating societies is largely in terms of the entrepreneurial opportunity and the number of such people in the society. I think everyone would agree that the most valuable 100 people to bring into a deteriorating society would be not 100 chemists, or politicians, or professors, or engineers, but rather 100 entrepreneurs."

–Abraham Maslow

1
THE ENTREPRENEURIAL REVOLUTION

Mike Callahan is a great entrepreneur. Right out of high school, he started a landscaping business and poured his heart and soul into it. After the normal struggles in the early stages of any business, he began to produce income at levels his friends and family envied. His business was succeeding by all accounts. Soon he married his girlfriend and life was going great.

As the business grew, it demanded more and more of Mike. Not just his time—it demanded his energy, creativity, and passion. He was happily growing the business, feeling a rush of excitement that's hard to describe if you haven't started a business that's succeeding. Most people have no idea what it's like to pour their energy, their finances, and their very identity into a business that struggles early on, starts to show promise, and then produces the cash and satisfaction the entrepreneur always hoped for. It is thrilling!

Mike was living the entrepreneur's dream. But things were out of balance at home. His wife was feeling neglected. So Mike did what most entrepreneurs do when wearing many hats in the business and running a juggling act in their personal lives. Mike did his best to be there for his wife as the business continued to grow. And yet important events were slipping. Little moments and opportunities were lost. Life was all about the business. Hobbies, friends, and personal interests had faded to the background. And Mike's marriage was going downhill.

On Valentine's Day, Mike got the devastating news. His wife was done. She was leaving him, feeling betrayed by Mike and the business he loved. No amount of apology would change her mind. They got divorced, both of their hearts broken by the growing and successful business that was taking more of Mike's time and energy than he ever anticipated.

Unfortunately, Mike's story is not unique. More and more people are drawn to entrepreneurship, as we will discuss in this chapter. They pour their blood, sweat, and tears into creating a successful business. Meanwhile, they are juggling all the responsibilities in their personal lives, trying their best to make it all work.

For some, their *struggling* business is overwhelming them, causing them to feel trapped and controlled by the business. For others, their *successful* business is almost an addiction, seducing them to spend every possible moment on the business. Most entrepreneurs are somewhere in between the struggling and successful ends of the spectrum. Nearly all feel like there aren't enough hours in the day. And so they make trade-offs and sacrifices that flirt dangerously with their health, relationships, and other personal priorities.

There is a better way. This book is about building a great business and a great life, in a balanced way. Too many of us entrepreneurs get caught up in the pursuit of success. And let's be clear: the success is so fun and exciting! And the struggles are demanding and unavoidable. Which is why we entrepreneurs need a guidebook to navigate the Quest for Success.

After 20 years of living it, observing it, and coaching it, this is my heartfelt attempt to guide entrepreneurs through it. If one entrepreneur reads this book and is helped by it, this book will be worth it. My hope is that many will be helped by it, achieving their business dreams in a way that serves and supports their personal lives.

Mike's story has a happy ending. In his sadness and resolve to find a better way to run his lawn care business, he found the Keys to Success. Sometimes he found a key by providence, sometimes by perseverance. It took time, but he found them. And the Six Keys allowed him to become an absentee seven-figure lawn care business owner and eventually sell the business as a turnkey operation that didn't revolve around him.

Today Mike is killing it in business and his personal life. His new business is coaching landscapers to run a successful business of their own, teaching them these very Keys to Success that he discovered on his journey. He's happily remarried, with the money, time, control, and impact—the true freedom—that entrepreneurs dream of.

Good for Mike! Let's spread that goodness to you and other entrepreneurs as we conquer the chaos using the Six Keys to Success.

THE PURPOSE OF THIS BOOK

This book is for the entrepreneur who went into business looking for freedom and instead found chaos. This book is for entrepreneurs who feel great tension between their business and their personal life. It's for entrepreneurs who feel trapped, controlled, and consumed by their business, not achieving the success they dreamed of. This book is also for entrepreneurs who are running a successful business but whose personal lives are out of balance. The purpose of this book is to help entrepreneurs build a great business . . . *and* a great life.

If you see yourself in this picture, know this: you're in good company. The vast majority of small business owners are either struggling in their business or they're struggling in their personal lives as they pour their energy into a successful business. All the while, entrepreneurs put on a happy face, finding satisfaction in the many wonderful aspects of business ownership. But too often they are sacrificing what matters most—health, relationships, values, and other important life interests.

Over the past two decades, I have become well acquainted with the success and struggle of entrepreneurship. I have personally battled through the trials and celebrated the triumphs. More importantly, I've been fortunate to see up close and personal the stories of countless entrepreneurs—customers, partners, and small business owners around the globe winning in business and life. This is not easy stuff, but it's worth it, *if*—and that's a big if—the entrepreneur pursues success with a balanced approach.

As the CEO of Keap, I love entrepreneurs, and so do our employees. We love your tenacity, ambition, work ethic, innovation, and creativity. We love your grit and guts to cast aside fear and criticism in order to go out and do something bold and daring that will create a ton of value, bring satisfaction to your souls, and produce opportunity for yourselves and all those you employ. At Keap, our purpose is to "liberate and empower entrepreneurs" so they can strengthen families, communities, and economies.

We love helping entrepreneurs succeed! And we *hate* seeing entrepreneurs fail. We hate seeing entrepreneurs close their doors. We hate seeing them lose hope. We hate seeing their confidence squashed, financial lives ruined, and relationships shattered. We hate seeing entrepreneurs' creative fire doused when their business or personal life falls apart.

We hate it because we have been there ourselves. And we have shared in the tragedies of far too many entrepreneurs. We feel a tight bond with the entrepreneurs working each day to find the freedom and success that motivated them to start their businesses in the first place.

In the early days of our business, we experienced all of the monumental trials. We felt like quitting nearly every day. We were on the verge of personal bankruptcy, with health and relationship challenges that seemed too much to bear. But gradually, we began to discover the Six Keys to Success. It didn't happen quickly. It actually took many years. But once we discovered and practiced these keys, our business took off. And as we refined the keys over the years, we began teaching them to our customers, finding great satisfaction in *their* success. We want to spread that success to you.

A BETTER WAY OF LIFE
FOR ENTREPRENEURS

In addition to our own experiences, 20-plus years of working with small business owners brought us to some simple but significant discoveries. We watched the same mistakes being made over and over again. We saw how small businesses achieved success as they applied the Six Keys. And we saw "success" on the outside covering up struggles on the inside. Sure, we saw the triumphs. But we also saw the trials and tragedies brought about by the chaos.

We call the personal tragedies "The Dark Side of Entrepreneurship." Unfortunately, the nature of business is that it frequently whips the entrepreneur around, creating chaos that often leads to ugly results in the business and personal lives of entrepreneurs. These aren't just unfortunate business consequences.

The personal consequences are dangerous and sometimes tragic: leading in the extreme to death, divorce, or destruction, and more commonly to depression, drinking, and drugs to cope with it all. Think I'm being too dramatic? Perhaps. Just know that, almost always, there is imbalance, neglect, and regret with respect to personal health, relationships, and finances. That is not okay and it needs to be addressed. Entrepreneurship is awesome. And we want you to enjoy it without experiencing the heavy toll it can take when the entrepreneur does not have life balance.

We've all seen ultra-successful entrepreneurs—from a business standpoint—who are not "winning" when it comes to family, friends, health, and personal balance. Well, it's not just the high-profile entrepreneurs who suffer from this problem. Sadly, it's common across the millions of entrepreneurs in the world. This imbalance is why I'm so passionate about the revised edition of *Conquer the Chaos*.

Over the years, we have learned that the keys to conquer chaos and build a successful business *and* life are not unique to one industry, company, or business owner. Success is determined by practicing predictable, repeatable, simple actions. But not just any actions—the right actions.

We also learned over the years that success in business doesn't really matter if the entrepreneur's personal life is a mess. What's the point of more time, money, and control if you don't like yourself or your family resents you or your health is lousy? Balanced growth. Business *and* personal success—the kind of success that brings great fulfillment to the entrepreneur. That's what we want for entrepreneurs. Because if it's just about business success, well, it probably won't last long. And even if it does, it's not worth the personal regret that comes with it.

I've lived this balancing act as we grew our business from zero to over $100 million in annual sales. I've been in countless masterminds, user groups, and conferences observing the very real struggle for business and personal success, brushing up against the Dark Side of Entrepreneurship too many times. I've made my share of mistakes in the balancing act, trust me. I've seen far too many friends err on the side of business success. And I know there's a better way. I know it. It is my mission in business to help entrepreneurs find that better way. This is why I'm so passionate about sharing this book with you.

THE ENTREPRENEURIAL
REVOLUTION DEFINED

I'm also passionate about this because so many more people are joining the ranks of entrepreneurship. They need guidance to conquer the chaos and avoid the Dark Side of Entrepreneurship.

By the time you finish reading this chapter, 190 people will have started their own business. If you read the entire book straight through, another 2,200 business owners will have started a business. And that's in the United States alone. Entrepreneurship is exploding all around us. Once considered a profession for a few rare, risk-taking, perhaps eccentric souls, entrepreneurship is now a widely respected profession.

Certainly, as an entrepreneur, you've noticed the growing interest in business ownership. You have friends who are entrepreneurs. Perhaps a brother, aunt, or cousin has started a business. Your neighbor down the street owns her own business. And it seems like nearly everyone has a side hustle of some sort, gearing up for the point when they can quit the day job and go all in on their business.

At the time of this book's first publication 14 years ago, the entrepreneurial revolution had clearly started. But today, the revolution is in full force and has completely changed the landscape of the business world. What's driving the revolution?

For any revolution to occur, three factors must be present. (See Figure 1.1.) Within the last few years, the same factors that led to political revolutions made their way into the economy, creating fertile ground for the entrepreneurial revolution. These three factors are:

1. A loss of security
2. A power shift
3. The promise of something better

ANY REVOLUTION	AMERICAN REVOLUTION	ENTREPRENEURIAL REVOLUTION
Loss of Security	No Representation	Corporate Distrust
Power Shift	Continental Congress	The Internet
Promise of Something Better	The Declaration of Independence	The Overnight Success Story

Figure 1.1 The three elements of a revolution.

The Loss of Security: Corporate Distrust

In generations past, many folks spent their entire careers at a single company, retiring after 40 years of dedicated service to someone else. To these folks, long-term employment with the company was the safe, wise, stable thing to do. If you wanted to get ahead in life, you worked nine to five in a predictable and stable environment, your employer took care of you over the course of your career, and you received a nice retirement plan when it was time to call it quits.

Now, however, the days of loyal employment are over. Working 40 years for the same company is practically unheard of. College graduates don't expect to work for the same company their whole lives, and workers of all ages want a variety of opportunities and career challenges. Corporations simply don't provide the safety and stability perceived by generations past. Furthermore, bad corporate behavior has created corporate distrust. Stories of corporate scandals, shareholder fraud, and downsizing are the norm, sowing the seeds of distrust and breeding cynicism toward corporations.

As a result of this corporate distrust, more and more workers are seeking ways to create their own stability. They start businesses from dorm rooms, spin up side hustles, and scan the market for opportunities to generate extra income. In short, due to corporate distrust, more and more workers are leaning toward entrepreneurship. And the second ingredient needed to create a revolution is what gives them ample opportunity.

The Power Shift: The Internet Age

If you had to sum up the one big thing driving the entrepreneurial revolution, it is the age of the Internet. In the past 20 years, the Internet changed everything, igniting the revolution. And now advanced web technologies on our phones are accelerating the revolution, completely shifting power to the individual.

The Internet:

- Allows people to work from anywhere
- Gives open access to information and artificial intelligence
- Connects people and opportunities through social media
- Makes it possible for anyone to profit from their expertise
- Puts the power of automation in the hands of the little guy
- Lets entrepreneurs transact online, anywhere, anytime
- Opens up a global market our parents could never have imagined

And those are just a few of the ways the Internet age is shifting the power to the individual. For the entrepreneur, this shift in power puts small business ownership more easily within reach. It opens up a world of possibilities that simply weren't possible in the past.

So we love the Internet age. We love the value and opportunity it provides entrepreneurs. And we love the entrepreneurial revolution that is happening all around us because of it. But before we get carried away praising the Internet age, I'd like to issue one word of warning. As much as we love the Internet age, its technologies are a massive contributor to the chaos. More on that later.

THE PROMISE OF SOMETHING BETTER: THE OVERNIGHT SUCCESS STORY

Before we jump into the promise that sparks the revolution, let's do a little lesson in United States history. Trust me, this history lesson applies to the entrepreneurial revolution and it also applies to your specific business as an entrepreneur.

The Fourth of July, celebrated as Independence Day in the United States, is not the day the United States won its freedom. The American Revolution had only just begun on July 4, 1776, when the Declaration of Independence was signed.

We celebrate the *declaration* in the United States, even though that declaration occurred long before independence was actually won.

Imagine that. More remembered than the day the colonists won their freedom is the day they declared their independence. I believe this is appropriate and significant because the colonists envisioned victory. They declared it. They called their shot. And that gave them a cause. It gave them hope. After all their frustration, fear, and pain, finally *they held the promise of something better*.

For the entrepreneurial revolution, the concept is the same. If corporate disillusionment provided the fuel and the Internet provided the means to start a revolution, then all that was left was to light the match. And the match—the spark that ignites the bonfire, the promise of something better—is a little thing called *the perceived overnight success story*.

People look at the stories of successful entrepreneurs and they see "overnight success." They see all the benefits that come to a successful entrepreneur: time, money, control, impact, and freedom. But they don't see the chaos, the journey, the struggle to build a successful business and a successful life.

Instead, they see the flexibility they crave and they resent their boss for not allowing it. They see the successful entrepreneur buy a new car or home and they feel a twinge of jealousy. They see the blossomed creativity of entrepreneurs who advances their ideas in the market and they harbor feelings of resentment when their own ideas are not appreciated at work. They see entrepreneurs accomplishing their dreams and they kick themselves for not taking action when they "thought of that idea first."

Corporate distrust, the Internet age, and the myth of the overnight success story are the forces that created the entrepreneurial revolution. More and more people are starting their own business, spurred by corporate distrust, empowered by the Internet age, and longing for their own overnight success story. All around us, aspiring entrepreneurs reach for the promise of something better, a promise that sounds like:

> "I've always wanted to start a business; it's time for me to pursue my dream."
>
> "Joe went for it and look at him now. If he can do it, I certainly can."
>
> "With all the layoffs around here, now's as good a time as any."
>
> "I want the flexibility to work when I want and have more time with the family."
>
> "Honey, I just can't take it anymore. I *have* to start my own thing."
>
> "I'll start it on the side and build it up until I can afford to quit my job."
>
> "Let's line up health insurance, get a little more in savings, and take the plunge."

These are the conversations going on around us, fueling the entrepreneurial revolution. You probably said something like this yourself before starting your business. And if you haven't staked out on your own yet, you *feel* the reality of these statements, don't you?

THE COVID EFFECT

So the stage was set. The three factors had all combined to create revolutionary conditions. And the population responded by turning to small business ownership in droves. And then COVID-19 hit and turned this flame we call the entrepreneurial revolution into a roaring bonfire.

Over the past three years since COVID, businesses have been starting up at a record pace. COVID changed everything and it turbo-charged each of the three characteristics that lead to a revolution:

1. **Corporate distrust** increased as macroeconomic factors shifted, remote work became normal, employees reexamined their work lives, and employers scrambled to adapt to the changing environment by reducing costs and laying off employees. The Great Resignation became a thing as employees decided they wanted a better way of working.

2. **The Internet age** went to a new level during COVID. Web conferencing, digital marketing, automation, mobile technologies, and AI all advanced significantly, as lockdowns and remote work became necessary. The technologies created and popularized during the pandemic will continue to accelerate the entrepreneurial revolution.

3. **The overnight success story** is perhaps the factor that gained the most surprising surge during COVID. Of course, mainstream media still glamorizes the rags to riches stories. But the massive surge has come from social media, YouTube, podcasts, and other user-generated content sources that highlight entrepreneurial success. Everyone has a platform. The world had time to watch during the pandemic. And now it seems influencers and successful entrepreneurs are constantly in the spotlight.

With the entrepreneurial revolution in full effect, accelerated by COVID, record numbers of entrepreneurs are joining the ranks of small business ownership. And that is why this book is so crucial—to help entrepreneurs build a great business *and* a great life, without being swallowed whole by the chaos. To help more entrepreneurs avoid Mike Callahan's first story and achieve his second story.

To be clear, it is a *great* thing that so many people are turning to entrepreneurship. Entrepreneurs make the world a better place, just as Abraham Maslow called out when he said:

"The difference between the great and good societies and the regressing, deteriorating societies is largely in terms of the entrepreneurial opportunity and the number of such people in the society. I think everyone would agree that the most valuable 100 people to bring into a deteriorating society would be not 100 chemists, or politicians, or professors, or engineers, but rather 100 entrepreneurs."

—Abraham Maslow

Maslow is famous for his Hierarchy of Needs. And he was right about the value of entrepreneurs in society. Now let's put those two concepts together as we look at the Quest for Success.

Chapter 1 Summary:
The Entrepreneurial Revolution

- Entrepreneurship is attractive and exciting, providing an opportunity for wealth and freedom. But the chaos of running a business wreaks havoc in the lives of entrepreneurs. Both the struggling entrepreneur and the successful entrepreneur experience chaos.
- This book is about showing you a better way. This book shows you the way to build a great business and a great life.
- We are in an entrepreneurial revolution. Record numbers of people are starting businesses due to three factors:
  1. A loss of security—corporate distrust
  2. A power shift—the Internet age
  3. The promise of something better—the overnight success story
- These three factors were driving entrepreneurship in record numbers. And then COVID hit and the entrepreneurial revolution exploded.
- All of these entrepreneurs are eager to build a successful business, but the definition of success is unclear and the chaos of small business awaits them.

2
THE QUEST FOR SUCCESS

I n the early days of our business, when my son Tanner was 10 years old, we were talking about what Tanner wanted to do when he grew up. As I asked him the question, he quickly blurted out, "I want to do what Jake's dad does!"

Thinking Tanner was focused and motivated beyond his years, I said, "Great, Tanner! What does Jake's dad do?"

"I'm not sure. But he has a ton of money, and he gets to be home all the time."

Tanner's answer provided a rather blunt explanation of what most entrepreneurs are looking to achieve. Money and time are key motivators for driving people toward small business ownership. But they are not the only motivators. Control, impact, and, ultimately, freedom are also important motivators.

THE ENTREPRENEUR'S HIERARCHY OF SUCCESS

After years of working with entrepreneurs, it is clear to me that business success is based on a hierarchy. Like Maslow's hierarchy of needs, the entrepreneur's hierarchy of success makes clear that money alone doesn't equal success. Likewise, a business owner who is able to take a lot of time off is also not necessarily successful. There's more to business success than money and time. And the fulfillment we receive as entrepreneurs moves up in a hierarchy, just as Maslow laid out all those years ago. (See Figures 2.1 and 2.2.)

Figure 2.1　Maslow's Hierarchy of Needs.

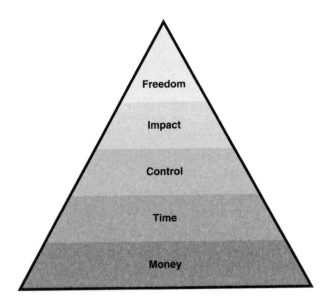

Figure 2.2　The Entrepreneur's Hierarchy of Success.

MONEY

Whether or not people admit it, money is one of the most attractive features of owning your own business. And it should be. For many people, it was the primary reason to leave the corporate world behind, where earnings are steady but essentially capped. In entrepreneurship, on the other hand, the opportunity to earn more money with no cap on earning potential is a powerful motivator. It's enough to get most entrepreneurs to take serious action.

If there weren't a monetary reward for owning a business, hardly anyone would do it. The financial rewards of success must be a part of the equation. It's not greed; it's capitalism. And it's what drives sharp people to solve difficult problems all over the world. Financial rewards, to the entrepreneur, are the fuel that makes the engine run.

Although money is a primary motivator for starting a business, too many entrepreneurs are in a bad relationship with money. They repel it instead of attracting it. They get caught up feeling greedy or unworthy of the financial rewards entrepreneurship offers. And that's such a shame because it locks them into the lowest level on the Hierarchy of Success. So I'd like to share a few thoughts about money that will hopefully unlock this first level and help you make great money in your business.

Let's start with the fact that money is essential and it opens up a lot of possibilities in life. As Zig Ziglar said, "Money isn't the most important thing in life, but it ranks right up there with oxygen on the gotta-have-it scale." And "Timid salespeople have skinny children." I love that one. I also love what my friend Joe Polish says about money. He calls money "fun tickets" and he says, "Money may not buy happiness, but it can buy fun."

Be proud of delivering a product or service that customers appreciate and value more than the money they give you in return. It's no small feat creating a great product or service that people exchange their hard-earned money for. We should be excited about the money we earn. And we should make no apologies for it!

One of my friends, Dave Ramsey, said it best when he spoke to my team at Keap several years ago. He said, "When you do a good job, your customers give you certificates of appreciation with presidents' faces on them." How great is that? Certificates of appreciation! The financial rewards of entrepreneurship are awesome and we can be humble and grateful for those rewards without being shy or apologetic about them. *When you value your product or service and proudly deliver it to serve your customers, you will attract money.* Lots of it. And that's a great thing!

As you increase your business and personal income, you'll be pleased with the financial success. But you will start to yearn for more time to enjoy it. You might bring in hundreds of thousands or even millions of dollars per year, but if you have to work 12, 14, or 16 hours a day to make it happen, your success will eventually feel hollow. In the long run, no amount of money can make up for the life you're setting aside to make your business work.

TIME

Time is a major motivator for starting a business. If you're like most entrepreneurs, when you decided to start your business, you wanted more time with friends and family. You had a desire to cheer on your son or daughter at their soccer game. You had a "to-do" list that you felt like you were never going to tackle. You wanted more flexibility in your work schedule so that you would have the time to do things that are important to you.

Yes, before actually starting their own businesses, many people believe that "being your own boss" means *entrepreneurs* get to decide when to work. If they needed an hour or two to watch a pee-wee football game, they could take it. If their family decided to go on vacation, they'd turn the business over to their employees, or simply stop doing business for the week. As an entrepreneur, they wouldn't be tied down by a nine-to-five job.

Unfortunately, it doesn't take entrepreneurs long to realize that being your own boss doesn't mean you can work whenever you want. Customers, financial responsibilities, and other factors dictate that you must work more than you thought would be necessary. And many times the entrepreneur's passion for the work drives them to spend long hours in the business. The truth is, there's so much to do that most entrepreneurs spend much more time in the business than they expected.

That's why entrepreneurs learn pretty quickly that time, not money, is their most precious resource. During the first few years of business, entrepreneurs usually work long hours to keep the money coming in. In fact, our experience at Keap has shown that it takes an average of three years for an entrepreneur's personal income from the business to match the income the entrepreneur earned before starting the business. That's one reason why the hours are extra long those first few years.

As the business starts to take off and the money is flowing in, smart entrepreneurs buy back more and more of their time by "doing what they do best and delegating the rest." The satisfaction that comes from being able to spend time on things you enjoy outside the business is one of the great rewards of entrepreneurship. And it's certainly the case that when you have money and time, the satisfaction rises. Just like Tanner pointed out all those years ago.

CONTROL

When we've polled entrepreneurs over the years about why they start their own businesses, right after money and time is control. They want to "be their own boss," call the shots, see their ideas and decisions play out in the market. They don't want their activities dictated to them by a boss.

Business ownership does offer the opportunity to be in control. But that control really comes when the entrepreneur achieves some success with time and money.

Until the business is producing the money and time the owner wants, the truth is that the business controls the entrepreneur more than the entrepreneur controls the business. Customers have demands. Employees need guidance. Expenses need to be paid. It often feels like the weight of the world is on the entrepreneur's shoulders and there aren't enough hours in the day.

As the business achieves more success in terms of money and time, the entrepreneur starts to feel the control they were looking for when they started the business: the control to step away from the business for a family matter, take a vacation, put some time into a hobby or other interests. It's all very fulfilling when the entrepreneur reaches the level of control on the Hierarchy of Success.

Furthermore, as the leader of your company, you get to hire and to delegate the things you don't love. You get to work on what you love most and do best. And that's an amazing reward of entrepreneurship. You'll know you've achieved the desired level of control when you can do what you want, when you want. That kind of control is truly liberating.

IMPACT

Of course entrepreneurs want to make money, have time, and be in control, but often their strongest motivating factor is the impact they want to have on customers, their community, and the world. They want to make a difference. They want to serve their customers in a way that changes their lives for the better. And they love getting the appreciation and recognition that comes when they have great impact.

Entrepreneurs often start their business because they want to have great impact, but they never ascend to this level of the hierarchy, getting stuck at money, time, or control. That's not to say they don't have any impact, but the level of impact they dreamed of is often lacking because they get caught up in the chaos.

FREEDOM

The greatest business fulfillment comes as entrepreneurs achieve all the benefits in the hierarchy: time, money, control, and impact. At the level of freedom, the entrepreneur is getting all those benefits and is feeling a liberation and capacity to create greatness. The entrepreneur can realize a level of satisfaction they could only dream of at the outset of their business. This level is like Maslow's "self-actualization" where the entrepreneur is living their best life and making a great impact on the world, fulfilling their business purpose and their personal purpose.

That is what the Hierarchy of Success is all about. It's the chance to do more than simply take care of your own needs at the lower levels of the hierarchy. It's the chance to live life according to your desires, ambitions, and dreams, having a great impact as you serve others. At the highest level of the Hierarchy of Success, entrepreneurs are able to create outcomes at will, bringing a measure of fulfillment and independence few individuals dream of, let alone accomplish. This is where the freedom and highest levels of fulfillment are felt.

It's easy to see how the Hierarchy of Success, as defined by money, time, control, impact, and freedom, has led tens of millions of people to small business ownership. The hierarchy is that "promise of something better." Yes, the entrepreneurial revolution is sweeping over the globe. But no matter how compelling the end goal may be, most entrepreneurs are not prepared for the reality of small business ownership.

Unfortunately, the entrepreneurial revolution will have grave casualties, like all revolutions. Of the roughly 2,500 small businesses that will be launched today, most won't be around in three years. Most of those businesses that *do* survive will

27

struggle mightily. Perhaps most importantly, of those businesses that are successful, far too many are led by entrepreneurs who make outsized sacrifices in their personal lives to achieve business success. That's why we need to take a closer look at the definition of success.

THE REAL DEFINITION OF SUCCESS

The Entrepreneur's Hierarchy of Success is a useful model to think about on our Quest for Success. We can all agree that success is more than just money or time. The elements of control, impact, and freedom are highly rewarding and need to be included in a definition of success. But even the Hierarchy of Success doesn't capture the full spirit of success for us as entrepreneurs.

An accurate definition of success must take into account the personal life of the entrepreneur. After all, small business is personal. The business life and personal life of the entrepreneur are intertwined. The entrepreneur's finances, identity, and ego are wrapped up in the business. And all of those forces tend to pull the entrepreneur away from health, relationships, and personal interests to invest more time and energy in the business.

With so many people flocking to entrepreneurship and with the chaos of business ownership lurking, we need to agree on a definition of success that encompasses the business and the personal life of the entrepreneur. We need a definition that will keep you grounded as you pursue your business goals and help you prioritize what matters most. The following definition of success will help us accomplish that:

Balanced growth in your business and personal life that produces more money, time, control, impact, and freedom.

That's success for entrepreneurs. Balance means we don't get sucked into the business to the detriment of our health and relationships. Balance also means we build the business profitably so that it works financially for the business owner. Many people assume a successful business means the business owner is making plenty of money, but that is not always true. Balance will ensure the business side of life is working *and* the personal side of life is working.

Growth means we are achieving our goals. It means we are building the business and attracting customers, employees, and the resources we need to fuel our business dreams. Growth also means we are improving personally, in our health, relationships, and finances. It means we are learning and increasing our capacity to have a greater impact on the world. Growth means we are becoming our best selves as we build a successful business.

When we are achieving *balanced growth in our business and personal lives* we are ascending the Hierarchy of Success. We are not sacrificing what matters most. We are avoiding the pitfalls of chaos. And we are living life in a well-rounded way that brings great fulfillment and contentment to us as entrepreneurs.

When "balanced growth" accumulates over time, it produces the purest form of freedom at the top of our Hierarchy of Success. But if we aren't intentional about that balance, the business will have a way of consuming everything we've got and we might achieve business impact without personal impact. On second thought, there may be personal impact, but it might not be *positive* personal impact if we aren't intentional about balanced growth.

Now some may say, "I don't want to grow." To that I will simply say that you are either growing or dying as a business. Inflation, competition, and your growing personal financial needs (bigger house, braces, college for kids, vacation desires, etc.) all require your business to grow. So please remove that counterproductive thought from your mind. Success, by definition, must involve growth.

Others may say, "My life and business are so interconnected that 'balance' isn't my desire. It seems like 'balance' is just semantics." I can appreciate that sentiment. It is, indeed, difficult to achieve balance. And because it's so elusive, many have concluded it's not important, desirable, or even possible. Well, just because it's difficult to achieve doesn't mean we should not strive for balance. The history of entrepreneurship makes it clear that if we punt on trying to achieve balance, we might be successful in the business. But at what cost? Life is more than the business. We want a successful business and a successful personal life. Therefore, we must take on the challenge of "balanced growth."

Here's the crucial point about balance: the win is in *striving* for balance. If you are striving for balance, you won't get too far off track. On the other hand, if you give up striving for balance, you will almost certainly find yourself way off course when it comes to important priorities in your personal life. I like to think of balance as a balance beam—but one that's actually on the ground. So you can't "fall off" the balance beam. When we strive to stay on that line, sure, we will wobble left and right of our goal. But we will maximize the time we are in balance, even though there will be many times we aren't quite on the beam. *The victory is that we don't stray far from the beam because we are always trying to be on it.*

"Balanced growth in our business and personal lives." That's our quest. That's the success we're after. And this book will show you how to achieve it. Before we move on, there's one last framework I need to share with you to help you in your Quest for Success.

THE STAGES OF SMALL BUSINESS GROWTH

When Scott and I wrote the first edition of *Conquer the Chaos*, we did a lot of research about small business growth. We had been observing for several years certain patterns of growth among our customers. We could clearly see their growth following a stair-step pattern. It became predictable and almost eerie that we could anticipate the inclines and plateaus as we worked closely with our customers. So we took the opportunity at the last writing to do some deep research on small business growth, as a complement to what we were observing in our customers' businesses.

Our primary source became the US Census Bureau data. I personally spent dozens if not hundreds of hours poring over the data to analyze the make-up of businesses in the United States. We made some incredible discoveries. When we combined these discoveries with our own experience and more importantly, the experiences of our customers, the lessons learned were eye-popping. Now, with another 14 years of experience, the lessons learned have only become clearer.

Let's start with some basic and interesting information found in the census bureau data:

- There are roughly 30 million businesses in the United States.
- 99.93% are small businesses, defined as under 500 employees.
- Only 21,000 of 30 million businesses have over 500 employees.
- **A whopping 99.6% are under 100 employees.**
- 3.8 million (13%) have 2–10 employees.
- 1.2 million (4%) have 11–100 employees.
- 24.6 million, or 82% of all US businesses, are solopreneurs (no employees).

Although the US government defines a small business as any business under 500 employees, I believe small business goes up to 100 employees. Our experience at Keap has proven that businesses with over 100 employees operate very differently than businesses with under 100 employees. In fact, businesses with 1 employee operate very differently than businesses with 3 employees. More on that in a minute.

At Keap, we define small business as 1–100 employees and mid-sized business as 100–1,000 employees. It's important to note that SMB is an abbreviation for "small and mid-sized businesses." But because many people think SMB is short for "small business," the possible definition of small business is even broader than the government's definition. Frankly, the world needs to get clear on this so we can serve small businesses better. With that said, let's focus on the small business data from the census bureau, with interest in businesses under 100 employees.

When you look more closely at the data, including the annual revenue of the businesses, some interesting points begin to emerge from the census bureau data:

- Solopreneurs' revenue averages of $47,000 per year.
- Revenue per employee gets up to $100k per year at a 10-person business.
- Revenue per employee grows to $150k per year in a 50-person business.
- Revenue per employee is about $200k per year in a 500-person business.
- There are 61 million small business employees, which is 46% of workers.
- Those 46% earn 38% of wages.

This is interesting stuff about the financial prosperity of small business owners and their employees as the company grows. As revenue per employee grows, the owner and employees tend to make more money, obviously. The point I want to make is that business growth clearly correlates to personal income for the business owner and employees. So let's not have any of this talk about not wanting to grow. Remember, our definition of success starts with balanced *growth*.

Now we get to the really interesting part about this data. When looking at the data combined with our observation of customers at Keap, we have learned that businesses grow in a very predictable pattern of stages. These "Stages of Small Business Growth" (see figure 2.3) have proven to be a useful guide to our customers and entrepreneurs everywhere. Let's look at a few important takeaways that will help you navigate your journey as you grow through the stages.

Clear categories created by the government. The government lumps small businesses into six categories: 1) Non-employers (solopreneurs); 2) Under 5 employees; 3) 5–9 employees; 4) 10–19 employees; 5) 20–99 employees; and

STAGE	1 & 2 Solopreneur Side hustle / Self-employed		3 New Employer	4 Steady Operation	5 7-Figure Business	6 Growth Company
Typical number of employees	1	1	2–3	4–10	11–20	21–100
Typical sales range	$0–3K /month	$3–10K /month	$100–300K	$300K–1M	$1–3M	$3–10M
# in the U.S.	18.4M	6.2M	1.8M	2M	750K	450K
Team size	Owner	Owner + Contractor(s)	Partner or assistant	One team	Multiple teams	Management team
Biggest hurdle	Time	Leads	Sales	Marketing	People & Systems	Leadership
Keys to success	Mindset, Vision & Rhythm		Strategy & Automation		Leadership	

Figure 2.3 The Six Stages of Small Business Growth.

6) 100–500 employees. Based on over two decades of experience, customer research, and observation of how small businesses operate, we adjusted the categories by dropping off the 100–500 category, splitting the solopreneur and slightly adjusting the other categories. The resulting groups gradually emerged over the years as clear stages of growth so we named this "The Stages of Small Business Growth."

Growth stages based on experience. We have spent the majority of our time at Keap serving small businesses with 1–10 employees. Why? Because we serve small businesses and that's where 94% of them are! We have learned a lot about these businesses. A solopreneur with a side hustle operates very differently than one who has quit the day job and is all-in on the business. Similarly, a two- or three-person business that is still figuring out its products, services, and cash flow operates differently than a business that has stabilized and has 4–10 employees. Businesses with 11–20 employees begin to get more efficient. And small businesses with 20–100 employees are scaling and growing, usually producing solid profits.

Plateaus and hurdles at each stage. One of the most interesting things we have learned is that entrepreneurs frequently get stuck at the stage changes. It is common to see the business grow in stair-step fashion, riding up in a thrilling burst of growth and then plateauing. Sometimes this plateau is intentional and needed to deal with "growing pains." But when an entrepreneur feels stuck, it's usually because one particular skill or hurdle must be overcome to unlock the next stage, which you'll see in the graphic. Additionally, it's important to understand that at all stage changes, you must assess your people, process, and products. Almost invariably, the hurdle that must be cleared is hampered by limitations of people, process, or product.

The 1s and 3s of revenue. This might be the greatest discovery that emerged from our research and experience. It turns out that a business changes quite significantly at the 1s and 3s of annual revenue. When a business grows to $100,000 per year, then to $300,000, then to $1 million, to $3 million and to $10 million, it goes through major changes. We repeatedly found our customers getting stuck at these revenue levels. We learned over time that savvy entrepreneurs gradually figured out the hurdle to clear, while others stumbled along, stagnating, backsliding, exiting, or selling the business. Still others yearn for the prior stage where they were more comfortable. They would sometimes downsize their business as the only viable way to increase their money, time, and control. *Caveat*: Revenue numbers are different in retail and manufacturing. For those industries, the number of employees is the best indicator of the stage change.

Growth of revenue and profit. As the data suggests, small businesses generally get more efficient and profitable as they grow. Sometimes entrepreneurs want to stay in the same stage and not grow to the next stage. If you choose to do that, it is perfectly fine *as long as you are becoming more profitable.* In fact, getting more efficient and growing your profits is a great type of "balanced growth," which is central to our definition of success. As mentioned previously, inflation, competition, and lifestyle will all require you to grow. So even if you aren't growing annual revenue and moving to the next stage, make sure you are becoming more efficient and growing profits *within* the stage you choose to settle into.

US businesses only. It's important to note that this data is based on US businesses. This raises two important points. First, the global market of small businesses is dramatically larger than what I've covered here. The world of entrepreneurs is massive! And second, although the numbers and averages may be different, we can safely assume the dynamics of business evolution are not unique to US businesses. Small businesses all over the world follow a similar stair-step pattern as their owners navigate the predictable plateaus and hurdles of small business growth.

Marketing investment mindset. We've seen very clearly that those entrepreneurs who view marketing dollars as investments are the ones who grow their businesses to $1 million and beyond. These entrepreneurs value and invest in copywriting, graphic design, and advertising. They want to grow sales and save time using technology to help them maximize their money, time, control, impact, and freedom. And because of this marketing investment mentality, their growth significantly outpaces other small businesses that don't have an investment mindset about their marketing.

The stages build on each other. As we've taught the stages to entrepreneurs over the years, we often hear something like, "I'm at Stage 4, but sales is still a hurdle for me!" Sure. It's not like once you clear the hurdle and unlock the next stage, the hurdle is cleared forevermore. The point of the hurdle is that it's the primary constraint on your growth that must be solved to unlock the next level. You must continue maintaining and improving that aspect of your business into future stages. Another way to say it is that as you get good at the hurdle that holds you back in one stage, it continues to propel your growth in future stages.

As entrepreneurs work to grow their business through the stages, the ambition and challenge of it can be so fun and rewarding! At Keap, we love helping small businesses grow through these stages. It's such a fun game to play. In Stages 1 and 2, the Personal Keys to Success are foundational to helping you manage time and attract leads. In Stages 3 and 4, the Strategy and Automation Keys to Success become critical to your growth. And in Stages 5 and 6, Leadership helps businesses grow from $1 million to $10 million. This is fun stuff—and it works!

So where are you in the stages? What do you need to do to advance to the next stage or to become more efficient and profitable in your current stage? The Keys to Success will help you move through these stages and achieve the balanced growth you want.

Now that we have set the table in our Quest for Success, with the Hierarchy of Success, our definition of success and the Stages of Small Business Growth, we are almost ready to jump into the Six Keys to Success. But first, let's get clear on the problem we want to solve: chaos and the Dark Side of Entrepreneurship.

Chapter 2 Summary: The Quest for Success

- Entrepreneurship is so challenging, exciting, and chaotic that it's easy to get lost in the Quest for Success. That's why we need three frameworks to guide our quest: 1) The Hierarchy of Success; 2) the real definition of success; and 3) the Stages of Small Business Growth.
- Just like Maslow's Hierarchy of Needs, there is a Hierarchy of Success for entrepreneurs:
  - Money for the things you need and want, with no financial pressure
  - Time to spend as you'd like and enjoy the financial rewards of your business
  - Control to determine what you do, when you do it, and with whom you do it
  - Impact that improves the lives of your customers, your community, and the world
  - Freedom to create, live your best life, and enjoy the highest level of the hierarchy
- The real definition of success for entrepreneurs is "Balanced growth in your business and personal life that produces more money, time, control, impact, and freedom."
- The Stages of Small Business Growth are the six predictable stages small businesses go through where people, process, and product must be adjusted at the 1s and 3s of revenue to unlock the next stage of growth.
- In stages 1 and 2, the three personal keys are critically important to success. In stages 3 and 4, Strategy and Automation are critically important to success. And in Stages 5 and 6, Leadership is critically important to success.

3
CHAOS AND THE DARK SIDE
OF ENTREPRENEURSHIP

Only those who have experienced small business ownership will ever be able to understand the chaos that comes from being a small business owner. I want to relate our own story to give a clear portrayal of small business chaos. But this isn't just our story. We have seen it in the lives of our customers and entrepreneurs everywhere. To conquer it, we must understand it. And make no mistake, there is a way to conquer the chaos.

Many years ago we found ourselves surrounded by chaos. We were working hard to get our new business off the ground. We had big plans for success, but at the time we were just trying to keep the lights on, overwhelmed by everything that goes into building a successful business.

One day, in the midst of that new-business chaos, our custom software company received an interesting phone call. It was Friday at 5:00 p.m. and the four of us were getting ready to wrap up a long and discouraging week. We'd ordered pizza, and it had just arrived when the phone rang. Well, the last thing we wanted to do was talk to anyone. But we needed sales, so I picked up the phone.

No sooner had I rattled off my greeting than the man on the other end shouted, "I have *pain*! Can you help me?" Then the man paused.

My mind was reeling with concerns. Was this a prank? Did this guy even know who he had called? Was this a customer?

What were we supposed to do about someone's pain? Shouldn't he call a doctor?

Eventually, we got to the root of this man's problem. The caller was searching for a software program that would more effectively manage his contacts. He was trying to follow up with his prospects and customers, but he was making a lot of mistakes. He was disorganized, his data was a mess, and he was in chaos.

This man's name was Reed Hoisington. On this particular day, his successful business had mistakenly sent a special, reduced-price offer to a group of people, including many folks who had already bought that product at full price. Customers were angry, demanding refunds, and he was in pain!

Well, at the time of that phone call, we too had pain! We were struggling to acquire new customers and our struggles were seriously impacting our home lives to the extent we faced the very real possibility of going out of business.

One business (Reed's) was dealing with chaos born out of success. The other business (ours) was dealing with chaos born out of struggles.

The fact is, we all find ourselves immersed in chaos at some point in our journey of entrepreneurship. It's part of the process. It can't be avoided entirely. But we can conquer it, get in control of our business, and operate the business calmly, predictably, and profitably.

WHAT IS SMALL BUSINESS CHAOS?

Imagine you walk into a gym for the first time, ready to work out and get fit. You've got your goals in mind and you're excited to get in shape. You jump on a treadmill and start a brisk warm-up walk. A trainer from the gym walks up and starts talking to you, asking about your goals. Then he starts turning up the speed on the treadmill. You begin jogging, slightly concerned you'll face-plant and end up in a heap at the end of the treadmill. But you adapt and you're fine.

Then the trainer turns up the speed some more. And he lifts the incline. You're struggling to keep up. You keep running because you don't want to quit or look bad. But the truth is, you don't quite know what you're doing and you're not sure this is what you had in mind when you walked into the gym. You *are* sure that the way you're working out is not the best approach for your fitness goals. And yet you keep running because you're stuck and you can't get off the treadmill.

Small business chaos is like the treadmill. Customer needs seem ever present. There are leads to work, projects to complete, bills to pay, and fires to extinguish. Technology is changing, customer data is scattered across systems and tools, and there's always some administrative or compliance work that you're not quite on top of. Your industry is evolving, competitors are encroaching on your sweet spot, and the economy is an issue.

And that's just the business side of things! Never mind the kids' schedules, your neglected health, personal financial management, home maintenance, oh, and your important personal relationships! The fact is, the moment you bring in prospects and customers, you start to feel the chaos. The inputs lead to disorganization, the priorities get blurry, and the overwhelm can easily set in.

In our business, overwhelm from the chaos didn't strike all at once. Business ownership seemed exciting at first. We talked about hiring employees, buying our own office space, and acquiring perks and benefits through the business. Our shelves were lined with books that shared the rules for business success. We dreamed about the life-altering breakthroughs we would experience and the financial freedom we wanted. We were all working together as close friends. Furthermore, we weren't being tied down by corporate jobs. That felt great!

But the chaos was steadily changing our reality. Within weeks, the amount of work required to run a small business forced all of us to reevaluate our situation. We began spending more and more time at the office, frequently working through the night to get projects completed. We forgot the meaning of the term "lunch break," and "nine to five" became a completely foreign concept. It didn't take long before our only option for business survival was to eat, sleep, and breathe our business.

Worse than the hours put in at the office was the financial stress. We were worried about our product, our clients, our sales, and whether we'd be able to pay our personal mortgages. The carefully avoided question was whether we could even make this business work.

As if that question weren't taking its toll, we also developed *small business paranoia*: that gripping fear that causes business owners to feel the business will topple like a house of cards if they step away for even a brief moment. We felt like we couldn't go on vacation (not that we could afford it), on a date, or to our children's soccer games without jeopardizing the business.

Life had suddenly taken on a whole new meaning. Like many new small business owners, we felt trapped, controlled, and consumed by the business. What had happened to the freedom we were seeking? We were propelled into the age-old "fight for survival," and the battle wounds were starting to show.

On a couple of occasions, we had to approach our employees and explain we couldn't make payroll. To our employees' credit, they stuck it out and worked hard to help us get through the tough times. Meanwhile, as the co-founders, we sometimes went weeks or months without taking home any money. Or paying any of our personal bills. For a period of about 10 months, we paid our mortgages 30 days late almost every month, because that was the soonest we had the money to pay it—just in time to avoid a 30-day-late ding to our credit reports.

As we went through these tough initial years in the business, the money would run out, and the creditors would come calling. I felt particular embarrassment one Sunday night when my eight-year old son asked, "Dad, why are you so mad?"

"Because a freakin' creditor called me at 8:00 on a Sunday night!" I snapped.

"What did he want?"

"He wanted to know why I haven't paid my bill."

"Well, Dad, did you tell him it's because you haven't made enough sales?"

My family all had a good laugh and I was glad my son understood how important sales are to a small business. But that wasn't much solace. The pain we were all feeling was suffocating. The chaos was burying us.

Another time, as my co-founder, Scott, sat in the hospital with his wife and brand new child, he was on the phone helping a customer. When his understandably irritated wife chided him, he looked down at the newborn baby and said, "You want to be able to afford the hospital bills, right?"

Our entire lives were wrapped up in a love-hate relationship with a struggling, all-consuming company. And although we had hopes and dreams of business success, the truth is there were times when we wanted to get out. But we couldn't because we had so much debt, pride, and identity wrapped up in the business.

After a couple years, we had invested so much time, money, and effort into the company that failure was not an option. So every day we trudged through one challenge after another. For the first two and a half years, our business was hanging by a very, very thin thread. In terms of our treadmill analogy, the speed was fast, the incline was steep, and we were sure this wasn't the workout we had signed up for. We were so out of balance, it felt like a face-plant on the rubber tread was imminent.

We rarely saw our families, and even when we were around, the business dominated our concentration. Not only were we not present when we were home, we were oblivious to our lack of presence. We had less patience, and little devotion to the people who meant so much to us. Our minds were busy, our stress levels were increasing, and we completely forgot what it meant to have a personal life.

Then finally, finally, the clouds started to break, and we knew the company was going to make it. A few critical experiences and a couple of good breaks eased the chaos enough for us to turn down the speed on the treadmill and achieve a sense of balance. Almost accidental realizations gave us the knowledge to start breaking through the chaos toward freedom.

We managed to formulate our business strategy as we went along. We found easier, less time-consuming ways of running the company. We brought on amazing employees who contributed greatly and helped build a fun, tight-knit, gritty culture. We also worked on controlling the chaos in our own minds. Eventually, we moved past the business-threatening problems. We were starting to think more clearly and we were starting to recognize that there is a better way to run a small business.

Now, as we recount this story, we smile at the crazy situations we made it through. We laugh about the funny things that happened back in those days. Like the time Scott and I took a client to lunch and we both forgot our wallets, which was probably a good thing because we were so poor at the time (Freudian slip). The client graciously agreed to pay.

Or the time we left the Arizona Farm Bureau Insurance offices after making a software proposal to their marketing director. We walked down to the parking lot, got in Scott's beat-up pickup truck (which was nicer than my beat-up pickup truck with no A/C—in Arizona!), only to find it needed a push start. Twice. Yeah, that was fun to do in the client's parking lot, right beneath the second-story conference room with floor-to-ceiling windows where we had just made our software proposal. Good times!

Although we are no longer crammed into a tiny little office space or driving beat-up old pickup trucks, we haven't lost touch with where we came from. These experiences intensified our passion and resolve to ease the pains of entrepreneurs who are struggling for balanced growth. Because it really doesn't have to be so hard.

THE CHAOS CONTINUES

New businesses experience a certain kind of chaos in the first couple years of the business. It takes a while for entrepreneurs to figure out their target market, product offering, pricing, and other strategic components of the business. There are so many decisions and foundational elements to put in place and the financial stress is so high that new business chaos is a real thing. That's what I have described here in our founding story. You have likely experienced, or are experiencing, something similar.

Unfortunately, the chaos doesn't go away after the business gets established. Even businesses that escape "survival mode" are plagued by chaos. So what is the problem? Where does the chaos come from? Once an entrepreneur gets out of survival mode, shouldn't everything be smooth sailing from there? How do small business owners find themselves gasping for air on the treadmill? Once you understand the answer to this question, you will understand why the formula for success is so powerful.

So let's look at the real causes of the ongoing chaos in an established small business:

- You're wearing all the hats.
- You don't know how to grow.
- You're growing the wrong way.
- You're drowning in technology.
- You lack a clear, central, guiding focus.

You're Wearing All the Hats

Think back to when you were working for someone else. Why was it so much easier? Because you had one job to do. Just one. Now that one job has transformed into 10 or 15 different roles. After selling products or services, handling customer service, managing employees, and paying the bills, small business owners really have little time left to spend on growing and improving their business. Their attention is constantly being pulled one direction after another. And by the time they do have a moment to themselves, they are often too drained to do anything more than run the same old gauntlet.

And it never seems to stop. If the toilets overflow, you'll add janitor to the roles you take on. Let me assure you, from experience, that no matter how in control you might feel, overflowing toilets have a way of tossing you back into the midst of chaos again. Because as an entrepreneur you play *all* the roles in the business—you wear all the hats. Even when you hire employees to take on some of those responsibilities, you have more than your fair share of roles to fill. Ultimately, the buck stops with you. And you get to make payroll to prove it.

You Don't Know How to Grow

Despite the popularity of entrepreneurship, growing a business is a tremendous challenge. You are always looking for customers willing to buy your products or services because without new customers, you can't grow a business. But most entrepreneurs don't start their business because they're great at sales, marketing, and growth strategies. They start their business because they know how to provide a product or service. There's no reason to be embarrassed if you aren't an expert at growing a business. Admitting it is the first step.

If you're a solopreneur, you are responsible for finding new customers, fulfilling on services for new customers, billing new customers, collecting payments, and much more. That's a lot of work for one person to do. And if you want to grow, you've got to do all this stuff simultaneously. Because if you aren't constantly filling the funnel with new prospects, the pipeline breaks and something or someone (probably you) doesn't get paid.

You Are Growing—The Wrong Way

An old adage says, "Your business doesn't have any problems that can't be solved by more sales." But that's not quite true. If your sales function outpaces your delivery function, you have big problems. Similarly, if you neglect other areas of the business, you will soon find an imbalance that can have business-threatening consequences. And this says nothing about the problem of growing by bringing in bad-fit customers or unprofitable customers. You can't "make it up on volume" if you're bringing in the wrong kind of customers.

If you're not prepared for growth, if you haven't got a process in place to manage it, then its arrival is going to demand more of your time and effort. And the result will be that the ball gets dropped, customers get angry, and you'll be running around frantically trying to make everything work. In short, you'll become intimately familiar with the term "growing pains." So yes, the business may be growing, but you won't be conquering the chaos, and you won't be anywhere close to finding your freedom.

You're Drowning in Technology

Remember in our discussion of the entrepreneurial revolution how we praised the Internet? Well, now we're about to tell you why it's not always our friend. In fact, the same technology that makes it easy to become an entrepreneur can in many ways become our archenemy and the primary culprit of chaos. Here's how:

Message overload. Email, texting, and social media are beneficial in so many ways, but they are also major contributors to the chaos. We are constantly bombarded with information and requests. If we don't have a way of managing this, it will manage us, causing us to operate in a reactive mode all day long. If we aren't careful, we are soon doing whatever the message senders want us to do instead of doing what will propel our business forward.

Too many solutions. The Internet has provided small business owners with too many solutions to their business challenges. That sounds a little strange, but think about it. Technology companies have developed every possible business "solution," from billing to scheduling to email marketing and everything in between. You didn't get into business to be a technology expert. But with all this technology, you must invest a significant amount of time learning about it, choosing what's best for your business, and then figuring out how to actually use it and stitch it all together to get the benefits of the technology. This takes a lot of time and expertise, and for many entrepreneurs it is a major headache and significant contributor to chaos.

Speed. When letters were used as the primary method of communication, business owners had several days of lag time to respond to a customer's request, concern, or situation. Now, a few days is insufficient for making things right. Customers and partners expect almost immediate responses. If a small business owner fails to respond in a timely manner, they appear to not care and they may lose a customer or partner. So the entrepreneur is consistently running, running, running just to stay caught up with the most pressing demands. This adds to the reactive mode and causes entrepreneurs to feel like they're on a treadmill that's out of control.

Scattered customer data. For most businesses, their customer data is spread out across many tools and systems. Some important information is in their billing software, other information is in emails, other key details are in text messages . . . or was that social media? It's hard to keep all of the information straight. The owner's brain is usually the glue holding it all together, which is taxing and chaotic (see figure 3.1).

Figure 3.1 Small business chaos.

You Lack a Clear, Central, Guiding Focus

If all those reasons weren't creating enough chaos, the lack of a clear business plan will tip you over the edge. Consider all the projects and tasks on your plate. Which one is most important? Where do you start? There are so many things that need to be done. And the day-to-day life of small business brings urgent issue after urgent issue to the top of your list. The fact is, without a clear vision, strategy, and execution plan, it is almost impossible to avoid "firefighting mode" where you put your time on the most urgent issue.

Firefighting mode is necessary at times. But when you get caught in that rut as the normal way of running your business, you're stuck on the treadmill of chaos and you aren't intentionally building your business. You're putting out fires, reacting to all that's required of you as the owner of your business. And just when you think you've got things under control in the business, a fire breaks out on the home front that requires your immediate attention.

Now, on top of all of those causes of chaos, consider how dynamic and fast-changing our world is. Economic trends, industry developments, and competition are constantly bringing change to our doorstep. And then we get an occasional cataclysmic change like COVID that puts chaos in hyperdrive. In our modern world, change is a way of life. And all of that change is a major contributor to small business chaos.

THE DARK SIDE OF ENTREPRENEURSHIP

The chaos is tough enough to manage in the business setting. But at some point, the chaos begins to mess with the entrepreneur personally—physically, mentally, emotionally, and socially. Left unchecked, the chaos can take the entrepreneur down a very dark path. Sometimes the darkness comes when the business is struggling. Sometimes it comes when the business is succeeding. The extreme consequences of the chaos are what I call "The Dark Side of Entrepreneurship." And this is what we must avoid in our Quest for Success.

Physical effects. Eating, sleeping, and exercising properly are all compromised as chaos sucks the time out of the entrepreneur's life. When this goes on for months or years, the body simply cannot withstand the toll. The common result is that either the body begins to break down or the entrepreneur's business begins to break down. Of course, there is a better way, and we'll cover that in the Personal Keys to Success.

Mental effects. Most entrepreneurs have deep doubts about their business at one time or another. Everyone around you, from friends and family to customers to casual observers, seems to be telling you that you cannot do this. Entrepreneurs are constantly hearing that they should "get a real job." Other times, the entrepreneur is on top of the world because the business is succeeding. But if the mindset isn't managed properly, the entrepreneur can go down paths of dark self-indulgence or personal neglect.

Emotional effects. The chaos wears people down. Disorganization and overwhelm, combined with the physical and mental effects of chaos, can bury the entrepreneur emotionally. On the other hand, when the business is successful, the entrepreneur is flying high. The rush is exhilarating but difficult to maintain. The point is that the highs and lows of entrepreneurship can be very hard to manage. Entrepreneurs often find themselves out of energy, out of belief, and out of sorts. Many entrepreneurs who get caught up in the chaos feel like they've lost themselves. And if *they* don't feel it, their loved ones do, as the entrepreneur is consumed by the business.

Social effects. Business ownership makes you different. Friends and family don't "get" what you're doing. You sometimes need to change your relationships to handle the chaos and grow your business successfully. And when the chaos is raging, you certainly don't have the time you once had to hang out with friends. Perhaps the greatest social toll is the toll on the family of the entrepreneur. So often, the aspiring entrepreneur starts the business in order to have more time for family, but the chaos consumes them and they have far less time and energy for their loved ones.

The personal consequences of chaos are dangerous and sometimes tragic. In the extreme, we see death, divorce, and destruction. More commonly, we see depression, drinking, and drugs to cope with it all—even when the business is successful! Nobody wants to talk about this stuff. It's ugly. And we entrepreneurs are a sunny bunch by nature, quick to point out all of the many positives of business ownership.

You might think I'm being too dramatic as I talk about the Dark Side. Perhaps I am. But I've seen too much to ignore it or downplay it. And I've come dangerously close to it myself, making many mistakes and wishing I had been more present at home over the years. Wherever you are on the spectrum of chaos and the Dark Side, just know that in almost every entrepreneur's story there are times of imbalance, neglect, and regret with respect to personal health, relationship and finances.

I want to help you avoid the Dark Side. If we can recognize and acknowledge the effects of chaos and the Dark Side, we can beat it. That's why I'm talking about it. And there's a sneaky little factor in entrepreneurship that works against us and makes chaos and the Dark Side particularly problematic.

EGO IS THE ENEMY

As entrepreneurs, we are driven to create, to build, to win. That ambition is a good thing because it helps us create amazing products and services that deliver value, create jobs, and improve the world. But we must be very careful about the ego inside of us because it will cause our demise if we aren't on high alert. The history books are replete with examples showing us that "Pride goeth before the fall." Jim Collins wrote a book about it called *How the Mighty Fall*. And Ryan Holiday exposed the ego in all its ugliness in his insightful book *Ego Is the Enemy*.

The ego is sneaky. It is constantly protecting us and preventing us from looking at the issues we must address. Sometimes those issues are in our business. Sometimes those issues are in our personal lives. And quite often they are character issues that we must address in order to improve and grow.

The ego is contentious. It wants to win at all costs. It argues, fights, bends some rules, and overlooks others. It sees the world as a zero-sum game. Another's win is the ego's loss. The ego is not satisfied unless it is bigger and better than fill-in-the-blank.

The ego is arrogant. It seeks validation. It takes credit. It looks for superiority and sufficiency. It revels in success and explains away failure. It won't admit mistakes. It elevates oneself above another. It is constantly comparing.

Perhaps most damaging to our success, and probably the biggest trick in the ego's book, is that *the ego avoids responsibility*. The ego justifies. It makes excuses. It rationalizes. It blames others. It criticizes. It turns a blind eye to the unpleasant feedback and evidence around us.

The ego is particularly hazardous for entrepreneurs because it can hurt us when the business is succeeding *and* when it's struggling. And because we are the leaders, people are naturally inclined not to tell us what our ego is hiding from us. That is a major hazard of entrepreneurship and we must actively combat it as we manage the Dark Side on our Quest for Success.

In full transparency, it took me a long time to realize how my sneaky ego was affecting me at work and at home. My greatest remorse over the years is that I didn't listen better to Charisse and others who were eager and ready to help me and who were hurt by my ego. Only recently did I come to really understand how to regularly check my ego. And because I don't trust that sneaky little ego inside of me, I remind myself daily that my ego might be deceiving me, even when I think it's in check. I'll give you some ideas and suggestions for checking your ego later in the book.

The entrepreneur's family members are usually impacted most by the ego. So as you pursue your Quest for Success with balanced growth, please check your ego—multiple times per day—for the sake of your family, your business, and yourself. You will avoid the downfall that so many entrepreneurs experience along the path of entrepreneurship. You will avoid the deepest and most tragic parts of the Dark Side. And you will accelerate your balanced growth and overall success.

ADHD

There's one last complicating factor of chaos and the Dark Side of entrepreneurship that we need to address. Many entrepreneurs have some amount of ADHD. It's part of what makes us effective as we generate ideas and execute our vision. However, it also makes it extra hard for us to be focused and present at home and at other times when people we care about need our presence.

We tend to be easily distracted and easily excitable. We also tend to put blinders on at times, missing important cues around us. Too often we are intense and quick to anger, hurting those around us and doing damage that sometimes we don't even notice. This is an especially combustible cocktail when combined with an unchecked ego and business success or business struggles.

This isn't discussed enough, which is why I'm covering it here. It doesn't have to cause so much darkness in the lives of entrepreneurs and their families. There is a way to manage it, which we will get to soon enough. But while we're on this topic, can we just acknowledge how amazing the families of entrepreneurs are? They are often behind the scenes while the entrepreneur is out front getting the accolades of success. The spouses and families of entrepreneurs deserve a special badge of honor for their support as we navigate our journey of entrepreneurship. We could not do it without them. And even if we could, it's not truly worth it without them.

Alright, enough of the heavy stuff. As we conquer the chaos in our pursuit of balanced growth, we can avoid the Dark Side, check our egos, and manage our ADHD. And I'll show you how, as we go through the Six Keys to Success. Now, let's get to the good stuff!

INTRODUCING THE SIX KEYS TO CONQUER THE CHAOS

These Six Keys are the proven way to conquer the chaos, with balanced growth in your business and personal life. They have been used by countless contented entrepreneurs. When you use these keys you will find renewed ambition, personal fulfillment, and the ability to transform your business into the success you've always wanted.

The Six Keys are broken into two sections: Personal Keys and Business Keys. A few notes as we introduce the Six Keys:

1. We start with the Personal Keys because you need to get this right to have long-term, balanced growth in your business and personal life.
2. The Personal Keys build upon each other and the Business Keys build upon each other.
3. The Six Keys work together in a virtuous cycle because as you build mastery of the Personal Keys, your capacity to implement the Business Keys will increase. Likewise, as you master the Business Keys, your ability to focus on the Personal Keys will increase.

THE PERSONAL KEYS: MINDSET, VISION, RHYTHM

The Personal Keys provide you with balance on your journey as an entrepreneur. As you fight to conquer chaos, the business will draw you in, you won't have enough hours in the day, your ego will mess with you in good times *and* tough times, and you will often feel overwhelmed as you scramble to do it all. Truth be told, you can't do it all.

The Personal Keys will help you prioritize and stay balanced, cultivating a Mindset of success and giving you a Vision and Rhythm to work toward your business and personal goals. Without adopting the Personal Keys, you may have strong business success for a season, even a long season. But it will be accompanied by personal sacrifice and disappointment as you struggle to get your priorities right in the face of the chaos. That's not our definition of success. Remember, we want "*balanced growth* in your business and personal life."

THE BUSINESS KEYS: STRATEGY, AUTOMATION, LEADERSHIP

The Business Keys give you the business growth and success you want, helping you achieve the money, time, control, impact, and freedom that bring you great fulfillment as an entrepreneur. The Business Keys give you the capacity to grow your business without getting consumed by it.

The Business Keys are the strategy and processes you implement to grow your business and keep it running smoothly and profitably. *If the Personal Keys give you balance, the Business Keys let you control the speed on the entrepreneur's treadmill.* With the Business Keys, we focus on fixing the flaws in your business that prevent growth and cause more chaos.

By putting the Six Keys together, you can achieve balanced growth in your business and personal life. And that's what we need to conquer the chaos and avoid the Dark Side of Entrepreneurship. Now, let's get started on the first Key to Success: Mindset.

Chapter 3 Summary: Chaos and the Dark Side of Entrepreneurship

- Small business chaos is like running on a treadmill. At times the speed is fast, the incline is steep, and it feels like a face-plant is imminent.
- The stress, urgency, and sheer volume of things to do can be overwhelming. And that's just the business side. The personal side only adds to small business chaos.
- The chaos affects both the struggling and the successful small business. It also affects brand-new businesses as well as established businesses.
- Small business chaos is a result of several factors:
  - You're wearing all the hats.
  - You don't know how to grow.
  - You're growing the wrong way.
  - You're drowning in technology.
  - You lack a clear, central, guiding vision.

- The Dark Side of Entrepreneurship—with its destructive physical, mental, emotional, and social effects—happens when the entrepreneur gets personally buried by the chaos.
- Ego is the enemy, causing entrepreneurs to fall in good times and bad. Ego is especially problematic for entrepreneurs because people don't tell the boss unpleasant truths.
- ADHD is a further complicating factor of small business chaos because many entrepreneurs deal with at least a little ADHD and anxiety.
- The Six Keys to Success help us conquer small business chaos and avoid the Dark Side of Entrepreneurship in our personal lives.

Part 2

THE PERSONAL KEYS TO SUCCESS

"Successful people do the things unsuccessful people are unwilling to do . . . even when they don't like doing them."
–Robin Sharma

4
MINDSET

mall business chaos is in the mind even more than in the physical world. That's why your ability to overcome the negative thoughts and emotions that inevitably arise inside of you as an entrepreneur is the number one Key to Success in your business and personal life. Neglect this key and it's only a matter of time until you melt down as an entrepreneur. I'm sorry to be so direct, but it's true. I would be doing you a disservice if I didn't tell it to you straight.

Wrapped up in the small business chaos, entrepreneurs are subjected to a tremendous amount of disappointment and negativity. If it were easy, everyone would do it. As you create a business, build your product or service, take it to the market, and serve your customers, there are so many pitfalls and challenges along the way. Then there's all the stuff you're trying to learn: you're drinking from a firehose, running fast, wearing all the hats as you try to make the business work. And we haven't even mentioned your personal life you're trying to balance. So how you deal with these challenges, mentally and emotionally, has everything to do with your success.

To overcome chaos and create order in our minds as entrepreneurs, we need to understand the concoction of thoughts, words, emotions, and beliefs that live inside of us. Because it's these thoughts and emotions that lead to our actions, which determines whether we are successful. When I was a teenager, my dad taught me a critically important life lesson. See figure 4.1.

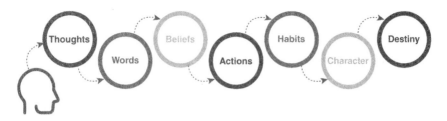

Figure 4.1 Our thoughts create our world.

It all starts with our thoughts. Over the years, I have come to see just how true this is. I've lived it. I've observed it in other entrepreneurs and in other professions. Top performers in every industry learn to manage their minds. My coach, Steve Hardison, has repeatedly shown me how important this is. He has walked me through countless dilemmas over the years. He likes to say, "The problem is not the problem. The problem is how you're thinking about the problem." He is right. But only every time. Our thoughts shape everything. And *we have the power to adjust our thoughts to serve us well.*

The words we speak follow our thoughts and create our world. If we understood how powerful our words are, we would take great care in what we say and how we say it, especially words about ourselves and those we love. Our words are great tools of creation. These words, spoken or unspoken, shape our beliefs, just as my dad taught me. And when we've cemented our beliefs through thoughts and words, every physical thing we create logically and naturally follows from those beliefs.

In Dr. Joe Dispenza's book *Breaking the Habit of Being Yourself,* he conveys it all quite simply: the thoughts we think and the feelings we feel determine the actions we take. Furthermore, it is habitual. We get into habits of thought, habits of feeling, and habits of action. So if we want to elevate our performance, improve our lives, we must elevate our thoughts and feelings, which lead to elevated actions. In other words, it's not just how we think about problems. It's how we think about everything!

So what thoughts are you thinking? If you are doubtful and uncertain about your business, you are likely to feel fear and discomfort. And you are therefore likely to take cautious and slow action. We don't have to be psychology geniuses to know whether that will produce high levels of success in your business! If deep down inside you question and doubt your ability to succeed, you will never conquer the chaos. Period. You've got to believe and have faith in the outcome first. As my dad taught me, the outcome follows the thoughts, words, beliefs, actions, and habits. Above all, you've gotta believe.

Alright so, how do you come to *believe* the right thoughts?

You must rewire your brain and program it for success. Left unchecked, our thoughts run rampant. But the truth is, we are the creators of our thoughts. You are the thinker of your thoughts. You are in control of what goes on in there. If you want to believe the right thoughts, you must create the right thoughts. *And you create the right thoughts by intentionally feeding your mind positive thoughts and removing, **or at least changing**, negative thoughts.* Then you dwell on the right thoughts, infuse them with positive emotion to form positive beliefs, and finally you ingrain those positive beliefs in your mind and heart so that you spring into motivated actions that will lead to success.

In other words, you must *cultivate* your Mindset of Success. Let's dive into how you do that.

CULTIVATING A MINDSET OF SUCCESS

When I was young, my dad constantly emphasized the importance of a positive mental attitude. Unfortunately, I didn't want to hear it as a teenager. Then, when I was mired in the challenges of growing a small business, humbled to the dust because we were on the verge of business failure and personal bankruptcy, a book he recommended in my youth jumped off the shelf at me: *The Power of Positive Thinking*, by Norman Vincent Peale.

That book changed my life. And it saved our business. Keap wouldn't be around if I hadn't learned to turn around my thinking in those early days when signs of business failure were all around us. I've talked with countless entrepreneurs who've experienced something similar. Because entrepreneurship is full of uncomfortable experiences dressed up as failure.

Every day, you must cultivate your Mindset of Success by intentionally engaging in thought exercises that will program your brain for success. There are countless ways to do this, but here are my Top 10 Tactics to cultivate a Mindset of Success:

1. **Your morning routine** must include time to feed your positivity and purge negativity. I highly recommend prayer, meditation, and journaling. This is a powerhouse trio to cleanse your mind of any unproductive thoughts and balance out your emotions. More on meditation and journaling in a minute because these things calm the chaotic mind and create order at the start of your day. Meditation and journaling in the morning are especially important if you have a little ADHD or anxiety, as many entrepreneurs do.

2. **Exercise daily**. The science is clear on the mental and emotional benefits of daily exercise. Entrepreneurs often neglect this critically important practice to their detriment, believing they are too busy. Nonsense. You can't afford not to exercise. Get your heart pumping and your body sweating at least 20 minutes per day and your thoughts and emotions will improve greatly. Your body will respond as you take control of it through your intentional decision to exercise it daily.

3. **Read inspiring material** each day. This is also a good thing to incorporate into your morning routine. Or you

can feed your mind, heart, and spirit with inspiration throughout the day with books, podcasts, and articles from thought leaders who elevate your thinking. Raise your thoughts and feelings to a higher plane by feasting on inspirational content instead of snacking on digital distractions that numb your mind and inhibit your greatness.

4. **Establish a clear picture of who you are** for the world. This is your identity. Some people call this your personal statement, affirmations, or "I am" statements. Whatever you call it, create your identity *intentionally* and recite it daily. It's the way to speak uplifting thoughts to your own mind and heart. It's the way to be and act like the person you intend to become. As you gradually and consistently upgrade your personal identity, your actions and performance will gradually elevate. We'll dig into the topic of identity in the next chapter.

5. **Review your business and personal goals** every day. Burn into your brain the clear intent you possess around your goals. Notice the progress. Convince your analytical mind you are achieving and will achieve your goals as you take stock of the little bits of evidence of success. Take the ups *and* downs in your business as opportunity. Remember this powerful advice Jim Collins, author and student of greatness, shared with me and my team: "The other side of the coin of success is not failure. It's growth." Profound. Reframe any perceived "failures" as growth.

6. **Practice three midday pauses and the ABC method** during your work day. Notice your thoughts and emotions. Accentuate the positive ones. Turn around the negative ones, which are those thoughts that are not productive for you, by using my ABC method:

   A. **Ask** yourself if the negative thought is really true.
   B. **Be** mindful of how you show up when you accept the negative thought as true. ("How's that working for you?")

C. Change the thought, even if slightly, so that you are less affected by the thought. A 180-degree change is best, but even small changes help. If your mind is stuck holding on to the counterproductive thought as true, remember that you can be right or you can be happy. Put the ego in its place and choose happy.

7. **Review customer success stories** and positive reviews. This is fuel for the entrepreneur's soul. It will remind you why you do what you do and keep you going in the tough times when you feel like quitting. It will give your analytical mind evidence of progress and success. And it will foster positive emotions in your heart and mind, which will fuel you to take the actions that will lead to more customer success.

8. **Give gratitude and compliments**. Gratitude is like a magic pill that makes everything better. Because when we stop thinking about ourselves and focus on others, everything really does get better. The Mayo Clinic has studied the positive effects of gratitude, stating:

> Expressing gratitude is associated with a host of mental and physical benefits. Studies have shown that feeling thankful can improve sleep, mood and immunity. Gratitude can decrease depression, anxiety, difficulties with chronic pain and risk of disease. *If a pill could do this, everyone would be taking it.* Your brain is designed to problem solve rather than appreciate. You often must override this design to reap the benefits of gratitude.

The magic thing about gratitude and compliments is that you feel better and so does the person you thank or compliment. Sam Walton said, "Nothing else can quite substitute for a few well-chosen, well-timed, sincere words of praise. They're free and worth a fortune." And, I might add, they also make *you* feel great when you speak them to others.

9. **Talk with a friend or family member** who can provide perspective. Sometimes we just get inside our heads and we need someone to listen and then snap us out of it. Make sure the person is unbiased *and* understands entrepreneurship. Be careful about who you get that pep talk from. Not only do you need someone who can hear you out and lift your spirits, but you also need someone who sees the big picture, has your best interests in mind, and understands the ups and downs of business ownership. Many well-intentioned loved ones steer entrepreneurs astray because they don't appreciate the facts and nuances of business ownership. Note: some of the best family members to snap us out of our funk are our kids. They have a knack for putting things in perspective and reminding us of what really matters.

10. **Spread optimism** to others and receive it from others. Don't dwell on the negative; learn from it. Don't turn a blind eye toward unpleasant feedback. Receive it with humility and accountability. Tackle it with grit and optimism as fuel for success. More on that in a minute. And be sure to surround yourself with people who do the same, while gracefully distancing yourself from those who don't. As an entrepreneur, you cannot afford to bring down your thoughts and feelings by surrounding yourself with skeptics, cynics, and doubters. Be optimistic. Life is wonderful. Entrepreneurship is amazing. Stay positive, go to work, and things will work out.

For entrepreneurs, it's vital to stay positive and build your confidence. Cultivate a Mindset of Success by practicing these Top 10 Tactics. If you want to go deeper on this topic, I recommend a book by long-time Keap customer Lewis Howes, entitled *The Greatness Mindset*. You are a creator, an achiever, and an important contributor to society. But you can't do all of that and unlock your greatness if you allow your thoughts and emotions to get the best of you. You are in control of your thoughts and emotions.

What you think and feel is your choice. We *choose* how we feel. We *make* our days. These things don't just happen to us. They are a choice. Choose happy. And make it a great day.

Above all, do not succumb to the cynicism and skepticism often lobbed at those who practice the techniques in this chapter. Cynics may say, "This soft stuff is a joke." But cynics never create anything great. They stand on the sidelines of life, pretending they are smarter than everyone, not emotionally smart enough to commit to the challenge. You are an entrepreneur. You are out to create something great. You cannot afford to be cynical. You are cultivating your Mindset of Success so you can conquer the chaos and achieve your goals. The faster you kick your inner cynic to the curb, the sooner you'll succeed as an entrepreneur.

I love this awesome quote by Bryant S. Hinckley: "Cynics do not contribute, skeptics do not create, doubters do not achieve." Cultivate the Mindset of Success so you can contribute, create, and achieve.

YOUR EMOTIONAL CAPITAL BANK ACCOUNT

As you cultivate a Mindset of Success, the goal is to turn the logical thoughts of your analytical mind into subconscious, powerful thoughts, emotions, and beliefs. When you add positive emotion to your thoughts, you create strong beliefs that drive your actions. It's true that seeing is believing. But it's also true—maybe even more true—that *feeling* is believing. In his 1944 classic, *Feeling Is the Secret*, Neville Goddard taught that how we feel about things is the real secret to how we shape our lives. We want to dwell on the positive thoughts, speak those positive thoughts, and bring positive emotion to them so that our positive beliefs drive our actions.

To do this, we must build up and store our emotions in a figurative emotional bank account inside of us. This "emotional capital" is intangible and tricky to wrap your arms around. Similar to a financial bank account, your emotional capital is stored in a depository of positive thoughts and feelings, and you'll need to withdraw from that account every day to take actions that lead to success. This means you must also make deposits into your emotional bank account every day. And you need to honestly evaluate your emotional account balance in the morning and at night. The truth is, most people don't pay much attention to this, and that's a shame. Because if you're not careful, you'll find yourself slipping into ruts of apathy, doubt, or fear. And those emotions will never propel you out of the chaos and into the success you want.

There is a simple way to determine the balance in your emotional capital account. Your balance is determined by the way you get out of bed in the morning and the way you go to bed at night. Do you jump out of bed, excited about the new day? Do you get ready for work in the morning thinking about the opportunities, the challenges, and the exciting work ahead of you? Do you hit the sack, eager to work on your business the next day, with a heart full of gratitude and excitement for what you get to do?

Or do you wake up worried and nervous? Do you go to bed with a knot in your stomach and the dreaded feeling you had when you were a kid on Sunday night, realizing after a fun weekend it was time to go to school the next day? It's normal and natural to have mixed emotions about your business. What we want to do is be conscious of our emotions and be guided by the positive ones. Each day, we want to engage in the practice of upgrading our thoughts and emotions, which leads to upgraded actions and performance.

So let's do a spot check right now. Ask yourself if you're "on fire" in your business like you were the day you started it. Have you fallen into the trap of "going through the motions"? Do you get easily disappointed? Are you clear on your short-term and long-term goals? Are you excited about your work and your goals? You want to notice how you're feeling, break out of the rut of just "doing what you do," and elevate your thoughts and emotions by practicing the Top 10 Tactics shared in this chapter. In particular, you want to infuse positive energy into your emotions, creating powerful beliefs and the emotional capital you need to fuel your actions for success.

With all this talk of positivity, you might think I'm an eternal optimist. It's quite true I'm optimistic. But I practice and teach a brand of optimism full of grit, faith, and determination. I call it "disciplined optimism" because if we don't apply healthy amounts of discipline to our optimism, we will get stuck in the chaos. Let me explain what disciplined optimism is and how it will help you cultivate the Mindset of Success.

DISCIPLINED OPTIMISM

To understand the basis of disciplined optimism, we need to introduce the Stockdale Paradox, a term coined by Jim Collins in his book *Good to Great*. In the book, Collins talks about Admiral James Stockdale, a prisoner of war in Vietnam. In the *seven years* Stockdale was held by his enemies in the infamous Hanoi Hilton, he was beaten repeatedly, but refused to succumb to the demands of his captors.

Because of his resistance efforts, Stockdale was eventually removed from other prisoners and held in solitary confinement. When he was released, Stockdale could barely walk or stand up straight. He went on to receive a Medal of Honor, serve for many more years in a distinguished naval career, become a successful businessman, and eventually run for vice president of the United States alongside presidential candidate Ross Perot.

Collins recorded a conversation he had with Stockdale. The answers Stockdale gave in his interview were profound and inspirational to me and many others. One of his statements left a particularly significant impression: "I never lost faith in the end of the story, *I never doubted* not only that I would get out, but also that I would prevail in the end and turn the experience into the defining event of my life, which, in retrospect, I would not trade."

When Collins asked who didn't make it out, Stockdale replied, "Oh, that's easy, the optimists. Oh, they were the ones who said, 'We're going to be out by Christmas.' And Christmas would come, and Christmas would go. Then they'd say, 'We're going to be out by Easter.' And Easter would come, and Easter would go. And then Thanksgiving, and then it would be Christmas again. And they died of a broken heart."

Stockdale then added, "This is a very important lesson. *You must never confuse faith that you will prevail in the end— which you can never afford to lose—with the discipline to confront the most brutal facts of your current reality*, whatever they might be" (Collins, 2001, 84–86).

That is the Stockdale Paradox: faith you will prevail plus confronting the brutal facts. The practice of disciplined optimism builds upon the Stockdale Paradox and applies it specifically to small business owners.

THE THREE COMPONENTS OF DISCIPLINED OPTIMISM

You can build disciplined optimism into your Mindset of Success by applying the Stockdale Paradox to your work as an entrepreneur:

1. Maintain an undying belief your business will succeed.
2. Confront the brutal facts of your current reality.
3. Go to work on those brutal facts because you *want* to improve your business.

There's a lot packed into that three-part statement of disciplined optimism, so let's dig into each component.

Maintain an Undying Belief in Your Vision

The first component is absolute belief that your business will achieve the long-term success you have envisioned. In Chapters 5 and 7, we will introduce the concept of your company Vision and Strategy, which will help your belief. You'll want to do these three things to maintain belief in your Vision:

Publish it. Write it down, post it by your desk, tell others about it, do everything possible to make it real and tangible. Revisit your goal constantly. When you give life to a goal in this way, you begin to believe (remember: Thoughts → Words → Beliefs). Publish the *words* that will help you build an undying belief in your goal and then speak your goal into existence. Treat it like your Declaration of Independence, as we discussed in Chapter 1.

Remember your progress. Take time to reflect and consider where you were last month, last quarter, and last year. Write down your achievements and celebrate your progress. Take special care to remember the challenges you've overcome and the things you've learned. The process of remembering and evaluating your progress will build your confidence and give you more momentum to achieve your goal.

Patiently, confidently, *work* at it. As entrepreneurs we don't always know *how* things will work out. But if we patiently and confidently work toward the goal, somehow it *will* work out. In other words, as entrepreneurs we need to have a little faith that if we keep at it, everything will work out in the end. Remember that most success looks like failure halfway through it.

Confront the Brutal Facts

The second component of disciplined optimism is the need to confront the brutal facts of your current reality. It's important to recognize that you must address these problems at the same time you are maintaining an undying belief in your goal. This "brutal facts" component has the effect of balancing your enthusiasm and focusing you on the work to be done. You must:

- State the problems facing you and your business.
- Accept that these problems won't magically go away.
- Reframe these problems as challenges to be conquered.

Again, you do this while simultaneously maintaining an undying belief that you will achieve your goal. That's the trick. You must not allow the unpleasant aspects of business to break your spirit. It's easy to get upset, discouraged, or numb when you deal with the brutal facts. Stay sharp. Stay positive. Stay focused on your ultimate goal and the realization of that goal.

Go to Work on the Brutal Facts Because You Want to Improve Your Business

Third, you must attack the brutal facts, and do so not because you have to, but because you *want* to. And why do you want to attack the brutal facts? Because you see these challenges, these obstacles, as the way to your success. You recognize that *The Obstacle Is the Way*, as Ryan Holiday taught us in his book by that title. When you find yourself wanting to talk with an angry customer or vendor, wanting to fix a process or system, or wanting to deal with a shortfall in payroll, you know you're going to work on the brutal facts, using them as fuel to improve your business and achieve success.

So that's the framework for practicing disciplined optimism. It is a powerful tool in your toolkit to build a Mindset of Success. No matter how much you practice the Top 10 Tactics and no matter how much emotional capital you store up, your business will give you plenty of opportunities to practice disciplined optimism when "stuff happens." Cash shortages, customer complaints, competitive pressure, missed goals, limited resources, and other unpleasant circumstances you encounter—all of these things give you an opportunity to practice disciplined optimism.

Before we wrap up our first Key to Success, I want to share one last important concept to help you establish a Mindset of Success. The concept is called entrepreneurial independence and it is a tool to help you manage the advice you get, your insecurities, and your ambitions as an entrepreneur.

ENTREPRENEURIAL INDEPENDENCE

It seems the moment you start your business, everyone has advice for you. Even friends and family who've never run a business suddenly become experts in their own eyes, eager to advise you in your new business. And the advice never stops coming. Sometimes you'll feel like the golfer being given 10 tips at once, all twisted up in knots, with no chance of hitting a good shot.

It can be tempting to tune out all the advice. But that has its pitfalls. Our ego wants to believe we have all the answers, even though we know there's so much to learn. We also know those who don't learn from history are doomed to repeat it. And let's be honest, there's a *lot* we don't know as we are learning to build a successful business. I'm guessing (and appreciating) you feel this way because you're reading this book! Thank you.

So what's an ambitious entrepreneur to do? Get tied up in knots trying to implement all the advice given? Tune it all out and stick to your gut, risking that your ego might steer you astray? Something in between? Yes, and that something in between is what entrepreneurial independence is all about.

Entrepreneurial independence requires you to strike the safe haven of confidence that lies between ignorance and arrogance. See figure 4.2. When arrogant business owners become

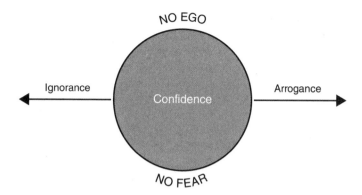

Figure 4.2 Entrepreneurial independence.

overconfident and believe too much in the value of their own thoughts, they are setting themselves up for failure. When ignorant business owners ignore the learning, advice, and wisdom of others, they can derail their own success. In both cases, the entrepreneur is blinded and sabotaged by the ego, whether by the ego's fear or cockiness.

Many years ago, my wise father-in-law taught me a lesson along these lines. He taught me that in business, a great motto to live by is "No ego, no fear." We have adopted that as a slogan and have found it to be a great guideline as we strive for the confidence that lies between the dangerous positions of ignorance on one side and arrogance on the other.

Listen to your gut. Trust yourself. But know that no one is perfect. You will make mistakes. And your ego is none too happy about giving ground to others. So how does the entrepreneur find that middle ground of confidence? By doing the following three things:

1. **Define your success.** As you take in learnings and advice from others, measure it against your plan, your picture of success. Get as clear as possible on what your success is so that you have a method for evaluating inputs. The second Key to Success is all about helping

you establish your Life Vision. The fourth Key to Success is about helping you establish your business Strategy. *Your Vision and Strategy give you the bearings you need to effectively evaluate the information you take in.*

2. **Believe in your decisions.** This boils down to one simple thing—don't do anything half-heartedly. Quite often, business decisions must be made based on limited data, before the business owner would prefer to make a decision. Just remember this: in almost every decision, the success is not so much a product of the choice you make; rather, it is a product of the way you carry out your choice. No matter what your decision, no matter how ill-prepared you are to make it, follow through wholeheartedly. Conviction is essential to making things happen. Stated another way, you can make almost any decision "right" by how you execute on the decision you've made.

3. **Avoid arrogance.** Because the ego is so sneaky and dangerous, it's best to err on the side of ignorance. Avoid arrogance like the plague. This means you'll want to listen more and talk less. If you're not sure whether to heed advice or ignore it, go ahead and take in the information, and then weigh it with all the other inputs. Being open-minded and "sleeping on it" when given advice is an effective way to avoid arrogance. The point is, better to be ignorant than arrogant because as I've already mentioned and as I'll describe in more detail later in the book, ego is indeed the enemy.

I want to share just a few more thoughts to help you practice entrepreneurial independence and strike that middle ground of confidence between ignorance and arrogance.

Get comfortable with conflict. You can't please everybody even if you want to, and conflicts will arise because people have different opinions. That's just part of being an entrepreneur and it shouldn't keep you from exercising your right and responsibility to make decisions and run your business. When you deal with others, be kind, but firm. For example, if your brother-in-law finds a building for your new office and it's not what you want, simply say, "That's kind of you to look. I'm actually searching in this area." He will have an opinion. He may try to change your mind. Just say, "No thanks. I'll keep looking." End of story. No debate. No discussion. No drama. You stand your ground and allow for differing opinions while staying in control of the decision.

Be open to changing your mind. You've had some interesting experiences since you first started your business. You know more about yourself, the business world, and human nature. You've learned a lot, and it's going to affect the way you think and what you believe. That's okay. Human nature is to grow. Be open-minded. Don't make decisions based on what you "used to do." Make the best choices you know how to make today, even if it goes against your previous ideas.

You may need to adjust some relationships. As you grow and mature, the trusted advisors you surround yourself with might need to change. This can be difficult for entrepreneurs who are used to taking advice from friends and family who do not understand how best to advise you. This means you may need to adjust some relationships or certain aspects of those relationships. You can continue seeking advice from those folks in other areas of your life, but for business advice, you may need to look elsewhere. And that may require that you get comfortable with disagreement.

Warning: If you haven't already done so, take some time now to determine which values, beliefs, and relationships you will hold sacred and which ones are safe to let evolve. In your growth as an entrepreneur, things will change. If you haven't taken the time to decide which values, beliefs, and relationships are untouchable, you may lose who you are and what matters most to you. And if you allow that to happen, no amount of business success is worth it.

At the end of the day, you are in control and you will determine your success. All the other voices will fade into the background over time. I love this quote from Ralph Waldo Emerson, which aptly describes what we face as entrepreneurs, receiving advice from every which direction:

> *"If you know you are right, stay the course even though the whole world seems to be against you and everyone you know questions your judgment. When you prevail—and you eventually will if you stick to the job—they will all tell you that they knew all along you could do it."*
>
> —*Ralph Waldo Emerson*

Getting your Mindset right is the number one Key to Success that will help you conquer the chaos. You'll need to:

- Cultivate a Mindset of Success using the Top 10 Tactics.
- Build up your emotional capital.
- Practice disciplined optimism.
- Exercise entrepreneurial independence.

All of that is a lot easier to do when you have a Life Vision that everything fits into. And that's our second Key to Success.

Chapter 4 Summary: Mindset

- Small business chaos is in the mind even more than in the physical world. To conquer the chaos, we must overcome the negativity and cultivate a Mindset of success.
- Your Mindset is a combination of your thoughts, feelings, and beliefs. Cultivating a positive Mindset is critical because your thoughts create your world.
- Cultivate a Mindset of success with the top 10 tactics:
  1. Use your morning routine to cleanse thoughts and feelings.
  2. Exercise vigorously every day for at least 20 minutes.
  3. Read inspiring material daily to elevate thoughts and feelings.

---

4. Establish and recite a clear statement of who you are for the world.
5. Review your business and personal goals every day.
6. Practice the three midday pauses and the ABC method.
7. Review customer success stories and positive reviews.
8. Give gratitude and compliments every day to lift others.
9. Talk with a friend or family member to get perspective.
10. Spread optimism to others and receive it from others.

- Monitor your emotional capital bank account regularly and make daily deposits to ensure you are executing with enthusiasm and positive emotion. Positive feelings are the secret that enables us to spring into positive actions that produce positive results.
- Practice disciplined optimism by: 1) maintaining an undying belief in your vision, 2) confronting the brutal facts, and 3) going to work on the brutal facts because you want to improve your business.
- Live with entrepreneurial independence by striking the safe harbor of confidence that sits between ignorance and arrogance.

5
VISION

Most entrepreneurs don't lack vision. They are visionaries in the business world, seeing things others cannot and creating solutions others will not. Entrepreneurs tend to have great business vision.

But what about the entrepreneur's Life Vision? Even though entrepreneurs tend to be good at business vision, quite often their Life Vision is lacking, leading to personal consequences that are dangerous and sometimes tragic. Entrepreneurs can feel like they're serving the business instead of their business serving them. Before long, we can feel trapped, consumed and controlled by the business, even when the business is "successful." This can create ugly results in the personal lives of entrepreneurs, as we've already mentioned.

Our second key to business and personal success is Life Vision. And after Mindset, Vision is the most foundational key to achieving balanced growth in your business and personal life. Because when your business fits into the bigger picture of your Life Vision, the business can serve you instead of you serving the business.

Before we get to creating a Life Vision that will set you up for balanced growth in business and life, let's dig a little deeper into why this business-life imbalance occurs.

WHY AND HOW DOES
THE IMBALANCE HAPPEN?

Obviously, small business chaos throws us out of balance. Although we've covered the explanation of chaos, its causes and symptoms, there's more subtlety to the chaos than we see on the surface. There's some powerful psychology at play here. In order to steer us clear of the Dark Side, we need to understand some of that psychology.

Business success is intoxicating, drawing us in and seducing us as entrepreneurs, blinding us to the other needs, demands, and interests in our lives. And business failure is suffocating, depriving us of the air to really breathe in life, conjuring up fear and worry, dominating our thoughts and emotions. The stress, pressure, and overwhelm can be too much to handle, causing us to neglect important priorities in life. Likewise, the challenging work, exciting rewards, and stimulating thoughts of the business can distract us from other crucial life pursuits.

In both cases—business success and business failure—*Ego Is the Enemy*. Ryan Holiday was 100% right when he wrote that book. And it especially applies to entrepreneurs, as I mentioned previously. We tend to have strong egos that drive us to create things others cannot or will not. That ego can certainly help us create and build a great business, but it is a sneaky sucker that can rob us of what matters most. We must constantly check our egos.

Finding balance is especially challenging for entrepreneurs because unlike most folks seeking work-life balance, entrepreneurship is just different, for so many reasons. We entrepreneurs love our work! We struggle to leave it alone. Our identity is often tied to and almost synonymous with the business. The success and failure of the business is personal. The business is uber-demanding. Personal finances are wrapped up in the business. The line between business and personal life is very fuzzy.

All of these dynamics create tremendous tension inside of entrepreneurs. As this tension plays out, little by little, we make decisions that relegate important people and things to lower priority. We skip a child's soccer game, miss a date, postpone or cancel a vacation, arrive late to a meaningful event. Our eating habits and exercise habits slip with tiny daily decisions as we feel too busy, too tired, too stressed, or too wound up. We rationalize our choices, sending hurtful messages to our loved ones, justifying our decisions and telling ourselves, "It's only for a short time," or "I'm doing it for the family," or "When XYZ happens, I can do things differently."

Unfortunately, there's always another thing that "requires" our attention. Always a good reason for our rationalization. Always something else that seems urgent or important. And so, just as we discussed in the prior chapter on Mindset, we create habits of busyness through our patterns of thoughts, feelings, and actions. But these are not the habits we want. We scarcely realize what we're missing out on, not noticing that what really matters is often the small stuff we can't see because we're so busy. And we're not actually present when we're home. We gradually sacrifice our lives for the business.

I am intimately and personally familiar with this inner tension. And I'm not proud of the fact that I battled it for many years, at times having my priorities out of whack in a way that hurt the people I love the most.

This is not what we truly want as entrepreneurs. And it's not what you will get if you embrace the second Key to Success: Vision. Because in order to achieve our definition of success, in order to achieve "balanced growth in our business and personal lives that produces money, time, control, impact, and freedom," we need to see the big picture. *We need a clear Life Vision that gives us perspective, purpose, and priority.* Without that, it's just too easy to get sucked into the business. Balance is impossible when your priorities are out of whack.

As you think about Life Vision, many of the tried and true axioms may spring to mind. Sayings like:

"Begin with the end in mind."
"Keep your priorities straight."
"To thine own self be true."
"Look at the big picture."
And as my coach, Steve Hardison, always says, "Don't fall for the booby prize."

What Steve means by that is "Don't get so caught up in the fame and fortune of business success that you lose what matters most—family, faith, health, and happiness." Well said. All of these clichés are recited for good reason. They apply quite nicely to Life Vision. Now let me tell you how we discovered this Key to Success and then I'll share it with you so you can implement it in your life.

THE EVOLUTION OF LIFE VISION

When Scott and I wrote the first edition of *Conquer the Chaos* many years ago, we did not include Life Vision (or Rhythm, for that matter). We had not yet discovered its power. Ironically, we couldn't yet see the results and effects of practicing Vision or not practicing Vision. And that's actually a very important thing to notice about this Key to Success: *It plays out over the long term, over many years, making it difficult to see the gargantuan benefits—and pitfalls—associated with practicing or not practicing this Key to Success.*

For quite some time, Scott and I were both practicing a version of Vision in our personal lives. We have both always lived very intentionally. We were students of Dan Sullivan at Strategic Coach (http://www.StrategicCoach.com); we gobbled up books on the topics of life balance and Vision; we masterminded with other entrepreneurs, trying to crack this nut one way or another;

and we were observing what our customers and other entrepreneurs were doing, or not doing, in terms of a Life Vision.

Gradually, we were learning and applying pieces of the Vision planning process, through practice and observation. The pieces were working for those who practiced them. And the results achieved by entrepreneurs who were implementing their Life Vision effectively were becoming irrefutable. It was just tricky to observe and discover this Key to Success because the results play out over an extended period of time.

It was also tricky to discover Vision as a Key to Success because not only does this stuff play out over time, it also seemed to be scattered across many different experts and sources. Over the years I sought out coaches, consultants, and spiritual advisors, picking up pieces here and there, putting them into practice in my own way. To be clear, I made all sorts of mistakes in my quest for balance, and I'm still very much a practitioner of this stuff—I practice it every day. But eventually I got to a method that works beautifully. And then I began sharing it with others, witnessing the profound impact it has on their lives.

In short, I have spent over $2 million and two decades studying, practicing, and establishing a method for creating and executing a Life Vision. I've used countless programs, taking bits and pieces of them to form a method that works gorgeously. Many people over the years have asked me about it. I shared it with people here and there, but until recently, I had not put it all together for others to consume. Which is yet another reason why I'm so excited about this book.

I'm giving you this Key to Success because I want it to help you as much as it has helped me and others who practice it. And I'm telling you this, not to draw attention to the money spent and effort invested, but because it is fantastically valuable stuff. It truly is a Key to your Success. But only if you practice it.

With that, let's get to Vision so you can design an amazing, balanced life that your business fits into.

THE FIVE PARTS OF YOUR LIFE VISION

When you put your Vision in place, it will give you clear *purpose, perspective, and priority*. It will help you live a well-rounded, balanced life. You will live life on your terms, purposefully, intentionally, and all based on the life you've designed. The awesome thing is that your business will fit into and support your lifetime goals, bringing even more meaning and value to your business. Your business supports your Life Vision and in turn, your Life Vision supports your business, creating a virtuous cycle of success. It's pretty awesome as you experience this playing out in your life!

Your Life Vision has five parts, which all relate to each other. The five parts of Vision, in order of importance, are:

1. Identity: *Who* you are for the world
2. Purpose: *Why* you exist on this planet
3. Values: *How* you live—the characteristics you espouse
4. Mission: *What* you will achieve in life
5. Goals: *What* you will do—physical, spiritual, social, business, financial

Identity, purpose, values, mission, goals—who, why, how, big what, and little what. These are the "big picture" questions you must answer to create your clear Life Vision. Let's jump into each one to help you do this. And, by the way, if you're wondering about the "where" and "when," those come into play in the next chapter as we get into the brass tacks of how you implement and execute your Life Vision using a Rhythm of Execution.

1. **Identity**. This is who you are for the world. It is a statement or collection of "I am" statements (sometimes called affirmations) that clearly articulate who you are. It is mostly an articulation of who you actually are, the real

you, with a little dose of aspiration sprinkled in. *In other words, it's your best self.* It's the place you come from when encountering situations in life. James Clear, author of *Atomic Habits*, teaches that when we get clear on our identity, the habits we want to adopt follow naturally. Some people have many "I am" statements. Some people have just a few. If you have many, like I do, you need a summary statement of who you are. I am a Christian, an amazing family man, and a billion-dollar-company CEO. That's the summary of who I am. Who are you? Work on this gradually, over time. Once you are clear on who you are for the world, once you know your identity and ingrain it into your mind, heart, and soul, you begin acting in congruence with your identity. As my coach would say, "You can be who you are, no matter what." And that's a powerful way to live.

2. **Purpose**. This is why you exist on this planet. It's a short, memorable, deeply meaningful statement to you that you stamp on your mind and in your heart to guide you through life. For example, my purpose is "To love, inspire, and enrich others." That may not mean much to some, but each word means a lot to me. When your "why" in life is clear, your success actions are easier, they have more meaning, and your business fits into the bigger picture of your life. There is a natural flow to things when you "start with why" in your personal life. Simon Sinek famously taught us this about business. It also applies to life. And it's even more important to "start with why" in life for entrepreneurs, because we are pulled to extremes by the business.

3. **Values**. These are the top five characteristics you embrace that guide how you live. This is pretty straightforward: one word each, five words that mean a lot to you. Top business thinkers and industry leaders have recognized that Jim Collins, Patrick Lencioni, and others are right:

great organizations are built on a strong foundation of values. Well, it's true of great individuals as well. Get clear on your top five personal values and they will shape your character and guide you to greatness through business and life.

4. **Mission**. This is what you will achieve in life. It's an opportunity to channel that entrepreneurial ambition into your life, not just your business. What do you want to accomplish during your time on planet earth? *How Will You Measure Your Life?* as Clayton Christensen powerfully asked in his book by that name. You have a mission to achieve that goes far beyond your business mission. What is your life mission? When you get clear on your life mission statement, there's an added energy and power to everything you do. You can draw on that power in challenging times and when making difficult decisions. And it will guide your goal setting, which is the fifth part of Vision. As Lewis Howes teaches in *The Greatness Mindset*, lack of a clear mission is the single biggest reason we fail to achieve greatness. Our mission propels us to greatness.

5. **Goals**. This is where the rubber meets the road, where things get exciting, where results start to pop. And where your philosophy turns into achievement. Divide your life into five areas: physical, spiritual, social, business, and financial. Look deep into the future. What does the pinnacle of lifetime achievement look like for you in each of the five areas? I recommend you write one lifetime goal in each of the five areas. Once you've written that down, create a corresponding 10-year goal for each of your lifetime goals. This gives you a tangible Vision of your future in the five areas—physical, spiritual, social, business, and financial—with a related lifetime and 10-year goal in each of the five areas. See figure 5.1.

Figure 5.1 Life Vision.

GUIDELINES FOR LIFETIME GOALS

We need to get clear on a few important high-level guidelines about lifetime goals. We'll cover goal-setting in more depth in the next chapter. First, we need to cover an important question: Why these five areas? Why not something else? Well, over the years, I've found through practice and observation that these five areas cover all the bases. Each is narrow enough to keep you focused and broad enough to give you a little flexibility to work on certain aspects of life as seasons change and life evolves. For example, you could work hobbies into the physical or social areas. I'll bet if you go back and look at your goals and New Year's resolutions over the years, you could probably fit almost everything into these five areas.

Second, we want to recognize the importance of these five areas individually and collectively. Each is important, and all work together. We don't want to neglect one area or another because these goals feed off of each other. So many times, progress in one area spurs progress in another area. A synergistic effect is at play here. Therefore, the opposite is true as well: often stagnation in one area blocks progress in another area. These areas of our life goals work together and this method of planning your life is intended to be a system, where all aspects work together to produce a magnificent, whole life.

Third, let's look closer at how each area helps us achieve the success we want. If we don't take care of our body, obviously we will struggle to succeed as we've defined success. Similarly, we need to feed our spirit so that our heart and emotions are tuned to perform at high levels. The social aspect is about relationships, service, and leadership that bring great joy and fulfillment to life. And we separate out business and financial goals because too often entrepreneurs overfocus on the business, and business success doesn't automatically translate to personal financial success. We want to make sure you're making it rain personally, so your personal finances deserve their own category of goals.

Finally, you want to get in the habit of thinking about each area of your goals as its own swim lane. Yes, I just explained that all areas of your goals work together, and they do. But it's also helpful to think of each area as its own swim lane so that you can break down a lifetime goal into 10-year, 3-year, 1-year, quarterly, and monthly incremental goals. More on that in the next chapter. For now, just get used to the idea that *each area of your long-term, lifetime goals is supported by mid-term and short-term goals*. Simple as that. Getting into the habit of thinking this way will serve your Life Vision and help you break down success into distinct and manageable areas of your life with short-term and mid-term milestones

PUTTING TOGETHER THE VISION PUZZLE PIECES

To recap, there are five parts of your Life Vision: identity, purpose, values, mission, and goals, in that order. And there are five areas of your goals: physical, spiritual, social, business, and financial. These puzzle pieces don't all come together overnight. But they do come together—gorgeously—as you work at it iteratively, through your Mindset work and your Rhythm of Execution, which we'll get to in the next chapter.

For now, the point is to know that you absolutely can achieve work-life balance as an entrepreneur when you look at life wholistically. And be assured that *you don't have to do it all or do it perfectly to get great benefits* from this method of life planning. I can't stress this enough: each piece of the Vision puzzle that you put into place will further your success and help you achieve balanced growth.

Many entrepreneurs have bits and pieces of the Life Vision scattered across different planning methods or loosely articulated in one way or another. I encourage you to articulate each puzzle piece and assemble the picture of your Life Vision. There is serious power in pulling it all together into a clear picture of your future because you build confidence and clarity when you can see it in one place. I call this "The Big Picture." You can get various tools and resources to help you assemble your Life Vision and Big Picture at www.ConquerTheChaosBook.com.

As you work on your Vision by applying the entrepreneur's visionary skills to your life, you will be amazed by the results. The balance and flow in your life will gradually improve. And over time you will begin to see and feel life-changing results. You'll be totally excited about the life you are creating. Your accomplishments and fulfillment will be off the charts, which is exactly what I want for you. I can't overstate this enough. I guarantee that as you start implementing this stuff, you'll see the power of it and you'll become a believer.

A while back, an entrepreneur I've known for years came to me, confidentially, to get some advice. He was leading a successful and growing business that was generating millions of dollars in annual revenue. By all accounts he was a very successful entrepreneur. And I can attest that he is and was at the time a very good entrepreneur, running a successful business. But there were some problems beneath the surface. His marriage was tense, to say the least. His family life was off. He had major team issues. The personal financial situation wasn't as strong as it could have been. His physical health was declining. He felt heavy, weighed down, and unsure of whether he even wanted to continue with the business. After listening to him, I could see he was missing a Life Vision and Rhythm of Execution.

After a couple conversations, he began implementing his Life Vision. He started by putting a few puzzle pieces into place. Gradually, his life began to change. Within weeks, he noticed he was feeling better physically and emotionally. He continued implementing more of the Vision and started working on his goals in the five areas. Within six months, things were significantly different in his life. As time went by, he implemented more and more of the Vision and Rhythm, loving the results that were flowing into his business and life. His team was happy. His wife was happy. And he was happy.

The fact is, in cases of both business struggles *and* business successes, we see the Dark Side of Entrepreneurship when the entrepreneur is not guided by a clear Life Vision. As things get totally out of balance, the stress mounts and entrepreneurs are known to do dumb things. I've certainly been there. "Stress makes us stupid," we like to say. If the stress is mounting and you don't have a Life Vision in place, do yourself a favor and adopt what I've shared here. You will love the *purpose, perspective, and priority* it brings to your business and personal life.

Your Life Vision is the second Key to Success and the real foundation for balanced growth in your business and personal life. The way to implement your Vision is to practice the third Key to Success: a Rhythm of Execution. Let's get to it.

Chapter 5 Summary: Vision

- Most entrepreneurs are pretty good at business vision, but a clear and compelling personal vision is needed to help them conquer small business chaos and give them purpose, perspective, and priority.
- When the Life Vision is well established, the entrepreneur's business fits into the Life Vision in a way that improves the entrepreneur's business and life.
- The results of an effective Life Vision—and a neglected Life Vision—show up over time, making it easy to overlook the importance of Life Vision.
- The five parts of Life Vision are: 1) identity, 2) purpose, 3) values, 4) mission, and 5) goals.
- To establish an effectively balanced life, goals need to be set in the five areas of life: 1) physical, 2) spiritual, 3) social, 4) business, and 5) financial.
- The five parts of Life Vision and the five areas of life combine to make up the puzzle pieces of an effective Life Vision that will create success: *balanced growth* that produces more money, time, control, impact, and freedom for entrepreneurs.

6
RHYTHM

Human beings are creatures of habit. And yet the chaos of entrepreneurship can throw even the most vital habits off kilter. At times when the chaos was most intense, I would run into the house at the end of a day, head straight for the bathroom, and then go to the kitchen to grab a quick snack. I would hurriedly say to Charisse, "I was so busy today I didn't have time to eat or even go to the bathroom," almost as if it were a badge of honor. And she would say something like, "Wow! Sounds like you're out of balance."

She was right. (By the way, Charisse is always right in her observations of my life as an entrepreneur.) I've seen a version of this over and over with entrepreneurs. The demands of the business are so great, the opportunities so exciting, and the fires so constant, that even if you have a good Life Vision in place, the chaos of the business can take control and knock you out of balance. Before you know it, you're busy, but you aren't achieving your goals and dreams.

To make matters more challenging, many entrepreneurs have at least a little ADHD or anxiety, as mentioned previously, making us very susceptible to "shiny objects," high stress, and any number of distractions that can knock us off our Vision. Many entrepreneurs buck schedules and structure, unwilling or unable to stick to a regular program. There's nothing necessarily wrong with that. It's a character trait of many great creators. In many cases, it's the reason entrepreneurs are doing their own thing instead of working for someone else.

Given all of these facts, entrepreneurs need a way of operating each day—no matter how chaotic things get—that ties them to their Life Vision, giving them calm perspective and helping them achieve their most important business and personal goals. We need a way to operate that works with our own style, that takes advantages of strengths and minimizes weaknesses. We need a way to operate in the "zone" or the "flow" so we can achieve our business and life goals.

That's why the third key to business and personal success for entrepreneurs is a Rhythm of Execution. And it is this Rhythm that produces *calmness, confidence, and consistency*, the flow that enables us to achieve our goals and dreams in smooth and predictable fashion.

A Rhythm of Execution is more than a collection of habits. It's a recurring pattern of habits, designed with great intention, suited to your strengths and weaknesses, to help you achieve your important business and personal goals. In other words, your Rhythm of Execution is *how* you connect your days and weeks to your Life Vision, in a balanced way, that helps you calmly and confidently achieve your goals. Beats the heck out of the chaos most entrepreneurs settle for.

Think of it this way. *Your Rhythm of Execution is your Vision, plus your habits, schedule, and goalsetting method.* And here's the beautiful thing: when you put your Rhythm in place, it's fun to follow, like a perfectly choreographed dance that fits *you* and your abilities. It doesn't require extreme amounts of discipline or willpower because it is fun and exciting for you.

This is an important point. As human beings, we resist change and we struggle to be consistent. Back to that "Ego is the enemy" thing, remember? This is even more true for entrepreneurs who are dealing with the chaos and the ambition and rush of running a business. It is common for entrepreneurs to be good creators but not great executors, to be good starters but not great finishers. In other words, *consistency* is not always a strong suit for us as entrepreneurs. And for that reason, some entrepreneurs might balk at or resist the idea of

Rhythm. But you're about to learn why Rhythm works and how it can help even the most maverick of entrepreneurs develop the kind of consistency that leads to balanced growth in your business and personal life.

The Rhythm of Execution works because it taps into our ambition as entrepreneurs. We are driven to achieve goals. We love to make progress. It is deeply fulfilling to win as we increase the amount of money, time, control, impact, and freedom in our lives. When we tap into ambition and start to get the benefits of the entrepreneur's Hierarchy of Success, we want to do more of that. And that's one reason why Rhythm works for entrepreneurs: *it fuels winning.*

The second reason Rhythm works is that it taps into our emotion as entrepreneurs. This is not drudgery. It is not stoic execution. It is energizing, encouraging, and exciting! Like a perfectly tailored outfit, it is ideally suited for you, designed to perfectly match your talents and interests as an entrepreneur. Sure, there are a few sacrifices you need to make. But the definition of sacrifice is giving up something good to gain something even better. And that's what happens in your Rhythm of Execution.

As you put your Rhythm in place, it will gradually become second nature to you. Our goal is to eventually get the entire rhythm running on autopilot so that you stick with your program under any circumstances. You're about to learn how to do that. And as you do it, you will draw extraordinary benefits and blessings into your life. This is life-changing stuff that helps you become your best self. It's pretty awesome to see it in action!

THE RHYTHM OF EXECUTION DEFINED

So, what is the Rhythm of Execution?

It's your rhythm of *essential morning, daily, and weekly activities that drive your monthly, quarterly, annual, and three-year goals in the five areas of your life.* Stated another way, it is a process for intentionally designing days and weeks that are exciting to you. As you stack these days and weeks on top of each other, you tie them into your monthly, quarterly, and annual goals. And you connect those annual goals to your 3-year goals, which, you guessed it, ladder up to the 10-year and lifetime goals in your Life Vision. Now you can see why having the five areas of your goals, each in its own swim lane, helps your execution. (See Figure 6.1.)

I know this looks like a lot of parts and pieces, and it is. But remember, you don't implement this all at once. You start simple and slowly build out your Rhythm. It will all come together gradually over time. Some people do this over the course of weeks or months. Others do it over quarters or even years. It's okay, however you implement it. Go at your own pace.

You'll find that the more you build out your Rhythm, the more benefit you'll get. So whatever you do, don't get overwhelmed or discouraged. Don't let the entire process prevent you from starting. *I'll show you how to start small so you can get on the path to success with minimal effort and quick benefits.* As you begin seeing the benefits, you'll crave more benefits. The snowball effect will kick in and you'll be building out your Rhythm and executing your Life Vision in no time.

Now, let me explain the beauty of 3-year goals. All of the pieces of Rhythm ladder up to your 3-year goals. And the 3-year time horizon is the link between your short-term Rhythm of Execution and your long-term Life Vision. That is very important so I will repeat it. *The 3-year time horizon is the link between your short-term Rhythm of Execution and your long-term Life Vision.* Remember the components of Life Vision— identity, purpose, values, mission, and goals—where you have a set of lifetime goals and 10-year goals? Well, the 3-year goals ladder up to your 10-year goals, which are milestones to your lifetime goals.

Three years is a magic time frame. It's long enough that you can dream big and achieve big results in your business and life. And it's short enough to keep you focused and productive, feeling appropriate urgency. You might say the three-year time

Figure 6.1 The Rhythm of Execution.

frame allows you to get your head in the clouds, while also keeping your feet on the ground. It's this balance of *dreaming and doing* that makes for an effective Rhythm of Execution.

One last thing about the three-year time horizon. Your three-year goals have a fixed duration of three years, as opposed to a floating three-year period. So you're always working toward a fixed horizon three years down the road from when you started. A year later, you're working toward a two-year point in the future, and so on. This keeps you grounded in your three-year plan, as opposed to annually coming up with a new three-year horizon. We don't want a moving target. We want to get locked in on what we will achieve over a three-year chunk of our lives. And when we are in the final year of the three-year horizon, we begin to set our sights on the next three-year chunk of our lives.

THE RHYTHMIC HABITS AND SCHEDULE

The activities you engage in and the frequency with which you perform them are your habits and schedule. This is the raw material of your Rhythm. Your habits and schedule connect your vision to your goals to produce an extraordinary and effective Rhythm of Execution. Think of it this way: *daily and weekly habits help you achieve your monthly and quarterly goals, which further your annual and three-year goals.* So we want to focus on your scheduled daily and weekly habits and program this into your Rhythm to produce predictable results.

I refer to your daily and weekly habits as Morning Mastery, Daily Doses, and Weekly Winning. These are the building blocks of a great life. It follows logically that when you stack up elegantly designed mornings, days, and weeks, you can't help but architect a great life. And great days start with Morning Mastery. Let's look more closely at the building blocks of your Rhythm: Morning Mastery, Daily Doses, Weekly Winning. And then we'll look at your monthly, quarterly, and annual goals.

Morning Mastery. To paraphrase Ben Franklin, "Early to bed, early to rise, makes people healthy, wealthy, and wise." Straight truth. *This is the number one secret to success.* When I was a teenager, I noticed successful people seemed to wake up early. Over the years, I've come to see the correlation between early rising and success is extremely high, approaching the point of causation. In his book *The 5 AM Club*, Robin Sharma spells out in vivid detail all the benefits of waking up early. No further research on the subject is needed. I've lived it and observed it over and over. Your Morning Mastery is *the* most important part of your Rhythm of Execution. Invest at least one hour each morning exercising your mind, body, and spirit with seven edifying activities while most people are in bed. I recommend prayer, meditation, journaling, goals, reading, inspiration, and exercise. Your morning seven might be a little different. *Just make sure you exercise your mind, body, and spirit for at least one hour total.* Give it a try. It will change your life in amazing and beautiful ways.

Daily Doses. These are your seven critical building blocks of a great day, in addition to your Morning Mastery routine. These aren't the items you must do for business or survival. These are seven core activities that "make it a great day." They are the activities that can easily get neglected by entrepreneurs over the course of the day. For example, I recommend healthy diet, gratitude, service, pauses, connection with loved ones, monitoring your behaviors, and end-of-day journaling/ reflection. Your list of seven daily activities will look a little different. The point is, this is the stuff that normally gets crowded out, causing future regrets. Don't tolerate that. Set your daily seven and track it. Just like working out at the gym, over time these small Daily Doses of intentional activity will stack up to produce excellent results in the five areas of your life.

Weekly Winning. This is where you intentionally design and create great weeks. Set aside one hour to design and create a Winning Week, which includes: a) your top three personal and business goals for the week; b) seven important weekly activities that bring you joy and balance; c) an evaluation of last week's progress and learnings; d) a calendar for planning your upcoming week; and e) your Life Vision and Rhythm of Execution so that you're designing your week within the context of your goals and your big picture. As for the seven Weekly Winning activities, think of them as larger doses of your Daily seven. These seven activities fuel and fulfill you, bringing you balance and joy. When you've done them at the end of the week, you feel like you're winning and having fun. You feel like you're enjoying the good life! Similarly, when you nail your top three personal goals and your top three business goals, you get that winning feeling because you're advancing your monthly, quarterly, and annual goals. The little thrills of weekly winning, in a balanced way, get you excited to do more. *The hour per week you invest in designing a Winning Week is the second secret to success, only slightly less important than waking up early.*

You are probably thinking, "Whoa, Clate! So many parts and pieces to this puzzle. I can't keep it all straight!" Well, remember I spent over $2 million and 20 years working on this! But don't fret, I've distilled it all down to one 8.5×11-inch sheet of paper that ties together the Life Vision and all its parts with the Rhythm of Execution. This is your Weekly Winning Worksheet (WWW) that will help you pursue your personal and business goals in a balanced way. (See Figure 6.2.) It's a pretty awesome tool to help you execute your Vision and Rhythm. You can get it free at ConquerTheChaosBook.com. Grab it now so you can start working on your Vision and Rhythm through the habit of a one-hour Weekly Winning session where you design a great week. *Pro tip:* It is the iterative process of filling out this sheet each week that helps you hone and refine your Vision and Rhythm over time. So just do it, however clunky it feels at first.

Now I can hear some of you saying something like, "I'm not a morning person," or "I don't want to be tied down to a schedule!" Well, let me invite you to look at it another way. I don't want you tied down. I want you freed up. And this Rhythm will actually do that if you design it to suit you. Just as a car driver

MY IDENTITY: I AM...

MY LIFE PURPOSE

MY LIFE VALUES

MY LIFE MISSION

MY LIFE GOALS

10-YR GOALS

V
I
S
I
O
N

WEEK OF: _____ WEEK _____ OF 52

THE WEEKLY WINNING WORKSHEET

TOP 3 PERSONAL GOALS:

1
2
3

ANNUAL THEME & PRIORITIES: _____

1
2
3

TOP 3 BUSINESS GOALS:

1
2
3

	SUNDAY	MONDAY	TUESDAY	WEDNESDAY	THURSDAY	FRIDAY	SATURDAY
	5 - 6AM	5 - 6AM	5 - 6AM	5 - 6AM	5 - 6AM	5 - 6AM	5 - 6AM
	6 - 7AM	6 - 7AM	6 - 7AM	6 - 7AM	6 - 7AM	6 - 7AM	6 - 7AM
	7 - 8AM	7 - 8AM	7 - 8AM	7 - 8AM	7 - 8AM	7 - 8AM	7 - 8AM
	8 - 9AM	8 - 9AM	8 - 9AM	8 - 9AM	8 - 9AM	8 - 9AM	8 - 9AM
	9 - 10AM	9 - 10AM	9 - 10AM	9 - 10AM	9 - 10AM	9 - 10AM	9 - 10AM
	10 - 11AM	10 - 11AM	10 - 11AM	10 - 11AM	10 - 11AM	10 - 11AM	10 - 11AM
	11 - 12PM	11 - 12PM	11 - 12PM	11 - 12PM	11 - 12PM	11 - 12PM	11 - 12PM
	12 - 1PM	12 - 1PM	12 - 1PM	12 - 1PM	12 - 1PM	12 - 1PM	12 - 1PM
	1 - 2PM	1 - 2PM	1 - 2PM	1 - 2PM	1 - 2PM	1 - 2PM	1 - 2PM
	2 - 3PM	2 - 3PM	2 - 3PM	2 - 3PM	2 - 3PM	2 - 3PM	2 - 3PM
	3 - 4PM	3 - 4PM	3 - 4PM	3 - 4PM	3 - 4PM	3 - 4PM	3 - 4PM
	4 - 5PM	4 - 5PM	4 - 5PM	4 - 5PM	4 - 5PM	4 - 5PM	4 - 5PM
	5 - 6PM	5 - 6PM	5 - 6PM	5 - 6PM	5 - 6PM	5 - 6PM	5 - 6PM
	6 - 7PM	6 - 7PM	6 - 7PM	6 - 7PM	6 - 7PM	6 - 7PM	6 - 7PM
	7 - 8PM	7 - 8PM	7 - 8PM	7 - 8PM	7 - 8PM	7 - 8PM	7 - 8PM
	8 - 9PM	8 - 9PM	8 - 9PM	8 - 9PM	8 - 9PM	8 - 9PM	8 - 9PM
	9 - 10PM	9 - 10PM	9 - 10PM	9 - 10PM	9 - 10PM	9 - 10PM	9 - 10PM
	AM Mastery	AM Mastery	AM Mastery	AM Mastery	AM Mastery	AM Mastery	AM Mastery
	Daily 1	Daily 1	Daily 1	Daily 1	Daily 1	Daily 1	Daily 1
	Daily 2	Daily 2	Daily 2	Daily 2	Daily 2	Daily 2	Daily 2
	Daily 3	Daily 3	Daily 3	Daily 3	Daily 3	Daily 3	Daily 3
	Daily 4	Daily 4	Daily 4	Daily 4	Daily 4	Daily 4	Daily 4
	Daily 5	Daily 5	Daily 5	Daily 5	Daily 5	Daily 5	Daily 5
	Daily 6	Daily 6	Daily 6	Daily 6	Daily 6	Daily 6	Daily 6
	Daily 7	Daily 7	Daily 7	Daily 7	Daily 7	Daily 7	Daily 7

MORNING MASTERY	DAILY DOSES	WEEKLY WINNING	MONTHLY GOALS	QUARTERLY GOALS	ANNUAL GOALS	3-YR GOALS
R 1	1	1	1	1	1	1
H 2	2	2	2	2	2	2
Y 3	3	3	3	3	3	3
T 4	4	4	4	4	4	4
H 5	5	5	5	5	5	5
M 6	6	6	Notes & Reflections:			
	7	7				

Figure 6.2 The Weekly Winning Worksheet.

with no brakes must go slower, an entrepreneur with no schedule will progress slower. The brakes enable you to drive fast.

The schedule enables you to progress fast *and* it frees your spirit because you get to design the activities, and even the spontaneity, that lights you up. If a winning week includes a couples massage with your spouse, three nature hikes, a night out with friends, or whatever brings you joy and balance, build it into your week! If you want to water ski once a month, sky dive once a quarter, and travel internationally once a year, build it in! If you want space for spontaneity to soak up whatever life has to offer, build it in! The schedule is intended to free your spirit, not weigh you down. And most Rhythm practitioners sleep in a little on Saturday and Sunday, which is a good time to get some extra sleep.

Above all, we want to design our daily and weekly activities to help us achieve our monthly, quarterly, and annual goals. So when you choose your morning seven, daily seven, and weekly seven activities, choose activities that will advance the goals in your five areas of life. Now, let's look at monthly goals, quarterly goals, and annual goals.

Monthly goals. This is pretty straightforward. It's less about the small daily and weekly activities and more about the monthly goals you're achieving through those daily and weekly activities. Your top three personal and business weekly goals from your Weekly Winning Worksheet will drive the achievement of your monthly goals. Your monthly goals fall into the five areas of your life: physical, spiritual, social, business, and financial. This is where your goals begin to connect up to your Life Vision. *At the start of each month during the quarter, you break off another piece of your quarterly goals and set them as your monthly goals.*

Quarterly goals. Again, these are the important goals in the five areas of your life that you will accomplish during a three-month period. These goals are furthered by the achievement of your monthly goals and they ladder up to the annual goals in the five areas of your life. You can see why the swim lanes are important—because every goal ladders up to the corresponding goal as we move up the time horizon toward lifetime goals. *It's important that you set your quarterly goals as part of a quarterly planning retreat* where you get away from all distractions and you can think and feel clearly. Even if that retreat is getting away for a day or a half day, invest the time to envision and create an amazing quarter during your retreat. Get away from technology. Rise above the noise. Get in touch with your best self. Reflect on your prior quarter. Feed your mind and spirit. And create your quarterly goals. I recommend doing this retreat with your spouse if you're married so that you're in sync as you design the next quarter of life. Plus, it's a lot of fun to get away together and that will cause you to look forward to your quarterly retreat. Charisse and I have done this for many years and *it's the third secret to success.*

Annual goals. One year of your life. You can accomplish a lot in a year if you're intentional about it. Establish your annual goals that propel you to achieve your three-year goals. Do this planning work during the last quarterly retreat of the year. Then spend the end of the calendar year getting crystal clear on your annual goals in the five areas of life so you go into the new year clear, confident, and excited. And make sure your annual goals ladder up to your three-year goals. As mentioned previously, 3 years is a magic time frame because it's long enough to dream and do big things and short enough to keep you focused and grounded. Set your annual goals in the five areas of life that will help you achieve your 3-year plan, which ladder up to your 10-year goals and lifetime goals.

The morning, daily, and weekly habits and the monthly, quarterly, and annual goals are life-changing for entrepreneurs! This will help you achieve your business and personal goals in a balanced way so you can conquer the chaos and avoid the Dark Side of Entrepreneurship. And although this Rhythm of Execution that drives your Life Vision might seem like a lot, it all boils down to three habits that, if ingrained into your routine, will transform your business and personal life.

START SMALL: THE THREE TRANSFORMATIVE HABITS

I'm excited to share with you how to start small, and how to avoid feeling overwhelmed or discouraged by this. You don't tackle this all at once. Here's what you do. You commit to doing these three life-changing habits that make this Rhythm of Execution begin to flow, almost on autopilot:

1. **Wake up early** and invest one hour to exercise your mind, body, and spirit, eventually building up to doing your seven Morning Mastery activities.
2. **Plan your week** by investing one hour to fill out your Weekly Winning Worksheet where you design into your week the seven Weekly Winning activities, your Daily Doses, and your top three personal and business goals for the week. All of that ties into your Rhythm and Vision. I recommend you habit stack an hour onto your Morning Mastery routine on Saturday or Sunday morning to plan your week.
3. **Do a quarterly retreat** where you get away from distractions for a day or weekend (at least a half day) to reflect on the past quarter and set the goals for your next quarter, consistent with your Life Vision and Rhythm of Execution.

Figure 6.3 The three transformative habits (aka the three secrets of success).

Wake up early. Plan your week. Do a quarterly retreat. That's it! I sometimes refer to these three transformative habits as the three secrets of success. If you're committed to doing these three things, your Mindset of Success, Life Vision, and Rhythm of Execution will all come together beautifully over time. The main tool you'll use to manage this is the Weekly Winning Worksheet (WWW). You will fill it out during your one-hour Weekly Winning session.

It will take you longer than an hour the first time you fill out your WWW, but you will get faster over time. Fill it out for the week. Track your progress each morning during your Morning Mastery routine. Iterate and adjust day by day and week by week. As you stack up winning weeks, and evaluate each quarter at your retreat, you'll see the power of these three transformative habits.

I've recommended journaling and meditation as part of your Morning Mastery. I wasn't a journaling and meditating person until a few years ago. It has had a profound effect on me as I've worked it into my morning routine. If you want to go deep on meditation and how to really program your Mindset, Vision, and Rhythm for success, read Dr. Joe Dispenza's book *Breaking the Habit of Being Yourself*.

If you deal with any form of anxiety, ADHD, or other mental or emotional challenge (and many entrepreneurs do), the Morning Mastery routine—and specifically the practice of exercise, journaling, and meditation—will do wonders for you. And if you're still skeptical about meditation, just go straight to Chapter 10 of Dispenza's book and start practicing it. Give it a try for 30 days and see what it does for you.

GOAL SETTING THE SMART WAY

The last piece of Rhythm, and the part that ties together your Vision and Rhythm, is goal setting. As you engage in the morning, daily, and weekly activities that help you achieve your monthly, quarterly, and annual goals, you want to be very clear about what you're achieving. That's why you want to create SMART! goals You might have heard this acronym before, but it will have new meaning to you now that you understand the importance of Life Vision and Rhythm of Execution in your Quest for Success as an entrepreneur.

SMART! goals are the way to tie your Rhythm to your Vision. SMART! goals are what you work on in your Rhythm. They keep you focused and excited. They help you create the consistency and clarity that produce spectacular results in your life.

When you create SMART! goals that tie to your Vision, and when you work on them in your Rhythm of execution, things get really fun! To be SMART, your goal must be:

Specific: Clear and objective. No fuzziness or subjectivity.
Measurable: You can definitively say you did or didn't achieve it.
Achievable: Realistic and believable. (Higher belief lets you set higher goals.)
Relevant: It connects to your longer-term goals, purpose, values, and mission.
Time-bound: There's a clear deadline.

Notice the "R" does not stand for "Realistic." That's the "Achievable" part. The "R" of Relevant is what ties your goals to your Vision. It's powerful psychologically because it connects to your Why. "R" is for Relevant.

Here are some examples of SMART! goals

"Increase sales 20% in the next 90 days."
"Lose 10 pounds, going from 180 to 170 by December 1."
"Improve conversion rate from x to y by September 30."

You'd want to be sure the "R" is accounted for by evaluating how well the goal connects to your bigger picture, but you get the idea.

I like to add an exclamation point to SMART! goals because there's one last ingredient that skyrockets goal achievement rates: *excitement!* When you add emotion, energy, and enthusiasm—sheer excitement—to your SMART! goals it's amazing what happens. The excitement lifts our performance. The excitement gets us to take action and sustains us through any sense of drudgery. So set goals that excite you, and be excited about your goals.

Here are three ways to crank up the excitement around your SMART! goals:

1. **Envision achievement of your goals** in your Morning Mastery routine. *Feel* what it's like to have achieved them. Believe it is happening. Then spring into action with that vision in your mind and that feeling in your heart.
2. **Reward yourself** when you achieve the goal as well as the little wins of progress. Decide beforehand what the achievement reward will be. And surprise yourself with small rewards for notching the little wins along the way.
3. **Remember your why** behind each goal. Studies have proven that people who focus on the why behind their goals are much more likely to achieve their goals than those who focus on the goal itself.

When you envision achievement, reward yourself, and remember your why, your excitement soars. And that feeling is a secret to success in goal achievement.

I'm a big believer in discipline, consistency, and willpower. But let's face it: they feel like work and drudgery, which often break down over time. Excitement beats the heck out of willpower. And the cool thing is that when you combine exciting SMART! goals with your Rhythm of Execution, designing it all in a way that fires you up, the natural and almost automatic outcome is more discipline, consistency, and willpower.

Stated another way, SMART! goals and the Rhythm of Execution are the fun way to build the discipline and consistency that produce beautiful results in your business and life.

WRAPPING UP THE THREE PERSONAL KEYS TO SUCCESS

We've now covered the three Keys to Personal Success: Mindset, Vision, and Rhythm. I hope you're excited about this! Can you see how cultivating a Mindset of Success by managing our thoughts and feelings leads into establishing your Life Vision where we set our identity, purpose, values, mission, and goals? And how cool is this Rhythm that helps you execute it all? This is powerful stuff.

When you follow this process, you will create consistency and continuity in your thoughts, feelings, actions, habits, and goal setting, which will help you achieve your Life Vision. You will gradually build a beautiful life plan and Rhythm for running your business and personal life. This not only helps you conquer the chaos, but it also produces predictable, almost automatic, results in your business and personal life. *Remember that days and weeks invested intentionally are the building blocks of a great life.* We want greatness!

We have covered a lot, but to simplify it down and get you started, remember the basics. The foundation of the Personal Keys to Success are the three transformative habits I mentioned when I encouraged you to start small:

1. **Wake up early** and invest one hour to exercise your mind, body, and spirit.
2. **Plan your week** that excites you, filling out your Weekly Winning Worksheet.
3. **Do a quarterly retreat** where you get away from distractions, reflect on the last quarter, and set goals for next quarter. Make it fun so you look forward to it.

If you adopt those three transformative habits, the whole Rhythm will unfold for you over time. And if those three habits are still too much, I get it. Just start with the single most important habit for success: wake up early. And then begin "habit stacking," *Atomic Habits* style. After you start to wake up early, you will want to exercise, meditate, and journal. These activities work out your mind, body, and spirit. As you do this, you'll find that your Morning Mastery becomes a sacred laboratory where you cultivate your Mindset of Success, design your Life Vision, and iterate on your Rhythm of Execution. All of this produces remarkable results in your business and life.

Keep in mind that you don't need to apply this Vision and Rhythm rigidly. Be adaptable. There's no perfect method out there and I don't profess to be sharing perfection with you here. (It *is* pretty awesome, though!) So, feel free to treat this as a framework for designing success in your life. Adjust and adapt the Vision and Rhythm in the way that suits you best. I'm not hung up on how you implement it exactly. I just want you to implement and get the benefits that come from Mindset, Vision, and Rhythm because this is what brings balance to your Quest for Success. This is what keeps you from giving in to the chaos and falling into the Dark Side of Entrepreneurship.

The last thing I'll share with you regarding the three Keys to Personal Success is something another Keap customer, Robin Sharma, loves to say: *"Successful people do the things unsuccessful people are unwilling to do . . . even when they don't want to do them."* So stop making excuses. Stop justifying your actions. Put your ego—which doesn't want you to change—in its place. Remove the mental blocks ("I'm not a morning person," etc.). That's nonsense. You are a successful person. And successful people do the things unsuccessful people are unwilling to do. Even when—no, *especially* when—you don't feel like doing them.

You are successful. Let's get on to building great success in your business.

Chapter 6 Summary: Rhythm

- Chaos throws entrepreneurs off balance, so we need a method to find balance and produce that calmness, consistency, and confidence that lead to success. Rhythm is the method that helps us execute our Life Vision.
- Your Rhythm is an intentionally designed collection of habits and routines that are fun to carry out because they're tailored just for you and your exciting goals.
- The Rhythm of Execution is your routine of morning, daily, and weekly activities that drive your monthly, quarterly, annual, and three-year goals in the five areas of your Life Vision.
- There's no need to get overwhelmed by all the pieces and parts of an effective Vision and Rhythm. *Start small* with the three transformative habits (AKA the three secrets of success): 1) wake up early, 2) plan your week, and 3) do a quarterly retreat.
- Use the SMART! planning method and be sure to inject emotion and excitement in your goal setting to increase the likelihood of success.

Part 3

THE BUSINESS KEYS TO SUCCESS

"The first rule of technology used in a business is that automation applied to an efficient operation will magnify the efficiency. The second is that automation applied to an inefficient operation will magnify the inefficiency."

–Bill Gates

7
STRATEGY

Bill Harney is the son of an entrepreneur. He grew up around his family's business and hoped to take it over one day. He worked in the business, learned the ropes, became a valuable employee, and gradually moved toward taking over as president of the 12-person business. Finally that day came and he was overjoyed. He knew all about the business and was ready to take it to the next level.

As Bill began leading the company, he realized it was a lot tougher than he expected. He was putting in long hours, implementing systems, and trying to build a foundation for growth. These relentless responsibilities brought chronic imbalance and fatigue. There were so many fires to put out, so many issues to respond to, that he struggled to proactively build the business the way he had planned. Bill and his team were all working hard but the results didn't match their effort. They weren't working on the right things and they weren't working together.

In the verbiage of Michael Gerber, author of *The E-Myth*, Bill and his team members were constantly working *in* the business. They had very little time to work *on* the business. In other words, they were doing the work of the business, but they weren't working on the business itself to make the business run more effectively. And so they were stuck in a reactive rut, struggling to grow the business the way Bill intended.

Over the past 20 years of my career, if there's one phrase that characterizes small business more than anything else, it's the phrase "firefighting mode." We are constantly reacting to fires as business owners. This causes entrepreneurs to feel frenzied and fatigued over time. This firefighting mode is one of the primary outcomes of small business chaos.

Mike Tyson famously said, "Everyone has a plan until they get punched in the mouth." Well, small business chaos seems to be punching entrepreneurs in the face every day. And if it's not a fire in the business, there's something on the personal front preventing you from working on the business. So if you don't have a true strategy and clarity in the tactical steps to execute it, you're likely to get knocked off course by the chaos.

Entrepreneurs need a way to rise above the chaos and pro-actively work on their business. They need a proven method that helps them establish a strategy that ties to the day-to-day operations of the business. And then they must stick to that strategy when the chaos gets intense.

The fourth Key to Success is about putting your business strategy in place so you can conquer the chaos and operate your business proactively and confidently. Bill Harney was able to do just that. He implemented his Strategy several years ago and it transformed his company. Today, he has 55 employ-ees, revenue has increased 10 times, and in his own words, "I'm having fun again." His company, Keeping Current Matters, helps real estate agents become trusted experts for their cli-ents. Bill is experiencing the benefits of balanced growth, and he is leading his company powerfully and effectively.

Strategy is a tricky word. It means different things to differ-ent people. But I think we can all agree that when you don't have a Strategy in place, you are reactive, scattered, and inef-fective. When you do have a good Strategy in place, you are doing the right things at the right time. You are effective and efficient, with everyone rowing in the same direction.

For purposes of the fourth Key to Success, there are two parts to Strategy: 1) Company Strategy, and 2) Customer Strategy. First, we'll cover Company Strategy. Company Strategy is a powerful Key to Success, particularly for businesses that have

10 or more employees. As you may recall from "The Stages of Small Business Growth" in Chapter 2, it's at that point that strategy and leadership begin to be very important to business growth. Because that's when the team is no longer close enough that everyone is tightly in sync. It's at that point of 10 employees or so that the business owner has a hard time leading the whole team. Therefore, it's powerful to get everyone on the same page using the method shared here to establish and execute your Company Strategy.

COMPANY STRATEGY

Simply put, Company Strategy centers around how you organize and focus your resources to create a competitive advantage and win in the market. It's about aligning and focusing on what you do and how you do it with *why* you do it. Not surprisingly, you must "start with why."

I can't tell you what your Company Strategy should be, but I can give you a proven method for establishing it. We began using this strategy planning method in the early days of Keap. We hired consultants, read the best books, practiced it, adapted it, and eventually created and implemented our own strategy planning method.

Then our customers started asking us to teach them this method when they visited our office or heard about what we do. At first we resisted because, well, we wanted to stay focused on our strategy as a software company! After some serious arm-twisting by a group of customers, we decided to teach the strategy planning method at one annual, two-day workshop.

It went over like gangbusters. Soon we were teaching the workshop once per quarter. Customers were eating it up, but it was not aligned to our strategy as a software company. So we spun it out as its own company a few years ago and that company is thriving today, teaching this strategy planning method to help seven-figure businesses grow to $10 million and beyond.

We have practiced, perfected, and preached this method for over a decade. We created it by taking the best of what big companies do and turning it into a method small businesses can use to drive growth and free up the business owner, who is usually the bottleneck, and is definitely carrying too much weight in the absence of clear Strategy.

The fact is that the daily dynamics of business create chaos and confusion. But a good strategy planning method will turn that chaos and confusion into clarity and confidence. And it probably goes without saying that clear and confident teams win, as they take targeted, coordinated action to achieve their goals.

By the way, one of the things you'll notice is that strong strategy requires saying no to a lot of stuff. You'll also find that as your strategy gets clearer, it's easier to say no to good ideas that aren't the best use of resources. Thus, tightening your strategy and saying no more often becomes a virtuous cycle to achieve higher and higher levels of success.

With that said, what's the strategy planning method for Company Strategy and how can you benefit from it? (And, by the way, you don't have to be a seven-figure business to benefit from this strategy.)

Here's the condensed but effective version, presented in three steps, that any small business can use to clarify its Company Strategy.

Step 1: Establish the foundation of the company by articulating your Company Vision, consisting of:

- **Purpose:** A 5–15-word statement of *why* the company exists
- **Values:** Three to seven prized characteristics that govern *how* your employees work
- **Mission:** *What* the company will accomplish over the next three years, stated as "We will _____ (qualitative success criteria), by X date (three years away) with a, b, and c (three quantitative success criteria)"

It's important to get the right people on board, so you must hire, train, and fire to the purpose, values, and mission. Getting employees on board who "fit" your purpose, values, and mission makes all the difference. We'll cover this in more detail when we talk about Leadership, the sixth Key to Success (see Chapter 9). Also, make sure you're clear and specific about your Mission and what you will accomplish in three years. Fuzzy descriptions are not useful.

For simplicity's sake, the Mission is about clarifying your niche and putting a stake in the ground in three years that represents success in that niche. If there's one aspect of Company Strategy that produces either great rewards or great penalties, it is the clear establishment (or not) of your niche. Stop and think about it. Most small businesses flounder until they find their niche. Sometimes small businesses find a niche almost by accident, and things suddenly get better. There's a reason the phrase "riches in niches" caught on. Find your niche. Decide what winning in that niche means in three years. Call that out clearly in your Mission. Focus your resources on the niche. Say no to opportunities outside your niche. And rally your people around your Mission to make it happen.

Warning: Many businesses skip Step 1 and jump straight to Step 2, but that's a mistake. The Strategy must be tied to the foundation and long-term Vision of the company or it will break down. "Start with why" as Simon Sinek says, and your Strategy will be much more effective.

Step 2: Establish your Company Strategy by articulating these components of sound strategy that support your three-year Mission:

- **Target market, positioning, brand promise:** who you're for and what you deliver
- **Competitive differentiation:** top three things that make you different and desirable
- **Core competencies:** your top three to five strengths you will focus on and leverage

- **Critical issues:** the top three to five issues you must resolve to accomplish your Mission
- **Goals:** three-year and annual goals, which you will break down into quarters and months during the three years

You establish and articulate these strategy components through a series of specific strategy planning exercises (think SWOT analysis—Strengths, Weaknesses, Opportunities, Threats). Which exercises you choose to do is not all that critical. You don't need to overthink this. Simply get together as a leadership team and hash it out until you come up with a draft of your Purpose, Values, Mission, and strategy components. The critical thing is to get your team thinking strategically and working with collaboration and constructive conflict to arrive at an agreed-upon articulation of your Company Strategy.

Step 3: Establish your daily, weekly, monthly, quarterly, and annual operating rhythm to help you execute your Company Strategy and avoid wandering off course:

- **Daily:** quick team check-in to remove obstacles and maintain momentum
- **Weekly:** one-hour team meeting to cover one or two big topics and check in on goal progress
- **Monthly:** half-day team meeting to cover big topics, check progress, course correct
- **Quarterly:** one-day offsite to check annual progress and set quarterly goals and priorities
- **Annual:** two days offsite, check Mission progress, set annual goals, align everyone

The first thing business owners say when they see this recommended operating rhythm is "We can't spend that much time in meetings." To which I say, "Your company is spending far more time than this in debates, distractions, and dissension because your people are not clear and confident about the company's direction. So, you can either invest this time getting alignment or you can spend far more time than this over the course of a quarter."

So, there you have it. A succinct, three-step process for articulating your Company Strategy and executing it. It's not easy putting a Company Strategy in place. But it is so worth it. The clarity and confidence you gain is amazing. The alignment and execution of the team improve dramatically. You get out of firefighting mode and into company-building mode. Your likelihood of success goes up dramatically. And everything is just more fun.

Of course, there are still fires you'll react to during the quarter. But you'll find that with your Company Strategy in place, you are intentional about the company's direction and future. You are clear on your goals and *how* you will achieve them. You and your team will be in alignment, as you all work together to achieve your shared Mission, guided by your Purpose and Values.

You should notice some familiar terms here: Vision, Purpose, Values, Mission, as well as rhythm, daily, weekly, monthly, quarterly, annual, three-year. We covered these elements on the personal side under Life Vision and Rhythm of Execution. These are foundational principles of success that apply to both the personal side as well as the business side of things. They are evidence of intentionality, design, and focus. When we get clear on who we are, why we exist, what we're up to, and how we execute—personally and as a company—we attract success.

When you follow this proven strategy planning method by completing these three steps, you will connect your daily activities to your goals and long-term vision for the company. Waste and confusion go down. Results improve. And everyone works together to achieve the Mission, operating with clarity and confidence. Not to mention, the leader's load is lightened significantly, distributed among other leaders and team members who share in the goals. This "distributed ownership" of the goals comes from co-creation of the plan, which is an important underlying principle of the method.

I've watched this method play out in hundreds of companies we've taught, with fabulous results. I continue to be involved as an advisor to the company (Elite Entrepreneurs, https://GrowWithElite.com) we spun out that teaches this method. It can be tricky when you start practicing this method, so I've arranged for you to get some free resources at ConquerThe ChaosBook.com to help you implement your Company Strategy. The creation of your Company Strategy can be a bit challenging, so you might want to do what Bill Harney did and reach out to the awesome team at Elite Entrepreneurs to get a little guidance.

If your company is at or approaching seven figures in revenue, you should definitely check out these resources. And if you're like most small business owners and you're not yet at seven figures but you want to put this planning rhythm in place so you can get out of firefighting mode and be more intentional in your business, you can get a free planning rhythm resource at ConquerTheChaosBook.com.

The fourth Key to Success is Strategy. We just covered Company Strategy. Now we need to talk about your Customer Strategy.

CUSTOMER STRATEGY

When it comes to the three business Keys to Success (Strategy, Automation, and Leadership), *the most important driver of your business growth is your Customer Strategy*. I say that with full confidence, having observed, studied, and immersed myself in small business growth for over two decades. If you've got a good Customer Strategy, you can build a great business because your customers will lead you to the products and services that will result in your success. And when you serve your customers well, they become raving fans, which is very profitable for your business.

Right up front, let's get clear on what Customer Strategy is. Simply stated, *it is the carefully designed end-to-end process your customer goes through, from the time a new prospect becomes aware of your company until the point they are your best brand advocate,* gobbling up everything you offer, giving you raving reviews, and referring tons of customers to you.

That end-to-end process is called the Customer Lifecycle. And understanding it helps you create a solid Customer Strategy to grow your business. For over a decade, we have been teaching small businesses how to successfully build their business using the Customer Lifecycle. This framework is powerful and proven. I'm so excited to share it with you, along with the underlying principles of the Customer Lifecycle, because it will help you conquer the chaos and systematically grow your business.

By the way, it's probably obvious, but it's worth pointing out that most entrepreneurs don't proactively implement a sound Customer Strategy using the Customer Lifecycle because they're mired in chaos. They are in firefighting mode, wearing all the hats, constantly working *in* the business with no time left to work *on* the business. And that's such a shame. But you're not like most entrepreneurs. You're ready to do this. So, let's jump into the Customer Lifecycle.

As you can see, the Customer Lifecycle has three distinct phases: 1) collect leads, 2) convert clients, and 3) create fans. (See Figure 7.1.) When you understand your Customer Lifecycle and each of its phases, you can build a *Customer Strategy that systematically turns new leads into clients and then into raving fans.* And that is clearly and obviously a major key to your success.

So let's look at each phase of the Customer Lifecycle and then I will explain the critical factor you must master to implement a highly successful Customer Strategy in your business.

Figure 7.1 The Customer Lifecycle.

THE THREE PHASES OF THE CUSTOMER LIFECYCLE

1. **Collect leads.** To do this properly, you must *target* the right audience, based on the target customer you articulated in your Company Strategy. Then you must *attract* your target customers by offering something of value, ideally for free. We call this a "lead magnet." Once you've attracted your target customers, you need to *capture* the lead so you can build a relationship with them. In short, to effectively collect leads, you must *target, attract, and capture* them by offering them something they value.

2. **Convert clients.** Once you've collected the lead, it's time to *engage* the lead in a way that builds the relationship so they know, like, and trust you. At that point, you must *offer* them a compelling solution to their problem, so they want to buy what you're offering. Finally, you *close* the sale. In summary, to effectively convert clients, you must *engage, offer, and close*, which opens up the real goal: Create raving fans.

3. **Create fans.** The purpose of closing a sale is to give you an opportunity to create a raving fan. That's the leverage in any business—*raving fans are extraordinarily profitable because of the three Rs: reviews, referrals, and repeat business.* So once you have a customer, you must *deliver* on your promise. Then you must *impress* your

customer by finding ways to go above and beyond their expectations. At that point, you can *multiply* their impact on your business by asking for reviews, referrals, and repeat business. So to effectively create fans, you must *deliver, impress, and multiply* your fans' impact on your business.

When you take this orderly approach to your Customer Strategy, you can guide your customers through your Customer Lifecycle in a proactive way. They feel appreciated and cared for. You feel in control and on top of things. The chaos of putting out customer fires dies down significantly. I cannot emphasize enough how beautiful it is when you design and implement your Customer Lifecycle. It's like putting Henry Ford's revolutionary assembly line into your business. But instead of producing Model T Fords, you have a conveyor belt that produces customers and fans for your business.

Stated succinctly, *the goal of your Customer Strategy is to turn new leads into raving fans by implementing your Customer Lifecycle.* Now I'm going to share with you the critical factor you must apply to your Customer Lifecycle to establish a killer Customer Strategy that consistently turns leads into clients and fans, driving your business success through the roof.

What's that critical factor?

FOLLOW-UP

As I always say, "The fortune is in the follow-up." Why's that? Because when you look at the three phases of the Customer Lifecycle, you'll see that in order to turn new leads into raving fans, you must follow up all throughout the Customer Lifecycle, from lead to client to fan.

And this is where nearly all small businesses fall short. Even if they lay out their clear Customer Lifecycle, too often it breaks down due to lack of follow-up. Which is crazy because the math (and 20 years of experience with hundreds of thousands of businesses!) is clear that more follow-up equals more sales. Consider the following statistics, based on a small business survey we conducted at Keap several years ago:

- Only 2% of sales close on the first contact.
- 3% close on the second contact.
- 4% close on the third contact.
- 10% close on the fourth contact.
- 81% close on or after the fifth contact.

So according to this survey, keeping in touch with your prospects is critical to closing more sales. Thus, it would make sense for small businesses to stay in touch past the fifth point of contact, right? Well, that's not what's happening.

- 48% of businesses quit following up after the first call.
- 24% of businesses quit following up after the second call.
- 12% of businesses quit following up after the third call.
- 6% of businesses quit following up after the fourth call.
- 10% of businesses quit following up after the fifth call.

And this last piece of data, sums it all up perfectly:

- Customers buy after seeing a message an average of 7–12 times.
- Most small businesses follow up one to three times.

Small businesses are leaving a lot of money on the table, hampering their growth by failing to follow up properly. More follow-up. More sales. It really is as simple as that. And yet sometimes we make it so difficult. The real question is, "Why don't small businesses follow up more?" I've asked tens of thousands of entrepreneurs if they believe they would sell more if they followed up more. They almost always say yes.

When I ask them, "So then why don't you follow up more?" Their answers fall into three buckets:

- No time
- No system
- No knowledge of how to do it properly

Time. System. Knowledge. That's what entrepreneurs say when asked why they don't follow up more. But it's even simpler than that: they misunderstand follow-up. They feel like they already shared their message with the prospect or customer. They feel like they're bothering the customer by following up. *They overlook the fundamental truth that most people they communicated with didn't receive or understand their message.*

So for these reasons, follow-up breaks down and small businesses struggle to grow. We're not going to allow that to happen in your business. None of those issues—time, system, knowledge, misunderstanding—should prevent you from putting a great Customer Strategy into place. I'm going to address the time and system issues in the next chapter. We're going to address the knowledge and misunderstanding issues right now.

Here's what you need to understand. As we've worked with small businesses over the years helping them implement their Customer Lifecycle, we've consistently seen success when these Fundamentals of Follow-up are applied.

THE FUNDAMENTALS OF FOLLOW-UP

- **Timing**. People buy when they're ready to buy, not when you're ready to sell. Put timing on your side by following up with new leads several times over the first two weeks. Then nurture those leads who don't take action, as well as your customers, on a weekly or at least a monthly basis.

Stay in front of them so you're top of mind when the time is right for them.

- **Segmentation**. Not every contact you have is the same. The contacts on your list should not be treated the same. As the business owner, you need to make sure you're sending the right message to the right person at the right time. In other words, the messages you send to your customers and prospects should be targeted to their specific needs and wants. Far too many business owners throw all their prospects' and customers' email addresses together and send out a mass, generic message to everyone on their list. If you want your follow-up to be effective, you've got to craft messages that work for individuals, not entire databases.

- **Repetition**. People must get your message over and over before it sinks in. You know your products and services like the back of your hand, but your customers don't "get it" the first time they hear the message. Chances are they didn't even hear it. And if they did, they probably didn't understand it. And if they did hear and understand it, the timing probably wasn't right. Tell them again, and again, and again. Remember, prospects must hear the message 7–12 times, on average, before they buy. Yet most entrepreneurs follow up 1 to 3 times. Double or triple your follow-up to double or triple your sales.

- **Education**. The buying process can be confusing and intimidating to customers. They need accurate, insightful information. They need to be educated and their concerns and questions need to be addressed. Give real value to your prospects and customers. Give them the information they need, and they'll thank you with their business. Serve them with genuine interest and they'll come to know, like, and trust you.

- **Variety**. Communicate with customers through a variety of media—email, text, phone, social, video, mail. Some prospects respond to a call, others to email, others to a text.

The reinforcement of your message through multiple forms of media doesn't just add up. It has a powerful, compounding effect in the minds of your audience. It raises your credibility and authority. Big businesses and Madison Avenue marketers call this "omni-channel marketing." Small businesses call it smart.

- **Personality**. People read and consume interesting content and they tune out boring stuff. Inject personality into your follow-up. Your audience wants you, not a dull, corporate voice. Small business is personal. Keep it that way in your follow-up by keeping it personable and conversational. No stuffy or boring follow-up.

When you apply these fundamentals of follow-up to your Customer Lifecycle, you will grow your business in a durable way. But there's something more you should know to really super-charge your Customer Lifecycle and get the most out of your Customer Strategy. It's the real secret sauce that we discovered at Keap after working with top marketers and serving customers for over 20 years.

To be completely transparent, I debated whether to include this next part in the book because many people can't appreciate it. You know, the whole "pearls before swine" thing. Well, you're not swine. And you're investing time to read this book. So you deserve the pearls of wisdom we were fortunate enough to learn over the years from some of the greatest small business marketers on the planet. These are the real secrets of follow-up, the treasure trove of wisdom that, if applied, will cause your sales to soar.

We learned these secrets from top marketers and experts who have used our software over the years. From Dan Kennedy and Bill Glazer, to Don Miller and Amy Porterfield, *and hundreds of other influencers and top marketers using our software*, we have been blessed to have a front row seat to see what works. And now I'm sharing it with you. We have practiced this stuff over the last two decades, teaching it to hundreds of thousands of small businesses. Our customers who implement these follow-up secrets get dramatic and fantastic results in their business.

THE SEVEN SECRETS TO DOUBLE OR TRIPLE YOUR SALES

1. **Speak to their problems.** Your prospects don't care about you. They don't care about your product or service. They don't care about your marketing or follow-up. They care about their problems. So when you talk to them about their problems, you'll have an eager, interested audience that wants to know how you can help them. Don't talk about your product. Instead, *fill your follow-up messages with information about your customer's problems* that happened to be solved by your product or service. As my friend and long-time Keap customer Donald Miller of StoryBrand Marketing says, "All good marketing has a hook. And your customer's problems are your hooks." Focus on your customers' problems and you'll hook your target audience so you can serve them with your product or service.

2. **Get a response.** The smartest marketers know the objective of all marketing efforts is to get a response. Generate a lead. Engage them in conversation. Close a sale. You *do that by sending the right message to the right market at the right time **and asking for a response***. Ask real questions. Invite them to connect with you. Make an offer they can't refuse. Be sure you have a call to action (CTA) in your follow-up. And make it simple for them to respond. Finally, remember that any response is better than no response. An angry responder actually cares and can be turned around and served. And that's actually much better than an apathetic recipient of

your message who tunes you out. Get a response from your follow-up messages.

3. **Stop the cherry-picking.** A good marketing campaign will produce three kinds of leads: hot (those ready to buy now or soon), warm (those who will buy eventually), and cold (those who will probably never buy). It's hard to determine initially what kind of lead it is, so you or someone on your sales team calls the lead, sensing and sifting whether the lead is hot, warm, or cold. The natural tendency is to work the hot leads, drop the cold leads, and "eventually" get to the warm leads. That's right, the natural tendency is to cherry-pick the good leads and ignore the warm and cold leads. Why? Because *the warm leads take a lot of time to work and they require different treatment than hot leads.* And people conclude the cold leads will never buy. But what if they would buy, given the right message delivered to them at the right time? What if the cold lead's circumstances change? And what if those warm leads just needed more and different follow-up than the phone call or two they get from a salesperson harvesting hot leads? You need to stop the cherry-picking in your business so you can maximize sales.

4. **Maintain a customer database (CRM).** Which brings us to the next follow-up secret of master marketers. They maintain a customer database. They store all of those leads—hot, cold, and warm—as well as customer information. They track all important contact and customer information, all follow-ups, purchase history, interactions, and more. Smart marketers have done this for years, building their list in a customer database, long before this software came to be called customer relationship management (CRM) software. *Once you have all of this information in your CRM software, keep it up to date by tracking everything.* When done right, your customer database is like a magic money tree you can pluck fruit from whenever needed.

5. **Shift from hunting to harvesting.** As mentioned above, many entrepreneurs feel like they are an unwanted pest when they are following up. That's because they are in hunting mode, chasing prospects and customers, talking about their product or service instead of the customer's problem. More specifically, they are coming across as a vendor instead of an expert. Stop that. Instead, share your knowledge about the customer's problems, so they will see you as an expert instead of a vendor. When you do this, you make the transition from unwanted pest to welcomed guest. You no longer have to chase prospects and customers. The psychology shifts and they are interested in you. This becomes very powerful in your sales work, as you can move from hunting to harvesting, with an air of confidence that attracts customers instead of repelling them.

6. **Start a lead-warming department.** Every business has a lead-generating function (marketing). And every business has a lead-closing function (sales). But in between marketing and sales, there's a lead-warming function. And it's astounding how much value, how many leads, how many opportunities, slip through the cracks between marketing and sales. Sales says, "Give us the good leads." Marketing says, "Close the leads we're giving you." And the problem goes on and on. The best marketers recognize the need for a lead-warming function and are committed to it, turning all those warm (and some cold) leads into customers and raving fans. They do it by sharing the company's expertise, repositioning the company from vendor to expert, capitalizing on the customer database, and playing the long game of building customer relationships over time. So start a lead-warming function that positions you and your company as the industry expert and trusted advisor to solve your target customer's problems.

7. **Entertain them.** Your prospects and customers need information about their problems at the right time. They need repetition, education, and variety. They need an irresistible offer and a CTA. They need all of the stuff we've touched on to this point. And if you practice it, you will significantly increase your sales. But if you want to absolutely blow your numbers out of the water, give them what they want, not just what they need. And what they want is to be entertained. By you. They want your personality, humor, authenticity, and stories. So entertain them. *Because when you give them what they need and combine it with what they want, you've got something spectacular, even entertaining. You've got a relationship. You've got a following.* You've got permission to converse freely and follow up regularly, giving them the opportunity to gobble up your products and services that will make their life easier, better, more successful.

When you practice the fundamentals of follow-up in your Customer Lifecycle and you add these seven secret ingredients, you get a special sauce that turns leads into clients and raving fans. The reason is that *your audience knows, likes, and trusts you.* They are predisposed to do business with you. They are attracted to you as the expert so you can operate as a harvester, not a hunter. Your results shoot through the roof and it's a lot more fun than chasing sales.

BACK TO THE BASICS OF CUSTOMER LIFECYCLE

We've gone deep here on the Customer Lifecycle, the follow-up fundamentals, and the seven secrets of follow-up. All of that was to show you "the fortune is in the follow-up." But don't get lost in the details. Start with the basics of the Customer Lifecycle. Let's end this chapter by focusing on the primary follow-up programs every small business needs. They are "the core four," which are the three most basic follow-up programs and the "Swiss Army knife" of follow-up.

1. **New lead follow-up**, to maximize lead conversion
2. **New client follow-up**, to impress new customers, build trust, and create fans
3. **Long-term nurture**, to build relationships and turn leads into customers and raving fans that generate the three Rs—reviews, referrals, and repeat business
4. **Special offer broadcast**, to bring in sales when needed

These are the basic three follow-up programs to start with. Over time you will add specialized follow-up programs based on different products, services, lead sources, customer segments, business objectives, and more. When you discover the power of proper follow-up, you will want to apply it all across your Customer Lifecycle, in collections, no-shows, anniversaries, customer milestones, and more. But let's not get ahead of ourselves. Start with the basic three: new lead, new client, and long-term nurture.

The Swiss Army knife of follow-up, a tool that you can apply in lots of places throughout your Customer Lifecycle, is the special offer broadcast. This email or text broadcast is sent to a segment or even your entire customer database, making a special offer that uses the following direct-response marketing elements to maximize response:

- Attention-grabbing subject line about their problem that gets them to read (hook)
- Clear and compelling message or story about their problem (story)
- An irresistible offer that solves the problem your customers face (offer)
- Scarce quantity available to make this offer special for your customers

- Urgency, with a deadline that creates a little fear of missing out
- Social proof, with customer comments and success stories to build trust
- Risk reversal, using a guarantee to make it easy for your customers to act

Hook. Story. Offer. Then evoke their emotion to buy and help them justify the investment. These direct-response marketing elements will boost your sales from a special offer broadcast and remind you of the power of follow-up each time you send a special offer.

Caution: Don't fall in love with the special offer broadcast. Your primary objective is to build a trusting relationship with your customers. If you're always going to the well to sell them something, you'll lose trust, burn out your customers, and train them to ignore you

Of everything you learn in this book, the Customer Lifecycle—with proper follow-up—will grow your business more than anything else. It is the way to systematically collect leads, convert clients, and create fans. Those fans give you the three Rs—reviews, referrals, and repeat business—which make up the vast majority of *profit* in any small business. So whatever you do, if you're serious about growing your business, get your Customer Strategy right by building out your Customer Lifecycle. My team at Keap can help you do it the way we've done it with tens of thousands of others.

Now, let's move on to the next Key to Success: Automation. Because if Customer Lifecycle is the best key to produce money, Automation is the best key to produce time. And heaven knows, you want a little more time in your life.

If you want to go deeper on the science of follow-up and how any small business can double or even triple their sales with proper follow-up, you can get more resources at ConquerTheChaosBook.com. We've taught this to hundreds of

thousands of businesses and we can help you adopt this Customer Strategy to drive your growth and success. Never forget: "The fortune is in the follow-up."

Chapter 7 Summary: Strategy

- There are two parts to Strategy: Company Strategy and Customer Strategy.
- Company Strategy can mean many different things. Its main objective is to provide focus and clarity to help you run your business intentionally and confidently so that you succeed. Set your Strategy following these three steps:
  1. Establish the foundation of the company by articulating your company Vision, consisting of your Purpose, Values, and Mission (PVM).
  2. Establish your Company Strategy by articulating the sound strategy components that support your three-year Mission: a) target market and brand promise, b) competitive differentiation, c) core competencies, d) critical issues, and e) goals.
  3. Establish your daily, weekly, monthly, quarterly, and annual operating rhythm.
- Customer Strategy is the most important key to drive your business growth. The goal of your Customer Strategy is to turn new leads into clients and then raving fans by implementing your Customer Lifecycle.
- Follow-up is the critical factor you must apply to your Customer Lifecycle to consistently turn leads into clients and fans, driving your business success through the roof.
- The fortune is in the follow-up. The fundamentals of follow-up and the seven secrets are the way to properly follow up so you can double or triple your sales.

- The Customer Lifecycle basics (often called "the core four") are: 1) new lead follow-up, 2) new client welcome, 3) long-term nurture, and 4) special offer broadcast.
- Start with the core four and apply the fundamentals of follow-up and the seven secrets. Then gradually build out your perfect Customer Lifecycle over time.

8
AUTOMATION

everal years ago, a small family business won a contest we held for our customers and prospects. The prize was a year-long subscription of our automation software. When we first heard from the husband and wife, they were a two-person shop, maxed out and wanting to grow their business. They had about 5,800 contacts on their list and they were getting about 200 orders per month for their product. Although they were experiencing some growth, they knew their business had the potential to achieve more.

Well, we got them started with our automation software and then sat back to watch the results. One month after putting automation to work in their business, this couple began to see the benefits. First, their list of contacts grew, then their sales volume took off, and with the automation tools in place they were spending less time fulfilling orders.

Three months after implementing automation, their list size had grown to over 10,000 contacts, and they were receiving over 400 orders per month. The best part is that they weren't working longer hours, they hadn't hired any additional employees, and they were less stressed than they had been three months prior.

Unfortunately, one year after putting automation to work, the wife had surgery that knocked her out of commission and out of the business for a few weeks. Think about what would happen to your business if you were laid up with surgery. Would your business stagnate or thrive?

Here's what our customer said:

"I had to have surgery in June, and I wasn't sure how long I would be out. Since our follow-up marketing sequences were already set to run on autopilot, there wasn't anything I had to do business-wise in order to prepare for my time off. Even though I wasn't in the office, new prospects received the information they were looking for, and the follow-up emails helped make the sales. **It ran like a machine**. We had record sales in June, even though I wasn't personally there much of the time. It is nice to know that if I ever need to take off an extended period of time, our family would still have a nice income coming in."

That is the power of automation. More specifically, that's the power of automating your Customer Lifecycle. It's not just increasing sales, not just saving you time. Automation liberates and empowers entrepreneurs to live life on their terms. Oh, and by the way, at the end of the first year, with some basic automation in place, this customer's business had grown four times:

- Their list size increased from 5,800 to 29,600.
- Monthly sales volume went from 200 orders to 850 orders.
- Monthly revenue shot from $13,000 to $48,000.
- The only labor increase was some part-time help from their daughter.

At the most basic levels of the entrepreneur's Hierarchy of Success, we want more money and more time. Yet most small businesses are at odds with that basic desire. Why? Because most small businesses are trading hours for dollars in some form or fashion. Many professional service businesses literally do this, charging by the hour for their work. But it's also true for the vast majority of small businesses, especially service businesses, where the business puts forth more time in exchange for more money.

To produce more income, you can either hire more people (another form of trading hours for dollars) or put more personal time into the business. Either way, the business is on the trading-hours-for-dollars hamster wheel.

The fifth Key to Success, Automation, changes the value exchange. It literally changes the math because you don't have to give as much time to get paid. And when you do Automation well, you can not only free up more time, you can also sky-rocket your income and profits. Automation makes it possible to get stuff done while you sleep or play or spend time with family and friends. Or work on higher-value activities. Automation is a multiplier of your hours. The point is, you don't have to trade hours for dollars anymore when you auto-mate your business. This is why I always say, "Automation is the great game-changer for small businesses."

And it's why Automation is one of the six keys to your business and personal success. Automation will help you conquer the chaos by eliminating things from your to-do list, getting stuff done in the background. The Mindset Key to Success helps you conquer the chaos by reducing stuff in your mental and emotional world. Automation helps you conquer the chaos by getting stuff done in your physical world, knocking out tasks and activities automatically, which frees you up. You are creating time. You are getting paid. You are duplicating your-self and your employees.

If you're like most entrepreneurs, at one time or another you've wished you could clone yourself, be in two places at once, get more hours in the day. Automation does that for you.

What successful entrepreneurs realize is that time, not money, is their most precious resource, especially when we consider the high cost of entrepreneurship and the tendencies to slip into the Dark Side of Entrepreneurship.

When you get Automation working for you and your busi-ness, the benefits are off the charts:

- More personal time to take a break, be with family, go on vacation, or engage in a hobby
- More work time to focus on the activities you enjoy

- Better use of your time to do the high-value work that requires *you*
- Peace of mind that your business is running in the background
- More money, as you increase sales and reduce expenses to improve profit

This Key to Success is obviously central to what we do at Keap. So it should come as no surprise that I'm extremely passionate about the benefits of Automation. But it's not financially driven for me. In other words, it's not about selling more software for the sake of generating more revenue for Keap. It's purpose-driven. It's about our customers.

See, our company Purpose is "We liberate and empower entrepreneurs to strengthen families, communities, and economies." And we do that with Automation. I'm so passionate about Automation because of the way it liberates and empowers our customers to do great things in their families and communities. Nothing liberates and empowers time-strapped entrepreneurs quite like Automation.

The countless stories I hear from customers who use Automation to conquer the chaos and change the game are what really inspire me. I routinely hear from customers:

"I was traveling and didn't have to worry because my business is on autopilot."

"Our business is growing, I'm working less and I spend more time with family."

"Keap is my best employee. It doesn't call in sick or complain and it costs less."

"I was in the hospital, but my business was fine because of automation."

"Due to automation, we can finally get to important projects that were on hold."

"Now I'm getting all kinds of ideas about things I never thought we could do."

I love that last one. Much like a bank line of credit opens up possibilities the entrepreneur couldn't imagine because lack of capital foreclosed those possibilities, Automation opens up possibilities entrepreneurs couldn't imagine because lack of time foreclosed those possibilities.

Read that again. Automation makes things possible that were previously unimaginable because there weren't enough hours in the day to do them.

This is yet another reason why I say automation is the great game changer. So why isn't everyone doing it?

WHAT TO AUTOMATE

Many entrepreneurs think Automation is too difficult, too impersonal, or doesn't apply to their specific business. Wrong. Smart entrepreneurs in every industry are doing it. The technology today makes it extremely personal. With a little guidance, every small business can get the benefits of Automation. The fact is that more and more businesses are discovering the magic of Automation. And with all of the technology advancements, AI, and mobile capabilities that enable us to run our business on the go, it's a big mistake not to explore what Automation can do for you.

So what do you automate? "Everything possible," is the general answer. But more specifically, you automate your Customer Strategy. That's right. You automate your entire Customer Lifecycle. At Keap, we call this Lifecycle Automation (LCA). (See Figure 8.1.)

When you automate the follow-up throughout your Customer Lifecycle, you grow sales and save time. You collect more leads. You convert more clients. And you create more fans. On autopilot. It's not a pipedream; it's Lifecycle Automation. And it is a magnificent thing when you do it in your business.

Figure 8.1 Lifecycle Automation.

LCA takes everything we just covered in our last Key to Success on Customer Strategy (Customer Lifecycle, follow-up fundamentals, the seven secrets to double or triple your sales) and puts it all on autopilot to help you grow your business, in a balanced way.

156

As I look back over the years and consider the impact we get to have on our customers' lives, it's Lifecycle Automation that changes their lives more than anything else.

It's hard to put into words the impact on a mom who has more time for her kids because her CRM software is working in the background to deliver information to prospects and customers instead of requiring her to manually deliver that information.

It's hard to put into words the satisfaction a young entrepreneur gets when his software automatically charges his customer, deposits money into his bank (cha-ching!), and enables him to do things with that money that he couldn't previously do.

It's hard to put into words the contentment that comes when that same entrepreneur knows that after the sale is processed, his Automation kicks off and will execute a sequence of automated follow-up to nurture that new customer, and it tracks everything in the system and notifies his employee of the three tasks to be completed in order to impress the customer.

It's hard to put into words the freedom a successful entrepreneur experiences when she goes on vacation, truly leaves the business behind, and knows her automated Customer Lifecycle is systematically producing more leads, clients, and fans while she gets the rest and relaxation she wants so she can get back to the business rejuvenated and ready to create more impact and freedom.

When entrepreneurs automate their Customer Lifecycle, there is a satisfaction, a calmness, a peace of mind that is quite the contrast to small business chaos. Lifecycle Automation gives them the time and freedom to enjoy life on their terms and achieve balanced growth. Lifecycle Automation helps them make more money, gain greater control, and scale their business to have maximum impact on the world. *Lifecycle Automation is the key that unlocks the definition of success: "balanced growth in our business and personal lives that produces money, time, control, impact, and freedom."* Automation *is* the great game changer for small businesses.

The benefits of Lifecycle Automation are amazing! It's how you truly conquer the chaos. It's how you change your business and your life as an entrepreneur. It's how you go from the treadmill of small business chaos to an assembly line that produces customers and fans. On the treadmill, *you* are at the center of the business, running hard, juggling everything and keeping it all straight in your mind. With an assembly line, *Lifecycle Automation* is at the center of your business, systematically producing happy customers. This is what I want for you so that you can achieve the business success you want while freeing up time to achieve your personal goals. Let's look at how to do this.

FROM MANUAL TO AUTOMATED

As my friend Michael Gerber, author of *The E-Myth*, says, "You should be working *on* your business, not *in* it." Putting Automation in place is one of the best ways to work on your business. It is an investment that will pay recurring dividends over time. Because when you get right down to it, you have one of three choices:

1. Spend more time getting stuff done in the business.
2. Hire someone to take over these responsibilities.
3. Get an automated system in place to manage and execute it for you.

Obviously it's better to put Automation in place. Hiring employees is important, and as you grow, you're going to hire employees. However, that doesn't mean they need to be doing all the manual grunt work. Give *them* the benefits of Automation as well. If it's manual, eventually your employee will make mistakes and need your help dealing with the chaos. Besides, they won't care quite the way you do, so they'll tolerate the manual process more than you do. And then you're throwing good money after bad to put out fires and put Band-Aids on manual processes.

Do yourself, your employees, and your customers a favor. Automate your Customer Lifecycle. Because when you do, it will be more efficient, consistent, and effective than your current manual processes.

Be aware that automating your business requires a time investment. Just like "you need money to make money," it's true that "you need time to make time." So don't look for a magic pill when it comes to automating your business. The good news is that just as you don't build your Rhythm of Execution all at once, you don't automate your business all at once. You start small, investing a little time to start generating returns, and then you keep investing little chunks of time, automating more and more of your Customer Lifecycle, sowing the seeds of Automation that will enable you to reap greater and greater rewards over time.

We've watched this play out in countless customers' businesses, and the success path is to start small and pick some low-hanging fruit. You want to identify a discreet process that is highly repetitive and directly related to producing revenue in your business. Isolate that piece of your Customer Lifecycle and automate it. Because if it's a small enough process that's repeated a lot and directly tied to producing revenue, it's costing you time and inhibiting sales, and it's small enough that you can tackle it. That's the definition of low-hanging fruit.

Of course, once you automate the first thing and pluck some low-hanging fruit in the form of more time and sales, you'll be energized to automate the next piece of your Customer Lifecycle. And then the next, and the next, and so on. If you're wondering about how to do this, I'll show you some hacks to simplify it all. And you're always welcome to contact us at Keap, and we'll be happy to guide you through it.

For our purposes here in the book, the best way to show you the benefits of Automation is to use an example. This is just one of many "use cases" of Automation, but it's a pretty common one, and it shows up at the beginning of the Customer Lifecycle, so it makes sense to start with the Automation of Lead Generation and Conversion.

THE TYPICAL LEAD GENERATION AND CONVERSION PROCESS

Let's look at a typical lead generation and conversion program. Suppose your company spends $2,000 on advertising or some form of marketing with a call to action that drives prospects to get either a free report or a free consultation with you. These are two of the most common "lead magnets," but we could substitute any other lead magnet in our example (free trial, white paper, demo, webinar, newsletter, etc.).

Let's say you generate 10 leads that request your free report or sign up for a free consultation. Of those leads, 3 are hot, 4 are warm, and 3 are cold. In the typical situation, the small business will work the hot leads and close 1 or 2 of them. They'll follow up with the warm leads two or three times, maybe engage a couple, and maybe close one of them. The cold leads either never show up or go MIA or they're just bad leads that may never be ready for your product. Furthermore, let's assume each sale is worth $2,500.

In this typical scenario, the small business spends $2,000 on marketing, generates 10 leads, two new customers, and $5,000 in sales. These are pretty standard numbers and conversion rates. With a manual process, it's tough to follow up 7–12 times (remember that rule of thumb?). So the results are lukewarm and the business better be generating repeat sales with these two new customers or this is a losing proposition where nearly half of the revenue is spent on marketing. And, by the way, if your Customer Lifecycle is manual, it will be challenging to properly follow up with the two new customers, calling into question whether you'll turn them into fans and get reviews, referrals, and repeat business from them.

When you take this manual approach, there is a lot of risk in your marketing investment. Indeed, there is a lot of risk in the business. So, let's look at an automated process and see if we can de-risk this typical scenario for the business owner.

THE AUTOMATED LEAD GENERATION AND CONVERSION PROCESS

Applying the follow-up fundamentals and the seven secrets from the previous chapter on Customer Strategy, let's see how much better this is. You invest the same $2,000 and you generate the very same 10 leads. But you automate a proper follow-up program to produce dramatically better results. Here's what a 12-step automated process would look like for a free report lead magnet. A free consult automated process would be similar, but let's use the free report lead magnet in this example.

A visitor requests the free report and your automation system captures their name, email, phone, and address, kicking off a proper 12-step automated lead generation and conversion process.

1. **Immediate:** Email confirmation sent to prospect thanking them for requesting the report and asking them to call you after they're reviewed the report. Always have a clear call to action (CTA) with each follow-up communication.
2. **Same day:** Print fulfillment company receives notice to physically mail the free report to the prospect (will arrive with the prospect on day 3 or 4).
3. **Day 3:** A "Watch Your Mailbox" email is sent that tells the prospect to check for the free report arriving today or tomorrow.
4. **Day 4:** A "Watch Your Mailbox" text is sent reminding them the free report will arrive soon.
5. **Day 4:** Free report arrives by mail, along with a special offer that expires 30 days from the initial request and a CTA to take advantage of the offer or call you with any questions.

6. **Day 7:** Follow-up email asks if they read the report, and whether they have any questions. The email also contains customer comments and reviews that overcome common objections. And there's a clear CTA to take advantage of your special offer.

7. **Day 14:** Second notice letter arrives. This includes the free report again and reminds them that they have a limited time to respond. Also includes a special bonus offer for responding sooner.

8. **Day 16:** A quick (two or three lines), personalized follow-up text is sent to make sure they received the free report and asks, "Do you have any questions?" to elicit a response.

9. **Day 21:** Phone call to check in, see if they've received the free report, and find out how you can serve them. If prospect answers, they'll usually mention they're sorry for not yet responding and you can have a great conversation about their problems. If they don't answer, you leave a voicemail reminding them of their number one problem, the solution you offer, and a CTA to give you a quick call back.

10. **Day 23:** "Time Is Running Out" email helps overcome another common objection and reminds them they have only a few days left to take advantage of the offer.

11. **Day 28:** "Final Notice" text sent as a courtesy that the offer is about to expire, you want to help them, and "Is there anything I can do to help you solve XYZ problem?"

12. **Day 33:** "Why Didn't You Respond" email survey kindly thanks them for their interest and asks them to honestly share how you could have served them better. Keep the emphasis on what you did wrong to get no response from them instead of blaming them for no response. This survey will help you refine your offer and improve your process. And it will often bubble up renewed interest.

When the prospect responds, your system moves them out of the 12-step process and into a new client or long-term nurture program. At the completion of the 12-step automated process, your system moves unconverted leads into your long-term nurture follow-up program (one of the basic three follow-up programs) where they will receive regularly scheduled follow-up emails with useful information about their problems. These will be sent automatically, weekly or monthly, depending on how good your information is for 12–24 months. Then repeat the long-term nurture program so that your customers are always hearing from you as an expert.

Of course, you will modify this Automation to fit your company, but when you implement something like this, the results speak for themselves. The numbers on this type of a program (in the same business case mentioned previously in the "typical" scenario) will be $2,000 invested, 10 leads, four to six new customers, and $10,000–$15,000 in sales. You'll close a couple of the hot leads; two or three of the warm leads and even one of the cold leads may convert over the long term. That's one of the many reasons why your long-term nurture program is so important.

This example incorporates four types of media (or channels): mail, email, phone, and text. You can deliver the report digitally, but the report isn't viewed as having the same value and the program is not as effective. If you do choose to deliver it digitally, be sure to use at least three channels of follow-up: email, phone, and text. The idea is to combine multiple methods of communication. Your prospect won't receive all of them. But they will usually receive enough that your message gets through to them.

One of the great benefits of this example of Automation is that it shifts the psychology in your favor and gets you out of hunting mode and into harvesting mode, as mentioned in the previous chapter. You'll notice your prospects apologizing for missing calls, interested in your information, and willing to talk about their problems and your solution. Sure, many will not buy or even respond. And a few may tell you to back off. But I challenge you to stack this follow-up program against the typical scenario of making one or two calls and sending one or two emails and then compare the results. This program will generate two to three times more sales, with better efficiency, better conversations, and far greater enjoyment on your part!

Now you can see that even if you were a follow-up master, you could not do as thorough and complete a job as your automated follow-up system can. If there are multiple steps in your marketing campaign, you're bound to make mistakes at some point. How do you know which contact receives what, and on which day? If you're only managing a handful of prospects or customers, this can be done by a mere mortal. But once you have dozens, hundreds, even thousands of contacts to manage, you just can't do it anymore. *This is a big reason why proper follow-up with 7–12 steps is not done.*

With Lifecycle Automation, you get the benefits of follow-up without any of the pain or mistakes. Plus, you'll be building relationships that cannot be achieved any other way. As one customer told me, "Lifecycle Automation allows me to build relationships with hundreds or even thousands of people that weren't possible when I communicated in mass or spent the time to do one-on-one communication." Exactly. That's the power of personalized, automated follow-up that you get from Lifecycle Automation.

I do need to offer three cautions about this type of proper follow-up to address some concerns you may have:

Caution 1: You'll be tempted to say that your prospects will get upset if you follow up this much. Don't fall into that trap. First of all, they won't read or even receive most of the steps you send. Second, if you're boring and the information you provide is of no value, you might be right, so make sure you're giving them valuable information! And third, if somebody does get a little annoyed, you have an opportunity to talk with them and serve them. Remember, even negative emotion that drives a response is better than apathy that results in no response. Serve them cheerfully.

Caution 2: When you put this into practice, you *will* begin getting responses. Be sure you are ready to handle the responses—add them to your CRM, track the progress through their buying process, and have prebuilt automations and ready-made templates to fire off at a moment's notice to save you time. Of course, it's a good problem to have, and if you need to handle all the responses manually, that's fine. But it's better if you're well equipped to handle the responses efficiently and confidently as they come in so you can keep the psychology on your side and stay calm and confident throughout the buying process.

Caution 3: The fear and ego-driven part of our brains (the "lizard brain" as Seth Godin calls it) tells us all of the reasons why we cannot do this. Cast that aside. This works. But if you simply cannot get yourself to go with this full program I'm recommending, just apply the principles I'm teaching you and up your follow-up game to *at least* include three emails, three phone calls, and a text. Just doing *that* will significantly improve your sales. And then you'll have the ammo to silence the lizard brain and go all in on this program so you can achieve maximum results.

Now, here's the really cool thing about the example I just shared with you: your competitors won't do this. You become the expert, the trusted advisor in your industry. And you build really great relationships as you automate your Customer Lifecycle in a way that feels very personal to your customers. The best part of all is that because it's automated, you can execute it flawlessly. As new leads drop into your automated system, they get the right message at the right time, at the right point in your Customer Lifecycle, personalized just for them. That's the beauty of Lifecycle Automation!

WHAT ELSE CAN YOU AUTOMATE?

When you generate and convert leads with Automation, you'll want to look at ways to automate more of your Customer Lifecycle. And you're in a great spot to do it once you've got an automated lead conversion system in place. Think about it. In the eyes of your new customer, you're already positioned as an expert, not a vendor. So where do you want to take the relationship from there? That's right! You want to turn those new clients into raving fans that generate the 3Rs—reviews, referrals, and repeat business. When you do so, you will significantly improve your business profit and the ROI from your $2,000 marketing investment.

Just as we compared the "typical" lead conversion process with our automated lead conversion process, we could do the same for any number of processes across the Customer Lifecycle and throughout your business. Without going into too much depth, let's highlight a few of the processes that you'll want to automate.

New Client Follow-up

Let's consider a "typical" scenario of new client follow-up with one or two calls and/or emails and contrast that with an example of Automation. For example, what if your system automatically kicked off a new client follow-up process like this one when a customer bought from you:

Day 1, Email: Thanks for your purchase and set expectations.
Day 3, Phone: Check in to ensure initial expectations were met.

Day 8, Email: Thank you again and watch your mailbox for a gift.

Day 11, Direct Mail: Thank-you gift fulfilled by your fulfillment partner.

Day 20, Email: Follow up on gift and see if they have questions.

Day 30, Phone: Check in to ensure satisfaction, serve, and learn how to improve.

Day 45, Postcard: Refer a friend and receive a discount on future purchases.

Then, just as you did at the end of your lead conversion program, you drop new customers into your long-term nurture. This will help you continue building relationships to create fans.

REVIEWS AND REFERRALS

When my business partner, Scott, purchased a car a few years ago, he received a great new client follow-up campaign. It included a "welcome to the family" email, a survey, a thank-you call, a personalized note from the salesman, two dozen cookies from a local bakery, and a couple of email and text check-ins to make sure Scott was completely satisfied with his purchase. All of that happened over the course of his first 30 days as a customer. That new client follow-up campaign led into a campaign of emails and texts requesting reviews and referrals.

That's a good example of how to "create fans" that will lead to the three Rs of reviews, referrals, and repeat business. And as I've said several times, those three Rs are what make up the majority of profit in any small business because you don't pay customer acquisition costs for repeat business. Furthermore, referrals and repeat buyers have a higher close rate. That's why we want the three Rs. But can you imagine trying to execute a proper new client welcome campaign without Automation? It might work for the first few new clients, but when the chaos hits, if that new client follow-up program is executed manually, it will most likely break down.

Contrast Scott's car-buying experience with one where the relationship ends with the sale. Which customer experience is likely to produce reviews, referrals, and repeat business? I think we all know the answer to that. We want to make sure you've got an awesome, automated new client follow-up program in place so that you can maximize the ROI of your marketing investments and improve your profit.

REPEAT BUSINESS

When you look across your Customer Lifecycle, you'll see there are many places where you'll want to offer additional product and services to your customers. When you are automatically building relationships with long-term nurture, you're in a good position to ask for repeat business. And when you use the power of segmentation, you can send the right message to the right customer at the right time, with an upsell or cross-sell offer they can't refuse.

BILLING AND COLLECTIONS

If you're a service provider offering a recurring service to your clients, billing and collections can be a real hassle. This is something you'll want to automate because every payment collected and deposited saves you time and ensures you get paid. Too often, service businesses "write off" payments they should be depositing into their bank account because the hassles of collection are just too much.

Set up your client's credit cards to be billed automatically. Put automated email and text reminders in place. And set up automated follow-up for expired or unsuccessful credit card charges. All of the funds should go into your bank account automatically, with invoices created and stored in your system. Once you set it up, you don't need to do a thing. This really is "set it and forget it." A great Automation system will let you set up a payment plan for a particular client or charge your clients on a quarterly or annual basis, or cancel a particular service or payment. The point is that Automation can free you up in a big way here, helping you save time, collect cash, and avoid mistakes.

WORKFLOW

When you automate your entire Customer Lifecycle, you'll want to keep going. It's common for our customers to automate all sorts of internal processes and workflows. Once you experience the time savings, you and your employees will want more of it, and you'll see all kinds of things to automate. Here are just a few examples of what we see our customers automating beyond the Customer Lifecycle:

- Automate the process of hiring new employees.
- Be notified when a customer takes an action and trigger an automated process.
- Automatically assign and track tasks for sales reps.
- Track and automate internal checklists and processes.
- Build morale by automatically capturing and sharing customer success stories.

This doesn't even begin to scratch the surface of what's possible when you automate the workflow of your employees. With an assist from Automation, you can keep yourself and your employees on track and maximizing your time. Automation gives you the bird's-eye view of your business and saves you from running through a daily maze of mundane tasks. Bottom line, with Automation you are making your business more scalable. Because things are set to run as needed, it really doesn't matter how many prospects and customers you add; the system can handle it. And you don't need to worry about it.

MICRO AUTOMATIONS

We just covered major processes and functions that can be automated, but there's so much more you can do. Every little repetitive task can be automated. Your system can trigger automation based on a link clicked, a task completed, a stage change in your fulfillment process, and so much more. These little micro automations add up to create big efficiencies in your business. Your employees will love the time savings and it will free them up to do higher-value work. Once you feel the liberation of Automation, you'll be looking for all sorts of ways to put Automation to work for you.

Honestly, without Automation it's hard to see how small businesses break free from the treadmill of chaos. Automation can handle some of the most complex and time-consuming jobs a small business owner has to take on. And it can knock out tiny little tasks that are being done manually, repeatedly throughout the business. That not only gives business owners and employees time back in their day to do other important activities, but it also gives them peace of mind as stuff gets done automatically in the background.

PRO TIPS ON AUTOMATION

Hopefully, it's clear why Automation is a Key to Success. It produces money, time, control, impact, and freedom. But it takes work to implement this stuff. So let me give you a handful of suggestions and short-cuts. These pro tips will maximize your likelihood of success and simplify the adoption of Automation so you can get the benefits without the pain. Like I said before, there's no magic pill, and you do need to invest some money and time to get the amazing benefits of Automation. But it's worth it. And these pro tips will help you significantly.

Pick a flexible platform. Make sure you get an Automation platform that will grow with you over time and will not paint you into a corner. Some solutions help you get started quickly, but they are not robust enough to grow with you. As the CEO of Keap, I'm obviously biased, but I am confident our platform is the most flexible and robust Automation platform on the market for small businesses.

It's not just software. After doing this for 20 years, it's clear to me that small businesses need more than just a software to automate their business. They need the strategy to make Automation work. They need services to help them get the most out of the platform. We always say, "Software + Strategy + Services = Success." You need the full solution to be successful when you implement Automation.

Start with prebuilt templates. Building Automation is very valuable, but you want to avoid starting from scratch as much as possible. When you start with templates, you get a good idea of what you want and what the platform can do. And you avoid the "writer's block" scenario that often happens when you start from scratch.

Tailor it for your business. Although you want to start with templates, make sure you invest the time to customize the Automation for your business. You want your customers to have a personalized experience in your Customer Lifecycle. And you want to represent your business well in your follow-ups and all the content and assets that are a part of your Lifecycle Automation.

Work with trusted partners. There are many digital agencies and consultants who specialize in automating small businesses. It may be well worth it for you to hire someone who has great experience in this stuff. We have thousands of certified partners in the Keap Family who are passionate about helping small businesses grow with Automation. Many of them are brilliant and worth their weight in gold to their clients.

Implement vertical solutions. When possible, vertical solutions can dramatically speed up your time to value and increase your overall success with Automation. Be sure such a solution comes with the automated follow-up programs that will help you automate your Customer Lifecycle. A vertical solution that lacks Automation of the Customer Lifecycle does not drive the success we want. (Note: Many Keap certified partners specialize in verticals, and that combination of a partner plus a vertical solution is a particularly powerful combination when implementing Automation.)

Lindsey Ardmore knows the power of Automation. She started her business when her baby was three days old. She knew she couldn't invest as much time as a new business normally requires, so she designed her business around Automation from the beginning. She built out her Lifecycle Automation, with automated processes for generating leads, converting clients, and creating fans. It took time to set up, but she gradually built a great business helping other female entrepreneurs market their businesses more effectively.

Lindsey and her team at Star Tower Systems now help their marketing clients implement Lifecycle Automation using Keap. Star Tower Systems' clients get the benefit of being guided by an expert. And in many cases those clients are able to benefit from the templates and proven strategies Lindsey and her team have used to successfully grow small businesses over the years. This not only helps her clients make more money, but it also saves them a significant amount of time that would be spent building Automation themselves.

Lindsey is getting the benefits of Automation in her business and her personal life. After her business began to grow successfully, Lindsey was able to realize a lifelong dream of buying a horse farm. She and her husband are now raising their family on a beautiful property in Florida. Lindsey's grit and hard work made her business possible. Automation made her business so efficient that she could focus on her dreams.

And by the way, Lindsey also implemented Lifecycle Automation in her husband's business, which is another great story of Automation.

Chapter 8 Summary: Automation

- Automation is the great game-changer for small businesses, enabling them to grow sales, save time, and stop trading hours for dollars.
- You can and should automate as much as possible in your business. The most important thing to automate is your Customer Lifecycle. This is called Lifecycle Automation (LCA).
- LCA gets you out of the center of your business. It gives you peace of mind, makes your team more efficient, and boosts business profits.
- LCA helps entrepreneurs conquer the chaos by getting more done in less time as they automate their Customer Lifecycle. LCA is effectively moving from a treadmill of chaos to a conveyor belt that produces clients and fans.
- The typical manual lead generation and conversion program produces a lot of waste. The automated lead generation and conversion program shows the efficiency and profits that flow to small businesses when they use LCA.
- Automate everything you can in your business. Follow the pro tips in this chapter. Start with the core four of your Customer Lifecycle, then gradually build out automation across the entire Customer Lifecyle and your entire business.

9
LEADERSHIP

The sixth and final key to business and personal success for entrepreneurs is Leadership. The topic is quite broad, so we will focus on a certain brand of Leadership that is specific to the work of entrepreneurs.

When I talk about Leadership as a key to success, I'm referring to the entrepreneur's ability to lead the company to achieve its shared goals while growing people in the process. That might seem like an obvious definition, but trust me, it will help us stay focused on what really matters when it comes to Leadership for entrepreneurs: *leading the company to achieve its goals and growing people in the process.*

The smaller the business, the less Leadership skill is required. And because it can be challenging to develop and flex these Leadership muscles, many entrepreneurs settle for a business with limited impact. Worse yet, when entrepreneurs start growing their businesses but they don't grow their Leadership skills, they get buried by the business. The weight of it all becomes too much. It wears them down. Burns them out. And tragically, it causes them to scale back, sell out, or shut down.

And those are just the tragic business consequences. That doesn't even touch on the chaos it causes in entrepreneurs' personal lives when they don't build their Leadership skills. The fact is, entrepreneurs' underinvestment in their own Leadership development is the single greatest contributor to the Dark Side of Entrepreneurship, with all of its nasty symptoms.

That's why I want this to be a wake-up call to any entrepreneur feeling the weight of a growing business, not knowing if or how you can keep leading the business.

You can do this!

I've been there. I was certain that I would lose my family, my health, or the business in those early days when it was so overwhelming. But I figured it out. And you can, too. If your business has fewer than 10 employees, this is important stuff. And if your business has more than 10 employees, this is *critically* important stuff to keep the company growing and everyone rowing in the same direction.

Just as you learned how to sell, market, build a product, and serve your customers, you *can* learn to lead your company effectively. Don't believe the voices saying you aren't a "born leader," you don't have an MBA or the personality or the experience—blah, blah, blah. Nobody who accomplished something great knew how to do it beforehand. They figured it out. And you can figure out Leadership too!

At Keap, we have spent millions of dollars on consultants and Leadership gurus. I have personally invested large sums of money on my own Leadership development. As mentioned in Chapter 7 on Strategy, at one point my team and I put all of this great wisdom together into a program to teach entrepreneurs how to do it. Later we spun out that company, called Elite Entrepreneurs, and it's now thriving on its own. I get to play there a little bit because I love it so much.

What I'll share with you in this chapter is the summarized version of the Elite Entrepreneurs program that develops entrepreneurial leaders. We'll focus on how you can use your Company Strategy—the Purpose, Values, Mission, strategic plan, and goals—to lead your company to success, all while growing your people. My objective in this chapter is to shorten the learning process for you and save you tons of time, money, and hassles by guiding you to the activities you must do to become a great leader of your business and help others learn to be great leaders in the process.

When you practice these principles of Leadership, you open up a world of opportunity. Your business can have much greater impact. You will achieve a level of freedom beyond your wildest dreams, because this is the Key to Success that unlocks the highest levels of our hierarchy. This is where you gain deep appreciation and fulfillment for your work as an entrepreneur. This is where you get to really bless the lives of others.

To maximize your effectiveness as a leader, we need to get you thinking like a CEO. And not just any CEO—an effective CEO, one who focuses on the three jobs of a CEO in an enlightened, modern way.

THINK LIKE A CEO

Many entrepreneurs don't consider themselves CEOs, figuring that's a big business term. Other entrepreneurs are stuck with "hero syndrome," thinking they must do it all. And some entrepreneurs call themselves CEOs when they're the only person in the business. None of this is necessarily "wrong." But all of *it is limiting the entrepreneurial leader.* And most of it misses the whole point of a CEO.

A CEO is a chief executive officer. "Chief" means the CEO leads a group of executives. What do those executives do? They "execute" the vision and strategic plan of the business to achieve the company's goals.

In other words, *the CEO leads others to execute the strategy and achieve the goals.* The CEO *does* little else. The CEO mentality is always looking to *direct, delegate, and develop others,* while keeping everyone rowing in the same direction to achieve the company goals. Notice I didn't say to achieve *your* goals. Think about the company. That's what good leaders do. They separate themselves and their own goals from the business goals.

To summarize, to achieve the company goals, the aim of the CEO is to:

- Do less.
- Direct the work.
- Delegate everything possible.
- Develop others.

I can hear you saying, "Well, it would be nice to have a bunch of people to delegate stuff to, but I'm on my own, pal (or my team is really small)!" You can still *cultivate a mentality that directs, delegates, and develops others* to achieve the company goals.

Work on the mentality of a CEO and it will start to come to you more naturally. You won't feel weighed down by *your* goals. You won't feel like you have to do everything. You'll stop feeling like your employees "don't get it." Instead, you'll start to feel lighter. You'll view employees as true assets and partners in your shared goals. And you'll find the world will begin conspiring to help you achieve *your company's goals*.

THE THREE JOBS OF A CEO

Okay, now that we've got you thinking like a CEO, let's talk about the three jobs of the CEO. I learned this many years ago after raising capital from one of the most prominent venture capitalists in the world. My new investor said to me, "Don't forget the three jobs of the CEO: 1) set the Vision; 2) build the team to achieve the Vision; and 3) don't run out of cash."

That was really helpful. Good, clear, focusing advice. Over time, I morphed the CEO's third job to be a little broader than "Don't run out of cash." Here are the three jobs of the CEO:

1. **Set the Vision**. This is where you and your team (even if you're a solopreneur and your "team" is a friend, a family member, and your dog) establish your Purpose, Values,

Mission, strategic plan, and goals (PVMSG or, collectively, Vision), as mentioned in the fourth Key to Success when we discussed Company Strategy.

2. **Build the team** to achieve the Vision. This means both hiring people and developing people who will execute the Vision. As the leader, you must make sure to "hire, coach, and fire" to the PVM. And each employee must have a clear "top three" set of responsibilities that tie them to the company goals. This is how you get everyone rowing in the same direction.

3. **Get the resources**. It's your job to secure the cash, the partnerships, and the other resources required to achieve the Vision. This is why smart entrepreneurial leaders maintain good bank relationships and spend time with industry and other leaders to attract and secure the resources the company will need to achieve its goals.

So there you have it. Those are the three jobs of the CEO. It's not rocket science. It's just tricky to prioritize this and focus on it as the leader because you wear so many hats, there are so many different things clamoring for your attention, and you're used to doing it all as an entrepreneur. It's also tricky because your habits and ego pull you into the *doing*. It's foreign and uncomfortable to be *directing, delegating, and developing others*. The ego gets satisfaction from doing. But if you don't step back to direct and delegate, your people won't develop.

It's also tricky because, let's face it, this is more art than science. It's helpful to talk with people who are living this Leadership stuff every day because they can help you stay on track to set the Vision, build the team, and get the resources. That's why it's useful for leaders to join masterminds, peer groups, coaching programs, and informal networks to help you see what it looks like to practice this stuff well.

We're going to cover the Leadership Key to Success by using the framework of the three jobs of the CEO. But before we cover the Vision, build the team, and get the resources, we first need to explore two other concepts—conscious capitalism and enlightened entrepreneurship.

Conscious Capitalism

Several years ago, I came across an approach to business that really resonated with me. The conscious capitalism movement is all about doing business in a way that does good for everyone associated with the business. This resonated with me because my personal purpose as I mentioned previously is, "To love, inspire and enrich others." Capitalism is a great thing! We should not be ashamed of making money in exchange for the problems we solve and the value we create for others. But we want to make sure everyone benefits in the process.

When the CEO is practicing conscious capitalism, everyone has a chance to win. Customers' problems are solved. Employees grow and reap financial rewards. Partners gain opportunities to build their businesses as part of the ecosystem. Shareholders are rewarded as the stock price increases. And the community benefits as the business is solving problems with its product or service and doing good in the community. Everyone benefits in conscious capitalism.

Now, it's capitalism, not socialism. So none of these benefits are guaranteed. They are *possible*. They flow when everyone is working together, doing their part. It's the CEO's job to align and unify all the stakeholders, as much as possible, to increase the likelihood of winning when everyone does their part. And it's the company's job to help everyone do their part.

I love conscious capitalism. I always want Keap to be a blessing in the lives of our employees, partners, customers, shareholders, and everyone associated with the business. I hope this movement resonates with you as much as it does me. Because when entrepreneurs take this approach to their business, they can do so much good. And they are more likely to achieve the higher levels of the entrepreneur's Hierarchy of Success. My experience is that most entrepreneurs feel this way because entrepreneurs are some of the most generous, creative, caring people in the world. I believe conscious capitalism can ignite that natural tendency in entrepreneurs and magnify the good we do in our businesses, enabling us to achieve high levels of impact and freedom.

THE ENLIGHTENED ENTREPRENEUR

There was a day when many entrepreneurs ran their business for themselves and only themselves. That's kind of the opposite of conscious capitalism. And thankfully, that way of operating has mostly gone by the wayside. The world has changed and people want to be part of a cause. This is especially true for younger employees.

This means that as an entrepreneur, you want to get your people involved, really involved, in the business. You want to co-create with them. *When your people feel like they're working in your business, you will get subpar results, people won't grow much, and it's not as fun.* On the other hand, when they feel like they're working in *their* business, amazing things happen.

To unlock the greatest potential of your people, and to maximize the company's performance, make them owners. You might do that literally, giving them an ownership stake, stock options, or profit sharing. You might do it figuratively, giving them ownership and autonomy over outcomes and projects. You might do both. Whatever the case, the Enlightened Entrepreneur recognizes it's not about him or her. It's about the common good that everyone is working toward.

When you take this approach, your people act like owners. And isn't that exactly what you want as an entrepreneur? Isn't it amazing when your employees treat customers like *their* customers? Isn't it inspiring when employees make it *their* mission to finish an important project or accomplish a big goal? Isn't it so fun when employees improve a process or fix a system that was causing subpar results? And isn't it liberating for you when your people are partnering with you to achieve the company goals, freeing you up so you don't feel so burdened by the business?

If your business is still in the early stages and you haven't yet felt the rush I'm talking about, look forward to it as an Enlightened Entrepreneur. It is amazing. To this day, it's one of my favorite things to see a Keaper (as we call our people) solve a long-standing problem or improve something I always wish were better. I can still think back to the days when Scott, Eric, and I wore all the hats and did all the jobs (most of them poorly, I might add). It is a thrill to see Keapers bring their specialized skills and do something far better than we ever did it.

This combination of think like a CEO, the three jobs of the CEO, conscious capitalism, and enlightened entrepreneurship sets you up to lead powerfully. It requires you to check your ego and make the business about others. Now that we're clear on our objective as leaders and our philosophy of how we'll approach Leadership, let's jump into the three jobs of the CEO: set the Vision, build the team, and get the resources.

SET THE VISION

In Chapter 7, we touched on setting the Vision as part of our Company Strategy topic. Now we get to go deeper into your Vision, which is your Purpose, Values, Mission, strategic plan, and goals. The Mission, strategic plan, and goals are based on the three-year time frame. Let's look at each component of the Vision you'll set. And keep in mind that it's your job to *co-create* this Vision. You don't retreat to the mountain on high, set the Vision there, and then bring it down to the people etched in stone. As history teaches us, people tend to reject such plans. You'll want to co-create the Vision with your team to gain buy-in and maximize your chances for success.

Purpose-built. Your company will be strong and you'll invoke the passionate commitment of your team when you build on a meaningful Purpose that inspires your people. The Purpose is why your company exists. It does not change and should last the life of your company. It is a short statement that acts as a rallying cry for your team. It is the cause behind the company. And it will attract and inspire the people you want to work with when you do this right. I've included Keap's Purpose, Values, and Mission so you can see an example of this. (See Figure 9.1.)

Our Vision

Our Vision guides our company and ignites our culture.
Our Purpose, Values, and Mission, create the Vision and live at the center of our Leadership Model.

Purpose
We liberate and empower entrepreneurs to strengthen families, communities, and economies

Core Values

We Genuinely Care
We listen to, care for, and serve the diverse people central to our Purpose: our employees, partners, customers, and entrepreneurs everywhere.

We Own It
We are a culture of performance and accountability. We face challenges with grit and optimism to achieve our goals.

We Learn Always
We have a forever curious, learn-it-all mindset and we value learning over knowledge. We use data and experimentation to innovate and constantly improve.

We Build Trust
We build trust through transparency and open, authentic communication. We presume positive intent and we are the first to extend trust.

We Check Ego
We check our ego at the door. Humility and gratitude help us work collaboratively, serve others, and accomplish more.

We Dream Big
We empower the entrepreneurial spirit by believing in people and championing their dreams. We solve big problems with big dreams.

We Win Together
We are one team, unified in our Purpose and Mission. We all win when everyone does their part in service of the whole.

Mission
To simplify growth for a million small businesses worldwide by 2030

Figure 9.1 Keap's Purpose, Values, and Mission

Values-based. Like your Purpose, your Values are foundational and they should not change over the life of your company. They are a "social contract" on how you and your people behave. When you get this right, you've identified the characteristics of a star employee that you want all employees to emulate. Everyone practices these Values, from the business owner to the newest employee, so make sure these are an articulation of who your best people are.

Mission-driven. You need your people inspired, motivated, and driven to achieve your Mission, which is a clear three-year plan. Your Mission should be stated in terms like this: "We will _____ (qualitative success criterion), by such-and-such date (three years away) with X, Y, and Z (three quantitative success criteria)." For example, an industrial cleaning company might say, "We will be the leading corporate cleaning company in Arizona by (three years away), with 1,000 clients, $30 million in annual revenue, and a 4.9 client satisfaction rating." The qualitative success criteria fires up the team. The quantitative criteria are the agreed-upon criteria that would distinguish the company as the leader in Arizona. (Note: For larger businesses like Keap, the Mission is a longer-term view that is then broken down into three-year "current missions" that ladder up to the long-term Mission.)

Strategy-guided. The strategic plan articulates the three to five key objectives that must be accomplished to achieve the three-year Mission. It also articulates the main pillars of Company Strategy covered in our fourth Key to Success. Most importantly, the three-year strategy plan highlights the three to five strengths, or core competencies, the company will focus on and leverage in order to achieve its three-year goals. The three-year strategic plan is broken down into an annual plan before the start of each new year. This keeps the company focused and on the same page, emphasizing the company's strengths, guiding everyone in the work they do to help the company achieve its three-year Mission. As covered in the Life Vision, the three-year time frame is equally powerful in your business Vision.

Goal-oriented. You need your people focused on the results that drive the company's success. You'll want everyone's work to ladder up to the company's top three goals for the mission, which are then broken down into the annual plan. The CEO's top three goals are the company's top three goals. And the Leadership team's top three goals support the top three company goals. Everyone's goals cascade down from the top. And every employee's top three goals ladder up to the company's top three goals, as much as possible. This is how you get everyone working together to win.

As the CEO, one of your jobs is to set the Vision. Where there is no vision, the people perish (Proverbs 29:18). By co-creating your Purpose, Values, Mission, strategic plan, and goals, you help everyone see where the company is going. You inspire and motivate your people to achieve it. You get everyone rowing in the same direction. It becomes clear who is not pulling their weight and who does not fit your PVM. You coach people up or you move them out. You cannot tolerate and harbor people who are not pulling their weight. That isn't fair to all of your team members who are doing their part to achieve the company's Mission. *Be courageous and coach underperformers up or out.*

When you co-create a Purpose-built, Values-based company, with a team of inspired people driving on your Mission and guided by strategy to achieve your common goals, it is a joy to work at the company. It truly becomes a "great place to work." It frees you up as a leader, helps you conquer the chaos, and enables you to achieve the higher levels in our Hierarchy of Success. The impact you make and the freedom you find are super satisfying. So step up to the plate as a leader and set the Vision for your company. If you'd like help doing this, you can get free resources and expert guidance from the Elite Entrepreneurs team at ConquerTheChaosBook.com.

BUILD THE TEAM

The second job of the CEO is build the team. Isn't it fun building something with others? To me, this is one of the greatest rewards of entrepreneurship. We get to combine our skills with others to achieve a common goal. That teamwork, that shared Purpose, is deeply satisfying. Unfortunately, some entrepreneurs don't get to experience that because they're not sure how to do this Leadership work. Not you. You've already got a pretty good sense for it based on the previous section "Set the Vision." And you're about to get some additional tools in this section. We'll cover building the team by developing the organization and building the team by developing the people.

Caveat: I realize some entrepreneurs want to be solopreneurs. And that's fine, as long as you're choosing that intentionally. But, deep down inside, many solopreneurs don't actually want to be working alone. They settle for it or say they want it because they are wary of working with others. Whatever your situation, if you're a solopreneur by default or by design, I want to at least give you the tools to build a team if you decide to do that. Because if you build a team, you can have greater impact. And even if you remain a solopreneur by design, many of these principles will help you as you work with contractors, partners, and others to achieve your company goals. After all, we are all a leader of one at the end of the day. May we lead ourselves well!

BUILD THE TEAM: DEVELOPING THE ORGANIZATION

To achieve your company's goals, you need great people, aligned to the PVM, and organized to execute the strategic plan. That's easier said than done. My friend Dave Ramsey likes to say,

"Business is easy. . .until people get involved." Well, there's some truth to that. But it's also a lot of fun when you get everyone working together in a spirit of unity and camaraderie. And that's what we want to do as we develop the organization. Here are a few important principles that will help you do that.

Use a developmental org chart. For many entrepreneurs, the term "org chart" conjures up images of stuffy, big business, corporate ladder-climbing, brown-nosing politics. Yuck! That's not what we mean here. The entrepreneur's org chart is an amazing developmental tool. Here's how you use it:

1. Get clear on all the roles (boxes) on the org chart the company will have filled when it achieves its three-year Mission.
2. Note the top three job responsibilities in short-hand near the box.
3. Write into each box the name of the person (in the company today) responsible for that role. If you're a solopreneur, your name's in every box. If it's just a few of you, your name will be in many boxes.

No wonder you feel the chaos, right? Publish the chart in a visible place. Then begin working your names out of the boxes, hiring and developing others to take over one role at a time. Which box do you get out of first? The one you're worst at. Work toward "doing what you do best and delegating the rest."

Practice HABU religiously. Your human resources are extremely valuable. You want each person to be doing work that represents the "highest and best use" (HABU) of their time. Put Automation to work wherever possible. And make sure your most expensive resources are doing the most valuable work. With every project and task, you should be asking if a lower-cost resource could be used to accomplish that task. You can't do that 100% of the time, but you can be guided by this important Leadership principle as you develop the organization. I recommend doing an ICE exercise regularly (once per quarter in fast-growth companies and at least once per year in any small business).

For an ICE exercise you write down everything you do. Honestly rate yourself as Incompetent, Competent, or Excellent at each activity. Show your rating to an objective observer who can verify or adjust your self-rating. Stop doing the Is, work to eliminate the Cs, and do more of the Es. Direct, delegate, develop. This is another way to "do what you do best and delegate the rest."

Hire, coach, and fire to your Vision. Sure, you need to hire people who can do the job, people who can execute the strategic plan and help the company achieve its goals. But don't hire people who do not fit your PVM. They might have the skills to achieve goals, but they will destroy your company. As Patrick Lencioni teaches brilliantly in his book *The Advantage*, organizational health trumps everything else in business. It creates an environment where people solve problems, collaborate, and contribute at the highest level. So one of your most important jobs is to hire, coach, and *fire* to your PVM. Get them out of the business if they don't fit the culture. And make absolutely sure your hiring leaders are doing the same. When it comes to PVM fit, little cracks at the top of the org chart turn into gaping chasms at the bottom of the org chart.

Intentionally build a great place to work. When you set the Vision and hire, coach, and fire to that Vision, you begin to build a great place to work. The foundation of great places to work is trust. So you want to always build trust by being transparent, providing context, and helping everyone get aligned to the Purpose, Values, Mission, strategic plan, and goals. Believe the best in and of your people.

Empower them to do their best work by giving them context and the big picture. And invest in their growth inside and outside of the company. You'll create an amazing culture that attracts the right people and repels the wrong ones. And while we're on that point, "the wrong people" doesn't mean they're bad. It just means they don't fit your PVM. You want to build an amazing, inclusive culture. But you don't want to include people who don't fit your PVM. This is very important and perhaps controversial with some, so it requires a little more explanation.

Look at our Purpose, Values, and Mission at Keap. (See Figure 9.1.) You'll note that we are big fans of diversity and inclusion. But we do exclude on the basis of PVM. You'll note how clear we are about our PVM. So imagine what would happen to our culture at Keap if we hired someone who doesn't want to serve small businesses and instead wants us to serve businesses with over 100 employees. Or imagine if we hired someone who doesn't want to learn and grow. Imagine if we hired a leader who is uncomfortable dreaming big, extending trust first, or multiplying their people. See figure 9.2. Those are examples of a cultural misfit. They're not bad. They're just not good for Keap. And unless they adopt the Values, they will be much happier at another company that's a better fit for them.

It's also important to point out that this doesn't mean we lack diversity or that we all have the same Values. As I say all the time to groups of Keapers: "You might have 31 values and I might have 27 and the Keaper next to you might have 34. But we all share these seven Values. They are our core Values. And they guide us in our work at Keap." As you build a great place to work, attract the people who fit your PVM and repel those who don't. As you do so, your culture will become a huge strategic advantage for you. Indeed, as Lencioni says, it will become an advantage that trumps everything else in business. And aside from the business performance benefits, it's just a lot more fun to work in a place where everyone fits your PVM.

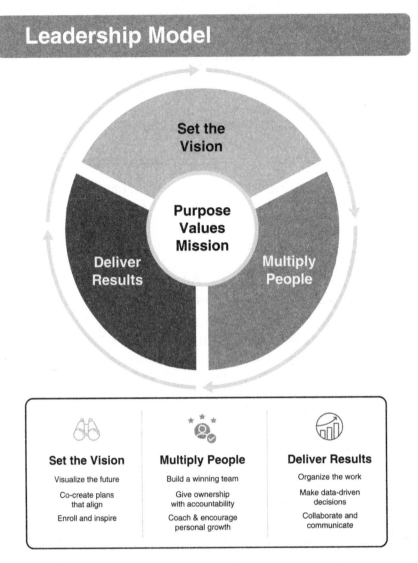

Figure 9.2　Keap Leadership Model.

BUILD THE TEAM: DEVELOPING THE PEOPLE

When developing the organization, we're focused more on the organizational structure, the philosophy, and the hiring practices of the company. When it comes to developing the people, we're focused on the growth and development of individuals in the company. We want them to do their best work and be their best selves. Here are a few principles to follow that will help you develop your people.

Grow yourself. It starts with you. If you aren't pushing yourself to get better in your role and to become your best self, you can't expect others to do the same. Lead by example. Work on your Life Vision and Rhythm of Execution to become your best self. Constantly work to upgrade your skills and capabilities. And improve your self-awareness, checking your ego regularly. You might invest in coaching, peer groups, or other development programs. Certainly you'll want to follow the advice of the Arbinger Institute's book *Leadership and Self-Deception*. You'll also want to regularly assess your productivity. The ICE exercise is a good one. Another is the five Ds exercise. When you feel overwhelmed:

1. Dump everything out of your mind and onto paper so you can see all the clutter.
2. Delete the stuff that doesn't actually need to be done.
3. Delegate what must be done but someone else can do it.
4. Defer the stuff that only you can do but it doesn't need to be done now.
5. Do the remaining stuff, in prioritized order.

Grow others. Give meaningful work to your people. Give them the objectives and involve them in the "how" of achieving the objectives. Challenge them. Clarify their role by agreeing with them on the top three most important business objectives they're responsible for. Quantify them as much as possible so they are clear and SMART. Help them get unstuck by showing them the bigger picture, explaining the why and walking them through ICE and five Ds exercises. Give your most ambitious team members opportunities to participate in strategic, company-wide projects so they can have greater impact as they develop perspective, skills, and relationships with others they work with on their projects. Delegate, relinquish control, and trust them. Perhaps most important, support them in their dreams and ambitions outside of their work responsibilities by encouraging them to implement their Life Vision and Rhythm of Execution.

Invest in development. Invest in role-specific and Leadership development programs to help your people grow and do their best work. These can be certifications, conferences, coaching programs, online learning platforms, or self-guided programs. Whatever the case, help all employees get excited about expanding their skills, increasing their market value, and contributing to the company to better serve customers. At Keap, we have found great value in offering our people an online learning management system that has literally thousands of courses and programs to help our Keapers improve their knowledge and skills. There are many such systems on the market. It's fun to see people roll up their sleeves and invest time in developing themselves. And it's a great thing for the company as our employees get better at serving customers and helping them grow with Automation.

Leaders are readers. One of the best and easiest ways to invest in Leadership development is to read books on business, Leadership, and personal development. This has been a staple of our Leadership development program at Keap over the years and I can't imagine where we would be without it. Good books really are the cheapest and easiest way to invest in leadership development.

To help you along, here is a suggested reading list of books that will help you build your capacity to lead. We have a much longer list of books that we give to employees and entrepreneurs who ask, but this list will get you started:

- *The Power of Positive Thinking* by Norman Vincent Peale
- *Think and Grow Rich* by Napoleon Hill
- *How to Win Friends and Influence People* by Dale Carnegie
- *The One-Minute Manager* by Ken Blanchard
- *Beyond Entrepreneurship* by Jim Collins

About 20 years ago, I began reading six books per quarter. Like you, I don't have a lot of time to sit around leisurely reading books, so here are a few tips:

- Always read books on planes.
- Listen to audiobooks (on two-times speed) while driving.
- Read books when traveling.
- Read one book at a time.
- Push yourself to read fast.
- Finish the book in one or two sittings.
- Listen to books on a service like Audible.
- Buy book summaries from a service like Blinkist.

Leaders of one. We believe all people are leaders. People don't need a title to be a leader. Some of our best leaders at Keap are individual contributors who are well respected by their peers for the high-quality work they do and the way they push themselves to get better at their role every single day. We all lead ourselves. We want everyone in the business working to become their best selves. To that end, ask yourself and your people, "What are you reading?" "What courses are you taking?" "What podcasts are you listening to?" "How are you becoming your best self?"

Create a happy environment. As leaders, it's our job to create an environment where employees can thrive. When employees are upbeat about their work, it spreads to others. I like to say, "Happy employees make happy customers make happy shareholders." So create an environment where you facilitate *and expect* your people to be happy. This is a two-way street. Remember back to our Mindset chapter (Chapter 4), where we each choose to create our own happiness. Do all you can as a leader to foster an environment conducive to happiness. It's fun and productive. Co-create it with your people. And don't tolerate the grouch who brings everyone down. That's unfair to all your team members who are choosing to be happy.

Whatever tactics you use to develop Leadership, please resolve to invest in it. This will spare you from the Dark Side of Entrepreneurship, as you and your team members grow through Leadership development. It will help you achieve balanced growth in your business and life. And it will increase the impact you can have on the world. Remember that all problems are Leadership problems. Invest wisely.

Leadership development is not easy work, but it's worth it to serve others and help them become their best selves. Plus, it creates a major competitive advantage as you build your company to be a great place to work. I love this great quote from the founder of Johnsonville Sausage: *"Most companies use their people to build a business, but we use our business to build people."* That's a great way to think as you build the team.

GET THE RESOURCES

The last of the three jobs of the CEO is get the resources. This means you're always building, always attracting, always networking, always serving. You've heard of the "ABC" sales mentality to "Always Be Closing"? Well, the ABC Leadership mentality is "Always Be Confidence-building." As you build confidence in your company, resources flow to the company. When I was in a business class years ago, the professor asked what a stock price measures. All the students threw out different responses. It blew my mind when he told us the answer: "Confidence. Stock price measures confidence in a company." Profound. "Always Be Confidence-building" and you'll attract resources.

Here are a few ways to help you get the resources you need in the areas of financial resources, human resources, and partnerships.

Financial resources. Most entrepreneurs are conservative and debt averse, which is perfectly fine. But if your business can generate higher growth and returns than the interest rate you would pay on a business loan, it's smart to get a business loan so you have the financial resources to grow your business. I recommend a line of credit because you only use it if you have a good investment opportunity and you can pay it down as the investment pans out. Establish and maintain a good banking partnership so you can secure a line of credit. If your Vision requires more capital, you'll want to get investors. And if you have a very big Vision that involves fast growth, you'll want to raise venture capital. This book is not the place for me to go deeper on financial resources, but I'll be happy to direct you if you contact me.

Human resources. Always be on the lookout for people who fit your PVM. When you project your PVM, people will be attracted to you. So speak about your PVM, share it with others, project it to your community, and get on stages and panels to share your PVM story. This will draw people into your business like a "talent tractor beam." For those who don't understand that *Star Trek* reference, just imagine a force field so powerful that when the right people are caught in your PVM story, it pulls them into your company and "resistance is futile."

Partnerships. You and your team can't achieve your PVM alone. You will want to bring in partners of various types. Sometimes they look like vendors. Sometimes they are educational, government, or industry organizations. Sometimes they even look like competitors. But there will always be people inspired by your PVM yet not in a position to work with you as an employee. You need partnerships. And you'll want to project your PVM to attract partners who can help you achieve your goals.

In all of these cases, your PVM becomes your primary tool to get the resources you need for the business. *Whether you're applying for a line of credit, attracting investors, or building partnerships, you'll want to use your PVM as a magnet and a filter.* Because if they don't fit your PVM, they will be a thorn in your side. So use your PVM liberally and wisely to get people on board with you and align everyone's interests.

Wow, we've covered a lot under the umbrella of Leadership. This is an important Key to Success. It will help you conquer the chaos because as you put your PVM in place, you will feel confident stepping back, taking vacation, and relinquishing some control to a team you trust that will pursue your shared goals in a way that's consistent with your PVM. I cannot emphasize enough how liberating this is, especially for conscious capitalists and enlightened CEOs who want to make an impact on the world.

Over the last six chapters, we've covered the Six Keys to Business and Personal Success for entrepreneurs:

1. Mindset: The mental stamina and emotional capital you need to win
2. Vision: The clear long-term view of your life that your business fits into
3. Rhythm: The daily, weekly, monthly, quarterly, and annual flow that ties to Vision
4. Strategy: The ability to do the right things at the right time for business success
5. Automation: The great small business game-changer that drives efficient growth
6. Leadership: The team- and culture-building skills to get everyone working together

Now let's look at how you can put all of the Six Keys into practice to conquer the chaos and achieve the balanced growth you want.

Chapter 9 Summary: Leadership

- You don't need to be "a born leader" to lead your company effectively. Just like you learned other aspects of the business, you can learn to lead well.
- You must think like a CEO: direct the company, delegate all you can, develop your people, and do less. This is counterintuitive because many entrepreneurs are used to, and find satisfaction in, the doing.
- The three jobs of the CEO are: 1) set the vision, 2) build the team, and 3) get the resources. As much as possible, stick with these three jobs and delegate the rest.
- By practicing conscious capitalism and enlightened entrepreneurship, you can build a meaningful company where people want to co-create and be part of something special.
- The way to build a great culture, and thereby establish a fantastic competitive advantage, is to establish your Purpose, Values, and Mission (PVM) as part of your Company Strategy, and then hire, coach, and fire to the PVM.

Part 4

PUTTING THE KEYS INTO PRACTICE

"The thing that makes all the difference, the thing that makes the difference between success and failure for entrepreneurs, is pure perseverance."

–Steve Jobs

10
CHANGING FOR GOOD

D obbin Buck is a changed man. In his 30s, he was destitute, on drugs, and devoid of any drive to live. By his own account, he was nearing a dead end. Dobbin snapped out of it, turning around his life in stunning fashion. As I write this very paragraph, Dobbin is enjoying a week with his family in Costa Rica, soaking up the good life in a gorgeous mansion on a picturesque, private beach in paradise.

Twenty years removed from those dark days, Dobbin now runs a successful business and he leads a beautiful life. He and his two business partners run a digital marketing agency called GetUWired. They have over 50 employees. They're on a mission to help small businesses grow more efficiently, helping their clients implement Lifecycle Automation, our fifth Key to Success. I've seen firsthand how GetUWired produces remarkable results in their clients' businesses. Dobbin loves what he and his team do to help small businesses grow with Lifecycle Automation.

What changed for Dobbin? Well, aside from getting a scare that he would end his life and throw away all possibilities and opportunities, he realized he needed to change for his family. Life "shook him by the lapels" and woke him up to who he could be and what he could become. To Dobbin's credit, he made swift changes and got on track to a productive life. *But it's the changes he made over time, gradually and consistently, that ultimately produced the success he is enjoying today.* And it will be the continued changes and improvements he makes over the rest of his life that will enable him to reach his full potential of greatness as a human being. Dobbin knows that. And he works every day on his Rhythm of Execution to stay on track and achieve his Life Vision.

The Six Keys to Business and Personal Success will transform your business and life gradually, just as they did in Dobbin's life. As you implement the Six Keys over time, you will grow in a balanced way, producing more money, time, control, impact, and freedom than you ever dreamed possible. You will conquer the chaos and avoid the Dark Side of Entrepreneurship as you practice the Six Keys:

1. Mindset of Success
2. Life Vision
3. Rhythm of Execution
4. Company and Customer Strategy
5. Lifecycle Automation
6. Leadership and Culture

"Practice" is exactly the right word. This stuff doesn't happen all at once. And it doesn't happen without sustained effort. But it does happen over time, as it did with Dobbin. And it's actually really fun and enjoyable when you follow some important principles as you practice the Six Keys to Business and Personal Success for Entrepreneurs. I call these the 10 Principles of Practice to help you implement the Six Keys to Success.

THE 10 PRINCIPLES OF PRACTICE

1. **Practice makes *progress*, not perfect.** Occasionally, an event or opportunity is so jarring that it snaps us out of our way of being and enables us to change ingrained behavior immediately. And some people—particularly

those who check their ego well and put it in its place—can change relatively quickly. We all want change overnight. But change usually comes gradually. *The trick is to stick with it by celebrating progress.* Incalculable New Year's resolutions are discarded because they focus on perfection instead of progress. As we celebrate the progress we are making, we can drop the perfectionism. We can put change in context. We can recognize that we have all the time it takes to create lasting change. And we can put it all in the perspective of our Life Vision, as we follow our Rhythm of Execution to create a successful business and life.

2. **"Tiny changes, remarkable results."** In *Atomic Habits*, James Clear taught us how important it is to start small when we are making changes. One percent better. Repetition. Habit stacking. Tiny changes lead to remarkable results over time. As Clear put it, "Each improvement is like adding a grain of sand to the positive side of the scales of life, slowly tipping things in your favor. Eventually, if you stick with it, you hit a tipping point. Suddenly, it feels easier to stick with good habits. The weight of the system is working for you rather than against you." That's what your Rhythm of Execution will do for you. Start small. Just wake up early. Then build out your Rhythm gradually. Tiny changes. Remarkable results.

3. **"The feeling is the secret."** In Neville Goddard's timeless classic, *Feeling Is the Secret*, he taught us how our emotions play a crucial role in determining our outcomes. Joe Dispenza's modern work has taken the concept to a deeper, scientific realm, helping us understand that we bring about what we *feel* about a particular topic. Elevate your feelings to elevate your performance. So when it comes to your Quest for Success, your emotions about your Life Vision, your feelings about where you're heading, are absolutely crucial. Every day, you must cultivate feelings of excitement, confidence, and positivity about

your Life Vision. Every day, you must root out the weeds of fear, doubt, and negativity. And every day you must upgrade your emotions to produce the spectacular results you are blessed to have the opportunity to pursue in this amazing life. Are you *excited* and *positive* about your life vision? Because if you are, I'm positive it will happen. And that's exciting!

4. **The joy of daily progress.** If practicing the Six Keys becomes drudgery and it requires superhuman willpower, forget about it. It won't happen. The Six Keys are not meant to be hard, back-breaking work. Do they require effort? Sure. But this stuff is meant to be fun and satisfying. Make your progress *"obvious, attractive, easy, and satisfying,"* those four characteristics of behavior change that James Clear taught us are bound to build good habits. With every little bit of daily progress, you want to cultivate a sense of accomplishment and joy. It's so awesome to get a little better each day. Celebrate it! Enjoy it. Talk about it. Laugh about it. Live it. And love it. In our family, we resolved to live our Mask family mission "in a fun, loving, cheerful way." And we've found that makes all the difference.

5. **The power of compounding changes.** James Clear also taught us, and I've seen and experienced how true it is, that tiny changes don't *add* up, they *compound* over time. Financial institutions and smart investors build fortunes using the powerful math of compounding interest. And smart entrepreneurs build success using the powerful math of compounding changes. *Just as compound interest builds massive stores of wealth over time, compound changes build massive stores of character over time.* So don't diminish the microscopic wins. Don't downplay the small improvements. And certainly don't deny the little adjustments you're making. They will pay big dividends over time. Just as the best time to begin earning interest is when you're young and the second best time is today,

the best time to make tiny changes is when you're young. And the second best time is today.

6. **Hard work, smart work, not long work.** You may have figured out by now that I'm a big believer in work ethic. Work is good for the soul. But we often mistake hard work with long work. It's quite possible to be working for a long time and not accomplishing much. It's also quite possible to work hard, but not smart. Robin Sharma's guidance here is some of the best I've found. Robin recommends working five great hours per work day, devoid of distraction, intensely focused on world-class work product. He says:

> "The old style of working is derived from an ancient era when people worked on factory lines. . . . We live now at a very different time. . . . Many of us are cognitive laborers rather than physical workers. . . . Working longer, therefore, does not serve us better, because working long hours depletes our creativity and degrades our mastery. . . . The most productive people work with supreme intensity. They do not snack on digital amusements or foolishly chit chat about TV shows. . . . They are serious. They are professionals, not dabblers. Specialists, not generalists. They go super deep versus really wide."

7. **Rest and rejuvenation.** As entrepreneurs, we tend to run our engines pretty hot. We tend to get a certain rush from the speed and activity of entrepreneurship. We tend to go, go, go in our passionate pursuit of progress. That's fine, but it is not sustainable, not to mention the risk of imbalance it poses, as we've detailed throughout the book. My advice to you is to "work hard, play hard and rest hard." As Dan Sullivan, creator of the Strategic Coach program for entrepreneurs, teaches, entrepreneurs must manage their time like pro athletes, with focus days, buffer days, and free days. Focus days are when we're doing our best and most valuable work. Buffer days are when we do our other "busy work." And free days are

when we rest and get rejuvenated for the focus days, which is where we create great value and perform at our peak. Brilliant stuff from Dan Sullivan. Robin Sharma looks at rest and rejuvenation similarly, advocating for *a practice of sabbaticals* that looks like at least one day off per week, gradually working toward one week off per month and one month off per year. I fully endorse this practice. I have taken Sundays off my whole career and I have experienced the rejuvenation that comes from this practice. By the way, to rejuvenate means "to make young or fresh again." Great advice for us in our Rhythm of Execution. One last tip on this: the transformative habit of a quarterly retreat is one of the best ways to get rejuvenated.

8. **Rewards and reflection.** Be sure to reward yourself as you achieve goals, milestones, and little wins. You've heard the phrase "Let the punishment fit the crime," right? Well, let the reward fit the win. Be honest about your rewards system. Just make sure you are rewarding yourself. You want to tie the reward to the win at the time you set the goal. You should give yourself appropriate rewards when you achieve milestones. And you should even "surprise" yourself with rewards when you discover or notice little wins along the way. The rewards can be money, prizes, time, experiences, recognition, and celebration with loved ones and accountability partners. Your system should be based on the Hierarchy of Success, rewarding you in the forms of time, money, control, impact, and freedom. You get the idea. Apply some of your entrepreneurial creativity to your rewards system to keep the game fun, exciting, and, well, rewarding. And don't forget to reflect on your progress during planning sessions in your Rhythm of Execution. The reflection often fuels the reward system. And sometimes the reflection itself is reward enough as you see all the progress you're making.

9. **Reframe failure as growth.** As you practice the Six Keys to Success, it's important to remember that all effort is growth. As Jim Collins, author on greatness, taught my team several years ago, "The other side of the success coin is not failure. It's growth." And as John Maxwell, author on leadership, teaches us, we improve in a virtuous cycle of 1) test, 2) fail, 3) learn, and 4) improve. As we move from step to step, it's our choice to see growth in the process when we finish step 4, moving to the next level of performance. Or we can see failure in the process and get stuck. Better to "fail" fast, and view the whole process as growth, not failure. All of it is fuel for success.

10. **Grace and self-forgiveness.** As driven entrepreneurs, we are hard on ourselves. And guess what? That slows our progress. We expect too much change, too fast. Our drive and ambition are seemingly never quite satisfied. We don't forgive ourselves for mistakes and slipups. This causes discouragement and prevents us from moving forward. Discouragement is the entrepreneur's Kryptonite. Combat it with grace, with self-forgiveness. As you apply the principles laid out in this chapter, you will see that practice does indeed make progress. And progress is worth celebrating. So go easy on yourself. Forgive yourself for judging yourself harshly. Believe in your best self. You're becoming that best self. Keep your head in the game by avoiding discouragement like the plague that it is.

Apply these 10 Principles of Practice to your Quest for Success. Come back to this chapter when you feel stuck or discouraged. These principles are derived from decades of practice, countless entrepreneurs, and leading experts on the process of change. Above all, stay positive. "You can do it!" are the words that ring in my mind, chanted to me over and over by my amazing dad, who programmed that phrase into my mind at a young age. I *can* do it. And you can, too!

THE EGO TRAPS THAT CATCH ENTREPRENEURS

As you implement the Six Keys, finding guidance from the 10 Principles of Practice, you will achieve great success. In order to sustain that success, you must avoid what I call the ego TRAPS for entrepreneurs:

- **T**imidity: "I'm afraid to fail" or "I'm afraid to succeed."
- **R**esignation: "I'm not enough."
- **A**mbition: "I want more, bigger, better."
- **P**ride: "I'm better than others."
- **S**abotage: "I'm not worthy or comfortable."

These sneaky TRAPS of the ego will try to thwart your efforts to achieve balanced growth. And they will certainly cut short the success you achieve if you don't recognize and dodge them. We want sustainable business results. We want you to achieve your stunning Life Vision. So we must check our ego and constantly be on guard for these Ego TRAPS.

TIMIDITY

Far too many entrepreneurs allow fear of failure to derail them. And some folks let fear of success take them out of the game. The ego is fearful. It doesn't want us to take action. It doesn't want us to try. We can't let it control us. We are entrepreneurs. We are better than that.

My favorite quote that speaks to this fear is one by Teddy Roosevelt that you've probably heard:

"It is not the critic who counts; not the man who points out how the strong man stumbles, or where the doer of deeds could have done them better. The credit belongs to the man who is actually in the arena, whose face is marred by dust and sweat and blood; *who strives valiantly*; who errs, who comes short again and again, because there is no effort without error and shortcoming; but who does actually strive to do the deeds; who knows great enthusiasms, the great devotions; who spends himself in a worthy cause; who at the best knows in the end the triumph of high achievement, and who at the worst, if he fails, at least fails while daring greatly, so that his place shall never be with those cold and timid souls who neither know victory nor defeat."

Strive valiantly. Don't be timid. Cultivate positive thoughts and feelings, and spring into action to create little wins. Get in the arena. Stay in the arena. Enjoy the triumph of high achievement. And learn from your failures to convert them into growth. Remember what Jim Collins taught my team: "The other side of the coin of success is not failure, it's growth."

Remember, it is not the critic who counts. Especially not the inner critic. Get into action. And silence your inner critic, that sneaky little ego.

Resignation

Discouragement is a normal part of entrepreneurship. Things don't always go our way. Stuff happens. Shoot, in the early days of Keap I used to say, "We have about one good day per month." It's okay that we get discouraged from time to time. What we can't do is allow that discouragement to paralyze us.

The ego feasts on discouragement and tempts us to stop trying, to resign ourselves to our current lot. The ego fools us into resignation by telling us we aren't good enough, smart enough, working enough. It tells us we aren't enough. This negative self-talk, rehearsing our shortcomings, dwelling on mistakes, it all subtly adds up. And if we aren't careful, the resignation happens in the back of our mind. We become resigned to accepting an undesirable outcome because our efforts aren't producing the result we want. The ego convinces us to stop trying.

Enough! We are good enough. We are smart enough. We are working enough. We are enough. We must chase away the debilitating discouragement that causes resignation. We must identify this trap of the ego and not allow it to control our thoughts, feelings, and actions.

We get on top of this by playing the long game. We remind ourselves that all problems yield to our sustained effort, that tiny changes produce remarkable results *over time*. We engrain Voltaire's quote in our mind and heart, that "No problem can withstand the assault of constant thinking." We keep our long-term goals firmly in mind. We are guided and inspired by our Life Vision. And we remember John Lennon's quote that "Everything works out in the end. If it hasn't worked out, it isn't the end."

Play the long game. Don't give up. Never stop trying. Tiny changes, remarkable results, compounded over time. Ditch the discouragement. You are enough. Don't let the ego tempt you into resignation. Sneaky little ego.

AMBITION

Ambition is a good thing for entrepreneurs, unless it is left unchecked. Once you have time, money, and control, you might be tempted to reinvest those rewards in the relentless pursuit of more. This is why you must bridle your ambition. Your ego is accustomed to being fed a certain way, with your ambition in the driver's seat. So as the chaos dies down and you get clear on your Vision, you must intentionally invest your time and money in ways that advance your Life Vision.

Your ego will have a hard time reconciling this, saying, "Wait a minute! You can't just take time off work. You always work. You shouldn't be spending money that way! How will we get more and look better? What will others think if you do that? This isn't how we do things around here. Stick with the program!"

No. You're building a better program. You're investing your resources more wisely than in the past. Your Life Vision provides purpose, perspective, and priority that you didn't have before. You're building an exciting future, executing your

Rhythm and achieving your Vision. Put the ego in its place when its unbridled ambition wants you to pursue more and more of what my coach calls "the booby prize." The booby prize is the fame and fortune, the accolades, the trophies, and the "stuff" people ooh and aah over.

I'm not saying there's anything wrong with those things. It's the pursuit of those things, the unbridled ambition to achieve those things and accumulate more, that blinds us to what really matters and traps us. The ego craves those things. We must check our ego, put it in its place, and be very aware that it's lurking in the background, trying to satisfy itself. It is fitting these objects of ambition are often referred to as "the trappings of success." Sneaky little ego.

PRIDE

"Pride goeth before destruction. And a haughty spirit before a fall" (Proverbs 16:18). Pride is, perhaps, the greatest of the ego TRAPS. When we begin to achieve great success, the ego subtly sets us up for a fall. The ego snares us, telling us how great we are, getting us to compare ourselves to others, elevating ourselves in our own eyes. As we believe the hype, obsess over "crushing competitors," and inhale our success, the ego begins to convince us that we are better, superior, or even invincible.

Far too often, the Dark Side of Entrepreneurship follows a period of beautiful success. In other words, those negative consequences we want to avoid are often unwanted byproducts of success. Why? Because we let the ego control us. We allow our pride to run rampant inside of us, fueling our actions, becoming the motive for what we do.

Jim Collins's book *How the Mighty Fall* sets forth how companies become full of this pride and begin to make decisions born out of hubris, which is defined as "excessive self-confidence." From legendary companies like Kodak and Blockbuster to smaller companies you wouldn't recognize, pride caused the fall. Let this be a warning to all of us as entrepreneurs, especially as we conquer the chaos and achieve great success. If we let the ego fill us with pride, we are setting ourselves up for a fall. Sneaky little ego.

SABOTAGE

As entrepreneurs begin to conquer the chaos, they sometimes feel like a fish out of water. They've been in chaos for so long, they've become accustomed to it. In some cases, we've seen entrepreneurs who need chaos to feel useful and valuable in their work, and sometimes they actually create chaos when it's not present in their business. They feel uncomfortable with success, even unworthy of it as something foreign to them. So when they start to break through by practicing the Six Keys, the ego engages a form of sabotage that throws them back into chaos.

That might seem crazy, but it's actually quite understandable. When you started your business, you were the glue that held it all together. Without you there wasn't a business. If you stopped working, the business stopped working. As you grow and succeed, not everything depends on you. And the ego doesn't like that. It wants you taking on new projects, big responsibilities, important things that only you can do. That's what satisfies the ego, deviously and subtly convincing us that we shouldn't stop the chaos.

Relax. Let go. You can take time off and enjoy the freedom. The business will be fine. In fact, we have found that it frequently thrives in the entrepreneur's brief periods of absence. Employees are glad to have a little more autonomy and decision-making power. The Automation still runs whether we're there or not. In many cases, we have seen record productivity occur in the entrepreneur's absence. It's not coincidence. The reality is that the business doesn't need you 24/7 like it once did. That's a great thing! But the ego doesn't like it, so it tries to reposition you into the middle of the business.

In *Breaking the Habit of Being Yourself,* Joe Dispenza lays out how this happens to many people unwittingly. He makes the point that we all get in the habit of being ourselves by the ingrained habit patterns of our thoughts, feelings, and actions. So when people are in the habit of chaos, they are thinking the thoughts, feeling the feelings, and acting the actions that keep them feeling comfortable in chaos. When a person tries to break free from those thoughts, feelings, and actions, the ego says, "Wait a minute, I'm not comfortable with that. Stick with the program and stop trying to change." Sneaky little ego.

We know the way to change is to elevate our thoughts and feelings about our success—to think it, feel it, and spring into action, creating tiny wins that further elevate our thoughts, feelings, and actions in a virtuous cycle of improvement. Don't let the ego sabotage your efforts. Be clear that the ego doesn't want you to change and will make you feel uncomfortable and unworthy as you exert effort to improve. Put your ego in its place, where it belongs, in the backseat, a willing and subservient passenger to you, the driver of this beautiful Life Vision you are creating.

GUARDING AGAINST EGO TRAPS

I suppose these TRAPS might apply to all people, but entrepreneurs are especially vulnerable to them. As we create in our businesses, building something that didn't exist before we apply our minds to it, we are out in front of the creative process. We are fueled by ambition and energized by the creative process. We envision something others can't see. And so we are particularly susceptible to the ego TRAPS.

Yes, the ego is sneaky, and the results of unchecked ego are a blatant driver of chaos. We must guard against ego TRAPS. We must have trusted advisors around us who tell the truth, who stand up to us. We need to listen to these trusted advisors. I can tell you from personal experience that when I haven't listened well, it causes problems and my ego is allowed to run the show. And that never ends well.

Because the ego is so sneaky with its TRAPS, I recommend you create a system to check your ego. Listen to your advisors (especially your spouse!). Check your ego regularly as part of your planning process. Perhaps you'll want to do a daily check to monitor whether your motives are selfish or serving. Whatever the case, be on guard and don't fall for the ego TRAPS that undermine your success.

I have come to find great value in ego checks throughout the day, where I honestly ask myself:

- Am I listening? To Charisse? To trusted advisors? To others?
- Am I eager to humbly receive feedback right now?
- Am I acting with a servant heart or a selfish heart?
- Am I acting with dominance or grace?
- Am I being 100% responsible?

Here are a few other techniques I've found helpful for me and other entrepreneurs who are serious about checking their ego:

- Work with a coach who will increase your self-awareness.
- Invite your team (regularly) to give you candid feedback about yourself.
- Build a stable of trusted advisors and ask them to help you see what you can't see.
- Manage your ego during a morning routine that includes meditation and reflection.
- Practice submission, service, and grace to build muscles of humility and gratitude.

Chaos is always waiting for the opportunity to slip back into place. But as long as you know that, and as long as you're watching your sneaky little ego, you can do something about it. When you need to, simply ask yourself what really matters in your life. What you'll find is that freedom is your true goal.

It always has been. But every once in a while, even the best entrepreneurs need a reminder.

When you read the title of this chapter, "Changing for Good," you might have thought this chapter is about permanent change. Or you might have thought it's about changing for the better. Either way, you would be right. Because what this chapter is about is the process of change. It's about the practice of change. Change is never "done." Change is "a mountain without a top" as my coach, Steve Hardison, likes to say. We don't arrive. We just keep improving, steadily and joyfully. We take the setbacks in stride. We take the advancements with gratitude and humility. We check our ego. And we keep getting better. Every. Single. Day.

Chapter 10 Summary: Changing for Good

- The Six Keys to Success will transform your business and life. There's no need to get overwhelmed by the Six Keys. Implement them gradually and practice them over time.
- The 10 Principles of Practice will help you implement and practice the Six Keys. You will see phenomenal results begin to stack up as you follow the 10 Principles of Practice.
- To achieve and sustain the success we want as entrepreneurs, we must avoid the ego TRAPS: timidity, resignation, ambition, pride, sabotage.
- As entrepreneurs, we must all guard against ego TRAPS by checking the ego regularly. Come up with your own methods and techniques to ensure your sneaky little ego is not running the program.

11
Keep Going

"The thing that makes all the difference, the thing that makes the difference between success and failure for entrepreneurs, is pure perseverance."

—Steve Jobs

That quote by Steve Jobs says it perfectly. The grit of entrepreneurs is what makes all the difference between ultimate success and failure. At Keap, we love you entrepreneurs for your grit and determination. We love it so much we named the company after you. Keap stands for the grit and perseverance of entrepreneurs. As in "keep going."

When I shared our founding story earlier in the book to illustrate small business chaos, I mentioned there were a couple of key experiences that turned the tide for us when we were struggling mightily. Let me share a very personal experience to underscore the point Steve Jobs is making about perseverance.

THE KEEP GOING STORY

The first three years of running Keap were brutally hard. About 18 months in, my co-founders and I were taking home a couple grand per month, going deep into personal debt, and struggling to make ends meet. I wanted to quit, but the personal guarantees on our computers, equipment, and office leases meant I would have to make those monthly payments while leaving my two partners for a "real job" as they tried to make the business work.

I decided to stick it out. We began making progress as we built our CRM software to automate marketing for our customers, but we still couldn't pay our bills. The tension was rising at home, yet I had begun to recognize that every day we survived made it more likely we would eventually be successful. My wife, Charisse, did not share my optimism.

In Charisse's defense, I was delusional. We had no money. Our credit was maxed out and shot. We couldn't feed our four kids we had at the time, let alone put them in soccer or take care of their dental needs. It's accurate to say we were rapidly approaching personal bankruptcy and Charisse was feeling the daily financial and emotional burden of our struggling business.

Meanwhile, I was beginning to see the power of our software, as customers raved about the effects of automating their follow-up. I had begun using our product to automate *our* follow-up and it was working. Revenue was increasing in the business, but we were in such a hole and we were trying to establish the business. There just wasn't much left for take-home pay among three partners.

So when Charisse and I would have tense conversations at night, I would tell her, "Things are getting better." Soon she started countering, "Well, they're not getting better for me!" It was getting bad.

Then one night we had yet another argument about the business. This one was especially rough. She was fed up. She had been telling me for a long time that I needed to look for a real job. I eventually caved and told her I would, but I couldn't bring myself to do it because I just knew the business would be successful. But on this night, she was adamant about me looking for a new job. She made me promise that I'd start looking for a job the very next day. I reluctantly agreed, reasoning that I could come back to the business when it could afford to pay us.

The next day, I went to work with every intention to look for a job. But as is so often the case for entrepreneurs, the business swallowed me whole that day. Customer fires, a hot lead to pursue, overdue bills, and who knows what else kept me completely occupied all day. By the end of the day I hadn't done a bit of job searching.

I felt a pit in my stomach as I drove home, partly because I hadn't kept my word and partly because I knew Charisse was at the end of her rope. As I walked into the house and found Charisse, she looked at me from across the kitchen and asked, "Did you look for a job today?"

With shame and embarrassment, I told her, "No." She walked toward me, gave me a big hug, and held on tight. I was worried and didn't know what it meant. Then I realized she was crying. I didn't know why. Then I started crying. I didn't know why. But all of the emotions of the prior two and a half years came pouring out as she held on to me tightly and I realized she wasn't mad at me.

Something else had taken ahold of Charisse's emotions.

After what seemed like an eternity, she loosened her embrace and stepped back enough to look into my eyes. I choked out the words, "What's wrong?"

She said, "Just keep going. God knows what we're doing. Everything's going to be okay. Just keep going."

I can't put into words what I felt when she said that. The years of pulling apart. The tension in our marriage due to the business. The intensity of the argument we had the night before. It all hit me so powerfully. And now she was with me. In my corner. We were a team. And I felt like we were unstoppable.

That day, Charisse's amazing faith, love, and support led her to have a life-changing experience. She knew God was aware of us. And she knew everything was going to be okay. Faith over fear. We just needed to keep going.

What has happened since that day 18 years ago is nothing short of a miracle. It hasn't always been easy. Truth is, you never "arrive" as an entrepreneur. There are always new challenges and opportunities. But our life has been incredible. The impact we've been able to have is greater than anything the two of us could have imagined all those years ago.

And it almost didn't happen. First, because I wanted to quit but couldn't due to financial obligations and personal guarantees.

Second, because Charisse was done and couldn't bear to keep going—until she had a deeply personal experience, based on her incredible faith, that made it possible.

Just keep going.

Every entrepreneur feels like quitting at times. Every successful entrepreneur has their "keep going" story. Every struggling entrepreneur needs to hear these stories. You can probably identify a "keep going" story or two in your own journey as an entrepreneur. You might be in the middle of one right now. The point of this story is not to shine a light on me and Charisse. It's to call out this critical ingredient of grit in entrepreneurship and to encourage and inspire you if you're in the middle of your "keep going" story.

I shudder to think what would have happened if we had thrown in the towel all those years ago. And I'm here to tell you that it isn't all smooth sailing once you get past those early years of struggle in your business. Just keep going. You can do it. It's worth it. Keep the faith. Keep believing in yourself, your business, and your dreams. Keep that Mindset of Success, no matter what. Maintain an undying belief. Your disciplined optimism will get you through the tough times. Faith over fear. Keep going.

KEEP SERVING

Along your journey, you'll have times when the joy is waning and the daily grind is wearing you down. You'll feel frustration about missing goals. You'll get off track on your Mindset, Vision, and Rhythm. And your Strategy, Automation, and Leadership will fall short or completely break down at times.

Would you like a surefire way to get back on track, recharge your batteries, and rediscover the joy of your business?

Just serve your customers. Dig in and solve a problem for a customer or multiple customers. Be of service. Purely serve out of a selfless desire to help them, not because of something you'll get in return. Just serve them.

In one of the great magic tricks of this world, we feel better when we forget ourselves and serve others. Entrepreneurship gives us this opportunity every day. Most of the time, we are caught up in the value exchange of business, thinking of what we get in exchange for our service. But nothing recharges our batteries quite like serving selflessly.

This magic trick works with employees, partners, and others, as well as with customers, family members, and neighbors. So, if you're feeling stuck as you practice these Six Keys to Success, ask yourself if you're serving or selfish. Where are your motives? Then do something out of pure, selfless service. The magic, as we know, is that it will lift others *and* get you back on track.

Before we leave this topic of service, I want to make a quick comment about self-care. I certainly believe it has its place in the world, as evidenced by the Mindset chapter and indeed the entire premise of this book: that success is about balanced growth in the business *and* your personal life. Yes, self-care has its place. But service to others is the surefire way to feel better about yourself and get back on track. We need to be careful that self-care doesn't cause selfishness in us as entrepreneurs, because the world needs our service and generosity. We can't afford to get overly caught up in ourselves, the way the ego tries to do with its sneaky TRAPS.

KEEP GROWING

Keep going. Keep serving. And above all, keep growing! Face each new challenge with grit and optimism. This journey of entrepreneurship is amazing. The business rewards of growing your company are incredible. And the personal growth is even more important.

We've talked about the importance of growth throughout the book. And our definition of success starts with "balanced growth."

There's one more reason why it's so important that you keep growing: conscious capitalism, the concept we covered in the chapter on Leadership.

Recall that conscious capitalism means that a business should be used to do good for everyone associated with the business. Customers, employees, partners, owner(s), the community—everyone benefits from the business. The business solves an important problem for customers. It creates jobs for employees. It provides opportunity for partners. It creates a positive impact on the community. It blesses the owner(s) financially and in so many other ways.

When a business stops pursuing growth, its impact is reduced in obvious ways: customers are not served well, jobs are lost, opportunities evaporate, owner benefits are reduced. The statement is commonly made that "small businesses are the backbone of a strong economy." But that's not quite accurate. The truth is, *growing* small businesses are the backbone of a strong economy. So keep growing, for everyone's sake. Society needs and wants you, the conscious capitalist, to be wildly successful in your balanced growth.

Small business growth is such a beautiful thing. As you go through this journey of entrepreneurship, you might want to take a break and stop growing, especially when you're experiencing growing pains. But that's a trap. Push through the growing pains. Growing pains are a necessary part of the process. Even if you're not growing revenue for a season, you must grow profits and you must grow personally. The mentality of growth is critical to your success. So don't let that slip. Keep growing!

FINAL WORDS OF GUIDANCE

It may be cliché, but it's true: success is a journey, not a destination. Thank you for allowing me to be your guide. As we've worked together through the Six Keys to Success for Entrepreneurs, I've tried to share a guidebook for your exciting journey as an entrepreneur. These Six Keys will help you:

- Make more **money**
- Find more **time** for yourself
- Take **control** of your business and life
- Have a greater **impact** on the world
- Achieve the highest level of entrepreneurial **freedom**

That's the Hierarchy of Success for entrepreneurs. And our definition of success is *"Balanced growth in your business and personal life, providing more money, time, control, impact, and freedom."* You'll achieve exactly that as you grow in and through the Stages of Small Business Growth by practicing your:

1. **Mindset** of Success
2. Life **Vision**
3. **Rhythm** of Execution
4. Company and Customer **Strategy**
5. Lifecycle **Automation**
6. **Leadership** and Culture

I want to share a few parting thoughts. In this awesome game of small business growth, so many entrepreneurs get caught up in *what they're making* **in** *their business*. But what really matters is *what they're making* **of** *their life*. My sincere hope is that this book has inspired you to create great success in your business, and to become your best self in life. A great business and a great life—that's what we want. You have greatness in you. And the world needs to see it.

I can promise you after over 20 years of personally practicing these Six Keys and observing them in practice among tens of thousands of entrepreneurs, they will transform your business and your life. They will help you achieve your goals and dreams. I deeply want you to experience this goodness and avoid the chaos and the Dark Side of Entrepreneurship. You just need to commit. These Six Keys work. They will work for you. It takes time to implement them. And it requires practice. But it's worth it. You can do it!

Start small. On the personal side, do the three transformative habits—wake up early, plan your week, and do a quarterly retreat. On the business side, do the core four of follow-up: new lead follow-up, new client follow-up, long-term nurture, and special offer broadcast. From there, everything else will unfold gradually and beautifully as you adopt the 10 Principles of Practice using these Six Keys to Success.

What an amazing life we get to live! It is a great gift, a privilege, and a blessing to be an entrepreneur. The lab of entrepreneurship is perfectly suited for personal development. This career of entrepreneurship enables us to apply our skills and talents in the market, do good for others, earn great rewards, and become our best selves. Entrepreneurship hones and polishes us in amazing ways. Entrepreneurship has blessed my life immeasurably and that's why I wrote this book—to share what I've learned, what I'm practicing, and what I know will bless your life as you practice it. Practice makes progress. Enjoy it!

Keep going, keep serving, keep growing.

Chapter 11 Summary: Keep Going

- As Steve Jobs said, perseverance is the thing that makes all the difference between success and failure for entrepreneurs. That's why we named our company Keap, as in keep going, keep serving, keep growing.
- My "keep going story" gives an inside view into the required grit of entrepreneurs and the power of faith from the entrepreneur's spouse. Every successful entrepreneur has a "keep going story" and every struggling entrepreneur needs to hear those stories.

- When things are difficult and you're feeling beaten down, have faith and just keep going. Things will work out in the end. If it hasn't worked out, it isn't the end.
- When you need a pick-me-up, find a way to serve a customer, a team member, or anyone, really. Service is a magic trick that makes things better in good times and bad. Keep serving.
- The strength of economies isn't small businesses, as we sometimes hear. The strength of economies is in *growing* small businesses. Your customers, family, community, and the economy need you to grow your business. Practice the business keys to keep growing.
- Entrepreneurship is an amazing laboratory where we get to practice becoming our best self. Practice the personal keys to become your best self. Keep growing!

Appendix

KEAP SMALL BUSINESS RESOURCES

K eap has been serving entrepreneurs for over 20 years. During that time, we've seen how much support it takes to succeed. That's why we offer so many amazing resources to help small businesses.

Our community of customers, employees, and partners, the "Keap Family," regularly helps entrepreneurs and their teams implement the Six Keys to Success. I highly recommend finding similar community and resources, because there is one thing we do know: growth is a team sport. You shouldn't try to do this alone.

CRM AND MARKETING AUTOMATION SOFTWARE

In Part 3, you were encouraged to find systems for running your business. Although there are many CRM solutions on the market, no other is designed to help you implement Lifecycle

Automation by practicing proper follow-up. As you search for a solution, look for something that:

- Is designed specifically for small businesses
- Enables you to fully automate your business
- Provides you with excellent support and services

What you choose is entirely up to you. If you would like to learn more about Keap's CRM and marketing automation software, please visit us at ConquerTheChaosBook.com.

THE SIX KEYS TO SUCCESS COURSE

This book provides you with the Six Keys to conquer the chaos. If you would like to implement these Six Keys, I highly recommend you join our course to guide you through the implementation process. In the course, you will:

- Gain access to tools and resources
- Interact with other entrepreneurs implementing the Six Keys
- Receive expert guidance from me and my team
- Gain the motivation and accountability to succeed

To learn more about the Six Keys Course, visit us at Conquer TheChaosBook.com.

SMALL BUSINESS GROWTH ROADMAP

You learned about the "Stages of Small Business Growth" earlier in this book. Are you curious what you can do to plan ahead and prepare for the next stage? Take Keap's small business growth assessment at keap.com/small-business-growth-assessment.

This assessment will give you customized recommendations on what to implement to break through to the next stage of business growth, including advice on what to automate, the right tech tools to invest in based on your growth stage, and more.

ADDITIONAL RESOURCES

Beyond our software and course, Keap has many resources available to entrepreneurs and their teams who want to practice the Six Keys to Success. From blogs and emails to tools and tips, you will find many free and valuable resources to help you grow your business. Join our Conquer The Chaos Facebook group to interact with other practitioners of the Six Keys. Visit us at ConquerTheChaosBook.com.

REFERENCES

Arbinger Institute. *Leadership and Self-Deception: Getting Out of the Box.* Berrett-Koehler Publishers, 2010.

Carnegie, Dale. *How to Win Friends and Influence People.* New York: Simon & Schuster, 2009.

Christensen, Clayton M., et al. *How Will You Measure Your Life?* Harper Business, 2012.

Clear, James. *Atomic Habits: An Easy and Proven Way to Build Good Habits and Break Bad Ones.* Avery, 2018.

Collins, Jim. *Good to Great: Why Some Companies Make the Leap and Others Don't.* HarperBusiness, 2001.

Collins, Jim. *How the Mighty Fall: And Why Some Companies Never Give In.* HarperBusiness, 2009.

Dispenza, Joe. *Breaking the Habit of Being Yourself: How to Lose Your Mind and Create a New One.* Hay House, 2012.

Doran, G. T. "There's a S.M.A.R.T. way to write management's goals and objectives." *Management Review* 70(11), 1981.

Gerber, Michael. *The E Myth Revisited: Why Most Small Businesses Don't Work and What to Do About It.* New York: HarperBusiness, 1995.

Goddard, Neville. *The Feeling Is the Secret.* Seed of Life Publishing, 1944.

Hill, Napoleon. *Think and Grow Rich.* London, UK: Createspace, 2009.

Holiday, Ryan. *Ego Is the Enemy.* Portfolio/Penguin Random House, 2016.

Howes, Lewis. *The Greatest Mindset: Unlock the Power of Your Mind and Live Your Best Life Today.* Carlsbad, CA: Hay House, 2023.

Kennedy, Dan S. *The Ultimate Marketing Plan.* Avon, MA: Adams Media, 2006.

Lencioni, Patrick. *The Advantage: Why Organizational Health Trumps Everything Else in Business.* San Francisco: Jossey-Bass, 2012.

Maslow, Abraham. *The Maslow Business Reader.* Hoboken, NJ: John Wiley & Sons, 2000, p. 134.

Maxwell, John C. *Failing Forward: Turning Mistakes into Stepping Stones for Success.* Nashville: Thomas Nelson, 2007.

Nomura, Catherine, and Dan Sullivan. *The Laws of Lifetime Growth: Always Make Your Future Bigger Than Your Past (Bk Life).* San Francisco: Berrett-Koehler Publishers, 2007.

Peale, Norman Vincent. *The Power of Positive Thinking,* New York: Prentice-Hall, 1952.

Roosevelt, Theodore. "Quotations from the Speeches and Other Works of Theodore Roosevelt." About: President and more, from The Theodore Roosevelt Association. http://www.theodoreroosevelt.org/content.aspx?page_id=22&club_id=991271&module_id=339333.

Sharma, Robin. *The 5 AM Club: Own Your Morning, Elevate Your Life.* New York: HarperCollins, 2018.

Sinek, Simon. *Start with Why: How Great Leaders Inspire Everyone to Take Action.* Portfolio, 2009.

Sullivan, Dan. "Business Coaching for Growth-Minded Entrepreneurs." http://www.strategiccoach.com.

US Census Bureau. Data referenced from 2018.

Suggested Reading List

- Blanchard, Ken. *The One-Minute Manager.*
- Carnegie, Dale. *How to Win Friends and Influence People.*
- Collins, Jim. *Beyond Entrepreneurship.*
- Hill, Napoleon. *Think and Grow Rich.*
- Peale, Norman Vincent. *The Power of Positive Thinking.*

ACKNOWLEDGMENTS

Wow. It seems impossible to thank all who've helped us along the way over the past 20-plus years. When Scott and I wrote the first edition of this book 14 years ago, our small company was just taking off. So many early mentors had an impact on us, from Reed Hoisington, Joe Polish, and Perry Marshall to Michael Gerber, Bill Glazer, Dan Kennedy, and Dan Sullivan.

As the years passed, too many people to name came into the picture to help us achieve our mission to "Simplify Growth for One Million Small Businesses Worldwide." Thank you to all who have played a role in the growth and success of Keap. I especially want to thank each past and present "Keaper" who has worked at the company, helping small businesses grow sales and save time with our software, strategy, and services.

When Scott and I wrote the first edition of *Conquer the Chaos*, we were greatly helped by a talented writer named Stephanie Fleming, who worked for our company at the time. As I've written this revised edition, I've come to appreciate how much she helped us with that original manuscript and it seems appropriate to thank her at this time because parts of her work have carried forward into this revised edition.

I also want to thank all of our partners and customers, who are Keapers in their own right, united in our Purpose: "We liberate and empower entrepreneurs to strengthen families, communities, and economies." We love serving you and working with you to change the world for entrepreneurs and their teams. And we salute you for the great work you do to serve your employees, customers, families, and communities. You, who are growing small businesses, create strong economies.

Our investors and board members also deserve a lot of thanks. There's no straight path to success when it comes to technology investments. There are zigs and zags in the process of building a company, and I want to thank Nancy Schoendorf, Scott Petty, Joe DiSabato, Geoffrey Moore, and others for believing in us and supporting us along the way.

It takes a great collective effort to create and publish a book. I am so excited about this book and what it will do for entrepreneurs and their teams, families, and communities. The book wouldn't have been possible without the efforts of the Wiley team and so many of our Keapers, who worked on and edited this book. There's no doubt this book is much better because of the efforts of all who helped create it. Thank you!

Finally, a shout-out to entrepreneurs everywhere, for having the grit to face the challenges, create value, and live the thrill of life as a business owner. We honor you and applaud you. My sincere hope is that this book will help you achieve the business and personal success of your dreams.

ABOUT THE AUTHOR

Clate Mask, the entrepreneur's guide, is the CEO and co-founder of Keap, the leading provider of CRM and marketing automation software for small businesses. His passion is helping small businesses grow using the Six Keys to Success. When Clate isn't serving entrepreneurs and building Keap, he loves to spend time with his wife, Charisse, their six kids, and their grandkids. He is intimately familiar with the balancing act of entrepreneurs, which is what drove him to discover and teach the Six Keys.

INDEX

Index

Index

keap

Conquer the chaos with the automation software built for growing small businesses

✔ Increase revenue without increasing marketing budget

✔ Respond lightning-fast and close sales before the competition

✔ Communicate with customers even when your team is offline

✔ Never drop the ball or miss out on opportunities

✔ Relieve your busy team from manual processes

Learn more at **keap.com/chaos**